Girls Like Us

Girls Like Us

40 Extraordinary Women Celebrate Girlhood in Story, Poetry, and Song

Edited by Gina Misiroglu

New World Library
Novato, California

New World Library
14 Pamaron Way
Novato, California 94949

Library of Congress Cataloging-in-Publication Data
Girls like us: 40 extraordinary women celebrate girlhood in
story, poetry, and song / edited by Gina Misiroglu.
    p.   cm.
ISBN 1-57731-084-5 (alk. paper)
1. Girls — Literary collections.   2. Women — Biography.
I. Misiroglu, Gina Renée.
PN6071.G53G571999
920.72 — dc21   98-53428
[B]   CIP

First Printing, April 1999
ISBN 1-57731-084-5
Printed in Canada on acid-free paper
Distributed to the trade by Publishers Group West

10 9 8 7 6 5 4 3

For Glenis

All of childhood's unanswered questions must finally be passed back to [one's hometown] and answered there, heroes and bogey men, values and dislikes, are first encountered and labeled in that early environment. In later years they change faces, places and maybe races, tactics, intensities and goals, but beneath those penetrable masks they wear forever the stocking-capped faces of childhood.

— Maya Angelou, *I Know Why the Caged Bird Sings*

Table of Contents

Girlfriends

Mentors & Heroes

Irreplaceable Moments

Mary Pipher, Ph.D.

Foreword

In *Reviving Ophelia* I write about early adolescence as the time when girls are in great danger of losing their true selves and becoming instead what they think others want of them. It is a time when girls crash into a girl-hurting, girl-devaluing culture. In order to survive, girls must resist the definitions imposed upon them. They must cling to the truth of their own experiences. This anthology is about the importance of girlhood in shaping the self. The storytellers are the resisters, the girls who fought the crush of culture, and became real people.

Girls Like Us is a perfect title for this collection of sparkling prose and shimmering poetry. The great paradox of human communication is that the deeper and more personal a revelation, the more it connects with the experiences of others. In our hearts, we are all the same. Over and over as I read this book, I felt that shock of recognition, "Yes, yes, this is me. This is us."

To my delight, the book doesn't focus on stories of boyfriends and popularity. The themes of the book are the universal coming-of-age themes for young women — identity, family, girlfriends, mentors and heroes, irreplaceable moments. These themes fit my own experiences as a girl. My important relationships were not with boyfriends, but rather with books, the natural world, pets, family, girlfriends, teachers, and neighbors. I laughed when I read Gish Jen's writing of a date, "I'm not in much danger of wrecking my life on the shoals of passion. His unmoving hand feels more like a growth than a boyfriend." I've been there.

This book tells the stories of all kinds of women — rich and poor, awkward and sophisticated, artists and social activists, actresses and world leaders, and athletes and scientists. To me the stories of immigrants are particularly interesting. Women from immigrant cultures look at America with fresh eyes. The work they must do to reconcile the world at home with the world outside builds cognitive and emotional complexity. Immigrants must both resist and accept the broader culture's power to define them and, in the end, they must fashion a complicated moral and social universe of their own.

The writers included in this anthology respected and learned from their pasts, but they didn't idealize or sentimentalize their experiences. They followed Raymond Carver's suggestion, "Why don't you just tell what really happened?" Henry James wrote that a writer is someone on whom nothing is lost. The women in this book are those kind of people. They wove their experiences into authentic, well-examined, and explained lives. Alice Walker's Story, "To Hell with Dying," is a good example of spinning the threads of past into gold. The vividness of details and her sharp, honest point of view allows us to see inside the rich world of her childhood.

Maya Angelou's great phrase, "the stocking-capped faces of childhood" took me back to my childhood in small-town Nebraska. I felt my town was a backwater place where nothing ever happened. I didn't understand that what happened to me there was my life and I waited for great adventures. Until I was a writer in my thirties, I didn't realize that my childhood was a great adventure, as formative as anything that happened later. I now realize that, in my small town, I knew a thousand people of all types and ages, and that I witnessed roughly the amount of drama that occurs in all of Shakespeare.

In the 1950s psychologist Lois Murphy did her important work on what she called "good copers." She found that they had in common a yearning, a sense of goals just outside their reach and that they strive to achieve. Murphy felt discomfort and unhappiness in childhood were not necessarily harmful. What mattered were children's responses to yearning and also their possibilities of success in reaching goals.

All the women in this book were yearners — for freedom, self-expression, knowledge, social justice, or transcendence. They didn't allow depression or anger to overwhelm them. Their responses were adaptive. Alice Walker and Gloria Wade-Gayles focused on what they felt grateful for. Georgie Anne Geyer chose compassion when she wrote of her father, "How can you honestly blame someone for not giving you what he didn't have to give?" These writers are not an angry group. They remind me of one of my clients who said, "I don't get mad, I educate."

This group of women resisted being defined as victims. Ani DiFranco writes, "I am not a kitten stuck up in a tree somewhere." They may have had help, but these women rescued themselves. They fought for their true selves in many ways, but whatever their process, the end result was growth. As Wade-Gayles says of the women from her childhood, these women were "sturdy oaks" who remained whole because they believed in their own goodness. And over time goodness prevailed. Happiness became the best revenge.

Many of the women in *Girls Like Us* are my age mates, experience mates, and soulmates. If we lived near each other, if we knew each other, we would be friends. Over and over, I was struck by how many stories we had in common. For example, like Ruth Colvin, I played a made-up globe game. I would shut my eyes, put my finger on the globe, and spin. Wherever I landed I would visit "in my mind." I'd imagine the sights, noises, smells, and music of those faraway places. I thought I invented this game. Maybe I did, maybe Colvin did, and so did other girls all over America, girls like us who needed to break through boundaries and find mystery and enchantment, girls like us who needed to put their difficult little worlds into perspective.

So many other stories could have been my own. Like Benazir Bhutto, I was the oldest, in charge when my parents were away. Like Wilma Mankiller, I had times when I hated my body, my town, and my school. Also like her, I spent time with grandmothers who saved me. Like Judith Wicks, I lovingly recall the holiness of family meals prepared by grandmothers. Can anyone talk of Grandmother without mentioning food?

Georgie Anne Geyer recalls a world in which girls were expected to be married before eighteen. Reading her powerful excerpt from her autobiography, I thought of my uncle's kind warning, "Don't get too much education or nobody will marry you." Like Joan Baez, I remember the first time I heard Belafonte and Pete Seeger. Like her, I recall great anxiety about public performances of any kind. Like Vivian Gornick, I was fascinated by adults with all their mysteries, moods, and conflicts. Like Marian Wright Edelman, I learned social responsibility from family. She writes, "I was always responsible to care for older relatives and neighbors. And everyone was our neighbor."

I remember the ugliness of small-town segregation. I recall cruelty to kids who were different and unable to defend themselves. The kids in my town played the germ game and wouldn't touch anyone who was "tainted." I can imagine the suffering of Jody Williams' brother who was deaf and schizophrenic.

Faye Wattleton lived less than one hundred miles from me, probably at the same time in another small Nebraska town. She was isolated by race and by her unusual minister mother; I was isolated by being non-Czech in all-Czech community and by my unusual doctor mother. Both of us recall the provinciality and clannishness of small towns as well as the bitter pain of rejection. Wattleton writes, "I cried a lot of tears in Nebraska." So did I. As I read her selection, I found myself wishing someday we could meet and tell each other our stories. In fact, I hoped this of many of the women in this book, and I think readers will feel the same way.

In *Girls Like Us*, the strongest connecting threads among the writers involve a love of reading. This anthology is written by voracious readers who all have similar stories, my stories. Like Agate Nesaule's, I remember my first awe-filled visit to a library. As a child, I read to calm down, to escape, to entertain myself. In books I found new worlds and, paradoxically, people more like me than my neighbors and family. I could identify with Geyer who writes, "As far back as I can remember I wanted to know — had to know — everything in the world." Like Geyer and Nesaule, I vowed to read every book in my small-town library.

Many of these women had lives "saved by books." However, so much passion aroused suspicion. I remember telling my dad how I loved books, even to hold them and smell them. He said, "Don't tell anyone that or they will think you are weird." When Nesaule read *Anna Karenina*, she was chastised by a teacher for selecting something too advanced. When I read certain books, I was accused of lying about them, of not really being able to understand what I claimed to have read.

In my small-town library, I found Pat Boone's book on teenagers, as well as *The Five Little Peppers and How They Grew, Black Beauty, The Hardy Boys, The Dana Sisters*, and *The Nancy Drew Mysteries*. I read biographies of athletes, war heroes, and presidents. All were good — I ate books. But the great books of my childhood were *The Diary of Anne Frank, Little Women*, and Betty Smith's *A Tree Grows in Brooklyn*.

Smith's book changed my life. She lived long before Carver ever wrote his first short story, but she told the truth about girlhood with all its pain, ugliness, complexity, intensity, joy, and beauty. I felt such comfort and pleasure in seeing some of my experience reflected, documented, and treated as important. For the first time in my life I felt that I was not alone. I was not the only one. The stories in *Girls Like Us* will do the same for a new generation of Ophelias.

Acknowledgments

It took many, many dedicated people to see this book realized.

For their encouragement, support, and words of wisdom, I would like to thank my team at New World Library: Marc Allen, Cathy Bodenman, Victoria Clarke, Marjorie Conte, Amy Garretson, Ryan Madden, Munro Magruder, and Tona Pearce Myers. A special thank you goes to Becky Benenate for spearheading this project and for her dedication throughout the creative process. Thanks are also due to Sue Arnold Mann and Judy Reeves, whose sharp editorial eye enhanced the words on the page, and to Kristin Fiore, whose research and sleuthing skills made the birth of this book possible. Peri Poloni and Mary Ann Casler helped create the identity of the book through their seasoned design skills.

Over the course of editing the book, many women spoke encouragingly of the concept and were particularly gracious with their time. Others generously donated their work because they believed in the message of this book. I would particularly like to thank Teresa Cader, Ruth Colvin, Toni DiFeliciantonio, Christy Haubegger, Dolores Huerta, Dorianne Laux, Anne Hitt Keiter, Dr. Shirley Ann Jackson, Devorah Major, Agate Nesaule, Dr. Antonia Coello Novello, Jane Shore, Katherine Soniat, Jane Wagner, Judith Wicks, and Jody Williams. I lift up all the contributors who willingly shared their experiences — without their messages there would be no book.

Extra doses of gratitude go to those who made the process of accessing some of the women and facilitating their discussions and interviews a relatively easy task, given amazing obstacles; specifically, Justin Arcangel, Laban Coblenz, Linette Lewis, Alex Marshall, Maj. Yvette Nonte, Gina Olaya-Quinton, Donelle Prado, and Ann Smith.

Finally, I would like to thank my family for loving me through my deadlines. Their generosity made writing time possible.

Introduction

When I started collecting stories of women's lives during their childhood and adolescence, I certainly understood that growing up is one of the universal themes of the popular culture. From fairy tales to feminist scholarship, you cannot escape the theme of childhood experience. But what I discovered through the course of assembling this anthology is what I trust is expressed through these pages: that growing up female is more than just a theme, it is a reflection of our reality — sometimes fictionalized, sometimes autobiographical, but always intensely personal. As these stories confirm, "growing up" is to grow up in the early decades of the twentieth century when phrases like the Great Depression had not yet made history. It is to grow up in the 1940s, or the 1950s, or the 1980s, when the definition of what it meant to be female — and express one's femininity — were in flux. It's to grow up in the Middle East, or China, or the United States, in diverse cultures amongst diverse social conventions, attitudes, and awarenesses. It's to grow up in a single-parent household, or a household of ten. Growing up, as expressed through these pages, is a universal collection of funny, heartfelt, and triumphant expressions of identity, family, girlfriends, idols, truths, and silly, one-of-a-kind moments — as told through the hearts and souls of some of the most interesting and progressive thinkers of the twentieth century.

As a whole, the collection is based on published writings, poems, songs, and letters that famous and not-so-famous women from diverse areas of life candidly share as their most memorable girlhood/womanhood experiences. Their topics of writing range from concepts of friendships to concepts of family, from sexual awareness to the awareness of the surrounding world, from true coming-of-age moments to indistinct pieces in time. There are both everyday experiences and true turning points in their childhood and adolescent years.

For many of these contributors, memories of childhood and adolescence are filled with the absurd and extraordinary. The rights of passage, lessons learned, and character traits claimed are deeply felt moments in their lives. In *Paula*, Isabel Allende tells of her parents' ingenuity in allowing her to express her creativity; Amy Tan explores the life of a young girl and her relationship to her mother and the girl next door in *The Joy Luck Club*; a girl named Martha attempts to define truth in Marta Salinas's short story, "The Scholarship Jacket." Whether autobiographical or fiction, many North American writers visit issues of identity and expression in their works, such as Bebe Moore Campbell's *Sweet Summer*, Margaret Atwood's *Cat's Eye*, and Georgie Anne Geyer's *Buying the Night Flight*. Likewise, mavericks — such as Faye Wattleton and Dolores Huerta — boldly speak out about how their checkered childhood has shaped them into being the determined leaders they are today. The lyrics, poetry, and other means of personal expression impart experiences unique to the women who have authored them.

As the voices of these pages struggle to conform to the expectations of their subcultures and grow into their womanhood, we too experience their confusion, love, joy, pain, and sorrow. We cry when Mr. Sweet dies in Alice Walker's short story "To Hell with Dying." We cheer on with Jackie Joyner Kersee's determinedness. We rejoice when Agate Nesaule learns to speak English. As participants who are allowed a glimpse of these women's lives or the girls whom they have chosen to write about, we remember, perhaps, similar feelings and experiences. And although ours may have been slightly bolder, or slightly more somber, experiences than say Vivian Gornick's transition through her preadolescence, we are propelled back into our childhood years and challenged to reclaim our own life stories, to reframe our own personal histories.

However symbolic of growing up, this anthology cannot possibly represent all the great stories of childhood — no single volume could. There are more than forty expressions of childhood and adolescence represented here as an accumulation of perspectives, heritage, and cultural or gender experiences. The collection organizes the material by theme, by some of the more common chords that writers touch on. The wealth of personal history and touching vignettes that have resulted from talks with and writings from these women is a testimony to how unique and yet universally true our personal histories can be. As almost a collection of "girlhood anecdotes," the book is meant to impart wisdom and perspective — we have only to look through these pages to recognize both the milestones and brief moments that have inextricably shaped us as women. How do the events of our youth affect our attitudes toward ourselves, our family, our community, and the global environment?

As women in this unique collection of writings convey, often there are no simple or uniform answers. But wherever we have grown up — whether a large metropolitan city in the United States or the farmlands of the European countryside — we can glean from these environments. We can embrace our childhoods as more than skipping rope or surviving high school, but as years of true discovery and transpiration, and a source of our strength.

— Gina Misiroglu
Los Angeles, California, Spring 1999

Identity

You grow up hearing things. I have an older brother, and when I was little we had this garage with a pinball machine, and all his friends would be over, and somebody would go, "Ah, she's psycho." Girls were always called psycho if they said to the guy, "Why did you break up with me?" or did anything like that. It was always, "Oh, she's psycho, she's a freak." So you grow up thinking that if you do anything, you're a psycho. And so I led my whole life being the pal, the buddy, the little sister with guys. And when I started to date, if they were awful to me, I'd be like, "Oh, that's cool. Sure, walk all over me. No problem." All because I never wanted to be called psycho.

— Wynona Ryder, as quoted in *Los Angeles Magazine*

Ani DiFranco

Not a Pretty Girl

i am not a pretty girl
that is not what i do
i ain't no damsel in distress
and i don't need to be rescued
so put me down punk
wouldn't you prefer a maiden fair
isn't there a kitten
stuck up a tree somewhere

i am not an angry girl
but it seems like
i've got everyone fooled
every time i say something
they find hard to hear
they chalk it up to my anger
never to their own fear
imagine you're a girl
just trying to finally come clean
knowing full well they'd prefer
you were dirty
and smiling
i'm sorry
but i am not a maiden fair
and i am not a kitten
stuck up a tree somewhere

generally my generation
wouldn't be caught dead
working for the man

and generally i agree with them
trouble is you got to have yourself
an alternate plan
i have earned my disillusionment
i have been working all my life
i am a patriot
i have been fighting the good fight
and what if there are
no damsels in distress
what if i knew that
and i called your bluff
don't you think every kitten
figures out how to get down
whether or not you ever show up

i am not a pretty girl
i don't really want to be a pretty girl
i want to be more than a pretty girl

—∘∘—

Ani DiFranco (1970 –) began singing and playing acoustic guitar when she was nine, moved out of her parents' home in Buffalo, New York, at fifteen, started writing songs about the same time, and founded her record company, the aptly named Righteous Babe Records, when she turned twenty. Twelve albums and well over a thousand concerts later, the *New York Times* now calls the twenty-seven-year-old "one of the country's most successful completely independent musicians." In recent years DiFranco has toured with Bob Dylan, collaborated with storyteller Utah Phillips, recorded with the Buffalo Philharmonic Orchestra, covered a classic hymn and a Bacharach/David pop hit, and paid tribute in concert to both Woody Guthrie and The Artist (formerly known as Prince). The result? Political, poetic, and intensely personal music that is impossible to pigeonhole. This song appears on the album *Not a Pretty Girl*.

Georgie Anne Geyer

Starting on the South Side

> "Women have a much better time than men in this world;
> there are far more things forbidden them."
> — Oscar Wilde

Like so many things, it all started with a small obsession. When I was only seven or eight, I used to lie in my comfortable old German bed at night, in every respect a most loved and blessed child, and think about it. What, I would wonder for reasons I have never totally understood, if only one person had the truth and that person was a woman? She would not voice it because the women I knew did not speak out; and so the world would be denied this crucial truth.

Years later a famous Chicago architect told me that when he was about the same age, he was tuning in to the same waves when he also wondered, "If I knew the truth, would I tell a woman?" Even to his mother? The male answer: "No."

The life I started with was circumscribed to create the perfect wife and mother. The expectations were clear, and until I was well into adulthood, I never knew anyone who questioned them. In the forties and fifties, there was no women's movement, and the old feminist movement of the twenties had left little residue for our type of world. Too, World War II had left the United States with men who craved the hearth and women who craved their men.

My future seemed engraved in stone. I would be the first generation of our family to receive a college education. I might work for no more than two or three years (but only as an "experience" in life, certainly not to support myself or for the joy of some desired work), and then I would marry some stable, nonabrasive, amiable, boy-next-door "good provider" with whom I would settle down (nearby) and raise no more than two children. They, in turn, would then proceed to replace my life just as I had replaced my parents' lives.

When I was a young teenager — interested in all sorts of young men — my aunts and cousins would assure me, with that intense certainty of women throughout history, that this brief time would pass and I, too, would be accepted as a wife in the world of men. "You will be married before you are eighteen," they repeated solemnly. It was a promise and at the same time a benediction; it was one's entire and only reason for living.

I remember with absolute clarity how I would look them straight in the eye and say, quietly and respectfully but slowly and stubbornly, "I will not!"

But then I had always been extremely willful and often blindly determined. When I was a baby, I in effect named myself. They would say to me, "Georgie . . ." and I would say back, "Gee Gee," and that was the name that always stayed with me.

Perhaps it all never would have happened if the women around me — women I loved very deeply — when asked their opinions on something, even something domestic, wouldn't have always said with such resigned submission, "I only think what Joe thinks." Or Jim, or Bob, or Louie, or whichever "good provider" they had opted for. I remember lying awake at night, not brooding but repeating to myself with a deep obstinacy, "They won't get me." It was T. S. Eliot's "Music heard so deeply that it's not heard at all."

Despite the fact that I was born in 1935 in the midst of the Depression and that my parents did not have the fifty dollars to pay the doctor, I was always what one would now call, like some bogus FBI poster, a "wanted child." My adored brother, Glen, was ten years old at the time, so I came as rather a surprise into a difficult world. The country was collapsing into bits, and our family was not spared. Relatives moved in with parents or with the one person in the family who had work. We were lucky because my father had his own business and helped everyone else in quite extraordinarily generous ways. Across the ocean, darkness was settling over Europe and my brother would soon almost be killed in the near-sunset of Western civilization, but our immediate world remained solid. There was always about our family, and inside us, like a hard rock of certainty, a strong sense of good and evil, of white and black, of sureness about the world and the generosity that comes from that. Moreover, in concert with this was the absolute assurance that the United States was not just "a" country — the United States of America was the lodestone, the central planet from which the rest of the world spun off.

Our house, too, was the center of everything, and this does certain very special things for a child. It was just a little house, a simple dark brick bungalow no different physically from the endless streets of bungalows and big comforting trees on the Far South Side, but it was very different inside. Everyone came to us. We did virtually all of the entertaining, and in the summer everyone came to our Wisconsin summer home. It seemed quite natural, and it also gave me a strong, secure sense of "being" very early on. Because of an odd mixture of personalities in the family — a mixture that could have been as disastrous as it was creative — we were the first ones to try everything. Much, much later, when we were both adults and he had children of his own, my first boyfriend, Richard Siegle, said to me, "Your family did everything first. You water-skied first. You were the first to slice open the hot dogs before you barbecued them." Big, important things like that!

When my mother died in 1979, handing me the one unsustainable blow in life that I never quite believed would or could come, the minister praised her so correctly as a "woman who created neighborhoods" wherever she went. This was so true; it was a gift of God that was hers. But we were so infinitely blessed in our neighbors, who became — and still are — our real extended family. There were the Siegle family next door, the Lengeriches across the alley (we had real alleys in those days too) and the Beukes and Bailleses next door. Our homes were extensions of each other. These wonderful people are still my rock and my solace.

But if ours was first of all a happy, prosperous family life, on the other hand hard work in the Germanic sense was expected of everybody, and everybody, moreover, was expected to enjoy it.

My father had a dairy business at 7749 South Carpenter Street that thrived precisely off the sheer amount of blood and sweat he and my grandmother, "Oma," poured into it. He would get up at three in the morning and run two of the most important routes, then come home for a big lunch that was really a European-style dinner, sleep, and go back to the dairy to work. Oma, who had come over from the German section of Poland near present-day Poznan in steerage when she was sixteen, heaved the milk pails around with the best of the men. But when she dressed up in her fine lace and beaded clothes, in her elegant big house with the Czechoslovakian china and the German crystal, she was the envy of any grand lady.

In contrast to the hardworking but fun-loving nature of the house, my religious life hovered like a slightly threatening angel. I was sent to a Baptist Sunday school with a straightlaced, terribly decent and highly puritanical family down the block. Not only did I believe in God, heaven, and angels, but I took totally to heart the Baptist maxim that one must "convert" and "bear witness to" one's loved ones. Whenever my mother's father and mother came out from the North Side, I became anxious and puzzled. My grandfather, Carl Gervens, a lovely, gentle, scholarly man from the Rhineland, was a German socialist and skeptic. He was not about to be "saved." I simply did not know what to do.

But this early experience with religious absolutism is not something I really regret. It helped me to gain a strong moral sense — and a sense that life was meant to be a dedication, not simply a pastime. When, during my university years, I gradually lost an organized faith, it was a great and disturbing loss for me; I have wondered since whether work, when central and crucial to us, does not become an internal search or a substitute for the lost or wayward outer God we now seek inside us. My propensity for otherworldliness fed by constant reading, I divided the world into two spheres, both of which were deep and sometimes terrifyingly real to me. One was the world here and now, the hearty bourgeois world around our breakfast table. The other world was the "heaven" of our Sunday school . . . the languorous clouds in the sky . . . the world beyond our worlds beyond the horizon. I remember how excited I became one day when both worlds collided with a great *Götterdämmerung* crash in my mind. I was poring over the atlas, one of my favorite pastimes, and I discovered that Bethlehem, which had always been a metaphysical concept for me, really existed. On a map! I was overcome with a throbbing excitement for days.

Juxtaposed to my literary daydreaminess was a very, very real world. There was Chicago with its political corruption, its racial hatred, and its Mafia operations and a citizenry that accepted all of this as natural. It was this tribal morality that fed the growing flames of my hatred for injustice and my desire both to protect myself from this parasitical world and to fight it and to try to change it.

Perhaps most important, hovering always just over the horizon, both terribly appealing and terribly threatening, was the black community. It hung there like a cloud on the horizon — but I had always loved the rain and the wind, and so I was fascinated by it. Most of the people in our neighborhood feared or hated blacks; to me they represented my first fascination with another culture. It was forbidden — and thus needed desperately to be known. I probed it, but carefully; occasionally I would venture a little way into it and sit on the stoops (we had stoops in those days and in those neighborhoods) and talk to the old "Negro" men and try to learn about them.

Much later, when I worked on the *Chicago Daily News,* I tried to repay the black community just a little for all it had suffered at our hands. I initiated and got printed the first series on the black community that any Chicago paper ever printed. We had thirty-eight parts to it — in fact, once we did it, we overdid it!

But in many ways life was also so snug and cozy that to this day my closest and most loyal friends are those from the "old neighborhood." We had "old countries" and "old neighborhoods" and "new neighborhoods" then, you see, and those who "made it" might move away but were never really hated for it — envied a little, maybe — because they always came back and never forgot their friends in the "old" neighborhood. Indeed, one success was everyone's in this basically tribal milieu.

In this environment my big, stubborn, honest father stood out like a beacon of honesty, if not of understanding. Both an admirable man and a difficult man, he was a typical "mountain man" of southern Germany. He had hands like great hams, and he stood well over six feet tall and weighed sometimes more than 250 pounds. He terrified my boyfriends.

He was absolutely incorruptible, with that dire, unforgiving honesty of self-made men whose honesty is both a heartfelt thing and a dare against the world they have bested.

In the midst of the Depression, before I was born, the dairy business on the South Side of Chicago was fraught with corrupt building inspectors looking for payoffs, with Mafia "enforcers," and with big dairies driving out small dairies like ours with bribes of five thousand or ten thousand dollars — substantial amounts of money at that time. If you were not Irish or one of the "machine" ethnic groups, you weren't in — especially Germans, with their individualistic tendencies toward their own businesses. My father had the dubious "honor," when he was a boy at Twenty-first and Lowe, of having to avoid the Reagan's Colts, an Irish gang that included such boys as Richard J. Daley and his cronies. This left him with a deep hated for "the machine" and its bullies. He overcame by being so big he simply threw Mafia bullies and others out physically.

I inherited this white, burning hatred. I was capable of being moved to tears when I was only seven or eight by the pictures in the paper of mobsters bombing union leaders' homes. I was never one of those suburban relativists, bred in suburbia where liberalism was easy; life for me was real because there was always a very real bully on every block.

In the early days of the Depression, before I was born, the White Castle route, a large and money-making route of hamburger stands all over the city, opened up for bids. They were little white-brick "castles" and the hamburgers were flat, good, and cheap — five cents in those days.

A story that became one of the little myths by which we lived was born when my father, Robert, went to Mr. Lewis, then president of the White Castle chain, and told him flatly, "I'm not going to offer you one cent in bribes. I couldn't, and I wouldn't if I could. But I'll give you the best milk and the best service you'll find anywhere."

Mr. Lewis, another rare, honest man, accepted the offer on the spot. The Geyer's Dairy chocolate milk was so rich that the White Castles just whipped it up and there you had creamy milk shakes. Thanks to all of those little white "castles," we became moderately well-to-do.

But my father worked so hard — and he had been forced to do so since he had to quit school at thirteen when my grandfather abandoned the family — that he had little time or few emotional resources for bouncing a blond little girl on his knee. Robert Geyer was an endlessly good man, but he was often, like many self-made men, remote, given to fitful rages, to lengthy soliloquies, or to endless silences.

I loved my father, and I never blamed him for anything, for how can you honestly blame someone for not giving you something he didn't have to give? I reacted with his same stubbornness and determination, by turning to work and accomplishment in order to "earn" love. I dealt with everything by going my own way, by doing, doing, doing. Later in my life it took me a long, painful time to figure out why my accomplishments didn't bring me love from other men, either, but instead only competitive resentment and rage of a new sort.

I guess I realize most poignantly what I missed when I was sixteen, already graduated from high school with highest honors, and we were out in Palm Springs visiting relatives. On a particularly pleasant starry night, after visiting relatives whom my father especially liked, we were walking across the moon-baked desert and my now more relaxed father put his arm around Mother and me. It was a singular, transcendent experience, just having my father put his arm around me. Although no one ever knew it, tears filled my eyes. It was the first time I could ever remember his touching me.

That a man was rough in manner and as remote in emotions as my father should have married my mother, a beautiful and refined young "lady" from the North Side, was still another curiosity. She was just as refined as he was rough; she was just as needing and giving of love and emotional expression as he was incapable of giving it. He was a "good provider," she always stressed, and he was certainly a good man; but he was a damned hard man to live with.

When I was born, for instance (and the birth took some forty-eight hours), my father used the time to put in the cement driveway beside the house, never once calling the hospital. He wasn't being intentionally cruel at all; he just thought that was a good time to put in the cement driveway.

It was my mother, Georgie Hazel, named after her grandfather, who taught me to read and write when I was four, sitting at a little table out in the sunlight at our lake house; it was my mother from whom I got affection and, generally, approval from my work. We traveled together. She laid the foundation for the curiosity that drove me to Siberia, up the Tapajoz, and down to Abu Dhabi (perhaps I did overreact a bit). And while the Geyers gave me their stubbornness and determination, I think it was her far more cultured family of Rhineland Germans who gave me whatever sensitivities I had.

But it was my mother, too, I think who quite unknowingly instilled in me a deep dissatisfaction with the "woman's role." She always insisted she wanted nothing except a family; yet she always complained bitterly about "all the work" at home. I realized much, much later that this tall, graceful, lovely woman was complaining not about "all the work" but about the fact that she was not rewarded by my father with the outward shows of affection that she, a tender and affectionate woman who would have bloomed under the lifelong gaze of a man capable of tenderness, so needed. In turn she became somewhat possessive of her children, wanting us by her side and wanting, I am certain, me to replace her in her position, as unhappy as she had often been with it. My choosing a profession, I am sure, struck her as a betrayal until late in life, when she came to understand and even prize it.

The third great influence on my life was my brother, Glen. Ten years older than me, tall, handsome, charming, and far too generous, Glen was in many ways a young, surrogate father to me. When I was just a baby, he took me under the long wing of his long arms and unwittingly prepared me for a world that would be a stage.

Glen, later to become a leading dress designer, had a genuine artistic sense that I never even approached; everything he touched turned to beauty. For me he created a marvelous fantasy world. He turned everything into a kind of theater for me, and so I learned early how to move in the kind of world of half-reality and half-fantasy that I eventually created for myself. I could have done little that I have done without him, his constant support, and his love.

But no amount of scrutiny of my childhood can explain why I wound up in Guatemala stumbling through the mountains . . . or in Cairo talking with Anwar Sadat . . . or in the rice paddies of South Vietnam . . .

or listening during a vicious sandstorm in Khartoum while American diplomats were gunned to death by Palestinian terrorists. . . . But as far back as I can remember, I wanted to know — I had to know — everything in the world. At ten I wrote a 110-page book (with myself as the heroine, naturally). In high school, in the absence of any guidance, I read right through the library. Even as a child I was terribly concerned about truth — truth, that is, in the sense of "what is" in the world. I was also concerned about those "couriers" who carried truth. I looked outward for truth, not inward, and broadcast it with the ardor of the missionary I once wanted to be. Eventually I chose journalism because — in opposition, for instance, to philosophy, where truth was theoretical — our truths were concrete and approachable, if only because they were small, relative truths.

—ɔ·ɔ—

Georgie Anne Geyer's (1935 –   ) syndicated column appears in more than one hundred newspapers in the United States and Latin America. A journalist since 1960, Geyer is a regular panelist on Public Television's *Washington Week in Review.* Throughout her years as the first woman foreign correspondent of our times, she has interviewed hundreds of world leaders, including Presidents George Bush and Ronald Reagan, Prime Minister Shimon Peres of Israel, PLO President Yassar Arafat, President Anwar Sadat of Egypt, Prince Sihanouk of Cambodia, King Hussein of Jordan, and President Muammar Khadafy of Libya. She was the first foreign journalist to interview Saddam Hussein of Iraq in 1973 in Baghdad, and the last American to interview Argentine President Juan Peron before his death. In addition to her column, Geyer is a regular contributor to magazines and has written seven books, including *Guerrilla Prince: The Untold Story of Fidel Castro* (1993), *Waiting for Winter to End: An Extraordinary Journey through Soviet Central Asia* (1994), and *Americans No More: The Death of Citizenship* (1996). She is currently at work on *The War against English: America on the Brink of Bilingualism.* This excerpt is from her autobiography, *Buying the Night Flight* (1983).

bell hooks

Bone Black

Good hair — that's the expression. We all know it, begin to hear it when we are small children. When we are sitting between the legs of mothers and sisters getting our hair combed. Good hair is hair that is not kinky, hair that does not feel like balls of steel wool, hair that does not take hours to comb, hair that does not need tons of grease to untangle, hair that is long. Real good hair is straight hair, hair like white folk's hair. Yet no one says so. No one says Your hair is so nice, so beautiful because it is like white folk's hair. We pretend that the standards we measure our beauty by are our own invention — that it is the questions of time and money that lead us to make distinctions between good hair and bad hair. I know from birth that I am lucky, lucky to have hair at all for I was bald for two years, then lucky finally to have thin, almost straight hair, hair that does not need to be hot-combed.

We are six girls who live in a house together. We have different textures of hair, short, long, thick, thin. We do not appreciate these differences. We do not celebrate the variety that is ourselves. We do not run our fingers through each other's dry hair after it is washed. We sit in the kitchen and wait our turn for the hot comb, wait to sit in the chair by the stove, smelling grease, feeling the heat warm our scalp like a sticky hot summer sun.

For each of us getting our hair pressed is an important ritual. It is not a sign of our longing to be white. It is not a sign of our quest to be beautiful. We are girls. It is a sign of our desire to be women. It is a gesture that says we are approaching womanhood — a rite of passage. Before we reach the appropriate age we wear braids and plaits that are symbols of our innocence, our youth, our childhood. Then we are comforted by the parting hands that comb and braid, comforted by the intimacy and bliss. There is a deeper intimacy in the kitchen on Saturday when hair is pressed, when fish is fried, when sodas are passed around, when soul music drifts over the talk. We are women together. This is our ritual and our time. It is a time without men. It is a time when we work to meet each other's needs, to make each other beautiful in whatever way we can. It is a time of laughter and mellow talk. Sometimes it is an occasion for tears and sorrow. Mama is angry, sick of it all, pulling the hair too tight, using too much grease, burning one ear and then the next.

At first I cannot participate in this ritual. I have good hair that does not need pressing. Without the hot comb I remain a child, one of the uninitiated. I plead, I beg, I cry for my turn. They tell me once you start you will be sorry. You will wish you had never straightened your hair. They do not understand that it is not the straightening I seek but the chance to belong, to be one in this world of women. It is finally my turn. I am happy. Happy even though my thin hair straightened looks like black thread, has no body, stands in the air like ends of barbed wire, happy even though the sweet smell of unpressed hair is gone forever. Secretly I had hoped that the hot comb would transform me, turn the thin good hair into thick nappy hair, the kind of hair I like and long for, the kind you can do anything with, wear in all kinds of styles. I am bitterly disappointed in the new look.

Later, a senior in high school, I want to wear a natural, an Afro. I want never to get my hair pressed again. It is no longer a rite of passage, a chance to be intimate in the world of women. The intimacy masks betrayal. Together we change ourselves. The closeness is an embrace before parting, a gesture of farewell to love and one another.

—❦❦—

Social critic, educator, and writer, *bell hooks* (1955 –) is an assistant professor of Afro-American studies and English at Yale University. She is the author of more than a dozen books, including *Sisters of the Yam: Black Women and Self-Recovery* (1993), *Teaching to Transgress: Education as the Practice of Freedom* (1994), *Outlaw Culture* (1994), *Art on My Mind: Visual Politics* (1995), and *Killing Rage: Ending Racism* (1995). Her memoir, *Remembered Rapture*, the third in a trilogy, was recently published, as was her first children's book, *Happy to Be*

Nappy (both 1999). Born Gloria Watkins, she writes under the name bell hooks, the name of her great-grandmother, to pay homage to the unheard voice of black women past and present. This excerpt is from *Bone Black: Memories of Girlhood* (1996).

Jane Shore

The Slap

In 1959, at Horace Mann Elementary
in North Bergen, New Jersey,
wearing white on Wednesday meant you were a virgin,
wearing red on Thursday meant you were a lesbian,
wearing green on Friday meant you were a tramp.

The gymnasium, with its locker room and showers
and drains, moldered in the basement.
Sanitary napkin dispensers were always empty,
and the changing room with stalls for privacy
had white flapping curtains that didn't quite close.
I undressed, and put on my grey cotton gymsuit
out in the open with the other girls.

The gym teacher, Miss Piano, wore a Dutch-boy haircut.
Her legs were as solid as a baby grand's.
She called us by our last names, like privates in the army,
and clapped, as each girl climbed the ropes
and disappeared into girders and beams
and caged light fixtures on the ceiling.
When my turn came,
I gripped the lowest knot and dangled down;
my legs drawn up, I looked like a dying spider.

On wooden bleachers, chummy as sorority sisters
the lucky girls who had their periods
gossiped and did their homework
after handing Miss Piano a note from the nurse.
Where was my excuse?

After gym class, I'd undress in my own stall,
stuffing my gymsuit back into its mildewed bag.
But first, I'd examine my underpants
for the red smear of "the curse."
The last of my friends, the last of the last.
No luck, I'd swathe myself again
in my neutral clothing.

When one morning, I woke up,
two black ink blots staining my pajamas,
I dragged my mother out of bed to tell her.
We squeezed into the bathroom
as if into our clubhouse,
as if she were about to show me the secret handshake.

Blushing, leaking, I sat on the tub's rim,
as if poised over the mikveh, the ritual bath.
Stuffed inside my underpants,
the bulky Kotex, safety pins, and elastic sanitary belt
I had stored in my closet for over a year.
My mother took a seat on the toilet lid.
"Ma," I shyly said, "I got my period,"
then leaned over to receive her kiss,
her blessing.

She looked as though she were going to cry.
In her blue nylon nightgown, her hairnet
a cobweb stretched over her bristling curlers,
my mother laughed, tears in her eyes,
and yelled, "Mazel Tov! Now you are a woman!
Welcome to the club!"
and slapped me across the face —
for the first and last time ever —

"*This* should be the worst pain you ever know."

An accomplished poet, *Jane Shore*'s (1947 –) first book of poems, *Eye Level* (1977), won the 1977 Juniper Prize, and her second book, *The Minute Hand* (1987), won the 1986 Lamont Poetry Prize, awarded by the Academy of American Poets. Her third book, *Music Minus One* (1996), was a finalist in poetry for the 1996 National Book Critics Circle Award. Shore was a Briggs-Copeland Lecturer on English at Harvard University and was a visiting distinguished poet at the University of Hawaii. Her poems have been published in numerous magazines, including *Poetry* (for which she received the Bess Hokin Award), *The New Republic, Ploughshares,* and *The Yale Review*. Her forthcoming book, tentatively titled *Happy Family*, is due out in fall 1999. Shore currently teaches at the George Washington University in Washington, DC. This poem is taken from *Music Minus One*.

Joan Baez
My Memory's Eye

I began the eleventh grade at Palo Alto High School, which did not have a Mexican problem because all the Mexicans lived in nearby San Jose. Aside from the expected bouts of nausea and anxiety that were simply a part of my life, I fit in surprisingly well. I was finding friends through a more unlikely source, too — the Quakers, or more specifically, their social action wing, the American Friends Service Committee. That year, along with three hundred other students, I attended a three-day conference on world issues held at Asilomar, a beautiful spot on the pine-speckled foggy beaches of Monterey. Not only did I fall in love with ten or twelve boys at once, but I was galvanized by the discussions, inspired in the way I had never been before. I found that I spoke forcefully in groups both large and small, and was regarded as a leader.

There was great excitement about our main speaker, a twenty-seven-year-old black preacher from Alabama named Martin Luther King, Jr. He was a brilliant orator. Everyone in the room was mesmerized. He talked about injustice and suffering, and about fighting with the weapons of love, saying that when someone does evil to us, we can hate the evil deed but not the doer of the deed, who is to be pitied. He talked specifically about boycotting busses and walking to freedom in the South, and about organizing a nonviolent revolution. When he finished his speech, I was on my feet, cheering and crying: King was giving a shape and a name to my passionate but ill-articulated beliefs. Perhaps it was the fact of an actual movement taking place, as opposed to the scantily attended demonstrations I had known to date, which gave me the exhilarating sense of "going somewhere" with my pacifism.

It was also through the Quakers that I met Ira Sandperl the following year. One sunny day at Meeting, in place of the usual sinking Sunday boredom, there was a conversation with a funny, brilliant, cantankerous, bearded, shaven-headed Jewish man in his early forties with immense, and immensely expressive, eyes. I couldn't know when I first met him that he would end up being my political/spiritual mentor for the next few decades.

Ira read to the teenage First Day School from Tolstoy, the Bhagavad-Gita, Lao-tse, Aldous Huxley, the Bible and other texts we had never discussed in high school. For the first time in my life I looked forward to going to Meeting. Ira was a Mahatma Gandhi scholar, an advocate of radical nonviolent change. Like Gandhi, he felt that the most important tool of the twentieth century was organized nonviolence. Gandhi had taken the concept of Western pacifism, which is basically personal, and extended it into a political force, insisting that we stand up to conflict and fight against evil, but do so with the weapons of nonviolence. I had heard the Quakers argue that the ends did not justify the means. Now I was hearing that the means would determine the ends. It made sense to me, huge and ultimate sense.

Ira adhered to nonviolence with a kind of ferocity which would eventually come to me as well. People would accuse us of being naive and impractical, and I was soon telling them that it was they who were naive and impractical to think that the human race could continue on forever with a buildup of armies, nation states, and nuclear weapons. My foundations in nonviolence were both moral and pragmatic.

One day it was announced at school that we were to have an air raid drill: three bells would ring in sharp succession, and we would all get up quietly from our seats and calmly find our ways home. We could call our parents, or hitch rides, or whatever we pleased, but the point was to get home and sit in our cellars and pretend we were surviving an atomic blast. The idea, of course, was as ludicrous then as it is now — despite the fact that in the atomic fever of the 1950s even some fairly sensible people were stocking their cellars with drums of water, saltines, and Tang.

I went home and hunted through my father's physics books to confirm what I already knew — that the time it took a missile to get from Moscow to Paly High was not enough time to call our parents or walk home. I decided to stay in school as a protest against misleading propaganda.

I was in French class when the three bells rang, and with pounding heart, I remained seated and reading. The teacher, a kindly foreign exchange teacher from Italy, waved me toward the door.

"I'm not going," I said.

"*Now* what ees eet."

"I'm protesting this stupid air raid drill because it is false and misleading. I'm staying here, in my seat."

"I don't theek I understand," he said.

"That's OK. Neither will anybody else."

"*Comme vous étes un enfant terrible!*" he mumbled as he left the room, shaking his head and tucking his multitude of disorganized notes higher under one arm.

The next day I was on the front page of the local paper, photograph and all, and for many days thereafter letters to the editor streamed in, some warning that Palo Alto had communist infiltrators in its school system.

Having opposed it before, my father now seemed pleased with my bold public action: I may have proven to him that I was serious about something aside from boys. My mother thought it was wonderful.

The action delighted Ira and cemented our relationship, to the great unhappiness of his wife. We'd walk for hours around the Stanford campus, talking and laughing until we were in tears at the folly of humankind, then we'd plan future actions to organize a nonviolent revolution to create a better world. I was enormously happy. My father was nervous about Ira and thought I should be paying more attention to school and studies.

"Doesn't this man have a wife?" he asked Mom. But Ira and I have such a unique and special relationship that neither of us has ever adequately defined it: a platonic, deeply spiritual relationship, bound by the commitment to nonviolence and tempered with loud and frequent laughter and a healthy cynicism about the state of the world.

Ira and politics didn't diminish the excitement I found in music. For fifty dollars of my own money I had acquired an old Gibson guitar. I don't know now how I ever got my fingers wrapped far enough around the neck to press down on the strings. When I stood up the belly of the guitar reached almost to my knees, and I had to hunch over to get a grip. (Not knowing much about guitars I never thought to shorten the shoulder strap.) There's an old photo of me singing at the college prom, dressed in a white evening gown with black straps that [my aunt] Pauline had sewn for herself the year before, topped with a silver lamé bolero my mother made especially for me. I have bare feet. My hair is in a pageboy, cowlick poking up gaily, sabotaging my attempts to look sultry. My mouth is a gob of lipstick and my eyebrow pencil is carefully tailored for the Liz Taylor look. The guitar is hanging down on one hip, which is appropriately cocked to balance it. I look sort of funny and sort of sweet. On the one hand I thought I was pretty hot stuff, but on the other, I was still terribly self-conscious about my extremely flat chest and dark skin.

I was offered my first out-of-town job by a teacher from Paradise High School who'd heard me sing at the Asilomar conference. Although I wasn't paid, my air fare was taken care of, and bumping through the clouds toward Paradise on a small aircraft (somewhere near Sacramento, California) I felt both very proud and very afraid. I was truly fawned over on this trip. Senior girls battled over whose house I should stay in and teachers wanted me to visit their classes. The father of one of the girls was a Shriner who dragged me off to sing at a dance hosted by members of his club. After three songs I sat down to have a Shirley Temple and a red-eyed old Shriner teetered over, put his arm around me and said in a kindly way, but with breath that could have withered a young oak, "You've got a helluva voice, kid. Don't sign cheap." I was far from signing anything, but I was blossoming in the attention.

I discovered the magnificent voice of Harry Belafonte. [My favorite aunt] Tia told me about a man named Pete Seeger who was the daddy of folk music and I went to see him when he came to town, and soon after that heard the music of the queen of folk music, Odetta. I was slowly drifting from "Annie Had a Baby" and "Young Blood" to Belafonte's "Scarlet Ribbons," Pete Seeger's "Ain't Gonna Study War No More" and Odetta's "Lowlands," all of which I attacked with deadly seriousness.

My mother and father loved me to sing at gatherings of friends and students in our living room, and I was happy to oblige. I had no idea what Pauline thought of my new role, but [my sister] Mimi liked it, and was herself soon to take up the guitar, which she would eventually play much better than I.

I was performing all the time. I sang at lunchtime and in the All Girls' Talent Show. I sang at other high schools' proms and in smoky dives for the parents of friends. And I was developing stage fright. Sometimes I was convinced that I had the flu — easy to believe with a headache, sore throat, nausea, stomach cramps, dizziness, and sweating fits. Once, at age sixteen, I had a terrible attack that turned my insides to water and had me crouching on the floor of the ladies' room in a dance hall where I was scheduled to sing a couple of songs. A kindly woman felt my forehead and proclaimed a fever, called my parents, and sent me home. As soon as I was safely in the living room, in front of the fire with a cup of tea, all my symptoms vanished, and I stayed up and plunked and sang happily into the night. That, to my memory, is the only time I didn't make it onto the stage.

Once I reached the stage, my voice usually functioned on cue, although occasionally the demons would strike during the concert. I would get short of breath, feel faint, or develop double vision; the words of the song would lose their meaning, or sound like a foreign language, and my terror would mount until I thought I would burst and evaporate into a dust cloud. By screaming silently to myself that I would be okay, I could usually overcome the sensations.

Still, singing helped me cope with the inevitable, overwhelming sexual tensions and excitement of adolescence. I flirted furiously from behind my guitar, sometimes staring into the eyes of one unsuspecting boy for an entire song. If he was tough, he'd look back the whole time. If he was with a girlfriend, the game was even more exhilarating. If the gaze really lasted, I'd feel myself go red and prickly from my toes to my scalp. There was no way to follow up on those forbidden stares, which was no doubt why I indulged in them so often. I flirted and sang, and developed a reputation for both.

By the time I reached my senior year, I had boyfriends: Sammy Leong, the only one my mother ever wanted me to marry (she wanted a Chinese Mexican grandchild); a football-playing born-again Christian with whom I tore around on motorcycles, squinting against the wind to see the speedometer top 110 while he shouted scripture over his shoulder; a millionaire Stanford student who bought me dresses and watches, and who would frown and pout when he was ticketed for speeding in his Ferrari, wait until the policeman had walked back to his car, then peel out from the curb with a great "HAH!" and race furiously into the next county, grinding his teeth and cursing to the accompaniment of screaming sirens. Through Ira I met Vance, whose name I thought was wonderful and who was an "intellectual"; I soon threw him over for Richard, who sat up all night necking with me on some streetlit steps where the air smelled of orange blossoms and gardenias. I didn't have friendships or affairs; I had escapades. I remained a virgin and kept myself in a psychic frenzy of unfulfilled crushes. My demons staged a powerful comeback, and finally, after a winter of seven colds and mounting attacks of nausea and despair, Mother packed me off to a psychiatrist.

I took a Rorschach test, identifying myriads of pelvises and skulls, and waited expectantly for the results so that I could be cured and feel better. To my great disappointment (I remember hot tears building up behind my downcast eyes), Dr. Heenen suggested that he did not have a crystal ball, and that all the inkblot test could do was help find a starting place. I was with him only a short while before we moved, but I shall never forget that one day, when I was so frightened and anxious that I had curled up on the floor of his office, he reached out and took my hand, and I felt as if someone had saved me from drowning. I didn't know then that my demons would never vanish, but I would have taken heart if I had known to what extent they could be placated, tricked, cajoled, and bargained with. The other day I gave a concert celebrating the twenty-seventh anniversary of my singing career. I looked out at the sparkling crowd of six thousand relaxed fans and marveled at how many years I had been walking out on stage. At that moment my stomach cramped up. I shook my head, laughed, and had a beer.

—❧❧—

Folk legend *Joan Baez* (1941 –) began performing in the Boston-Cambridge folk hotbed in the late 1950s; soon she was billed regularly at local clubs, and she played the first Newport Folk Festival in 1959. Her first album, *Joan Baez,* appeared in 1960, featuring her beautiful soprano voice and accompanied by her guitar. Within a few years her albums were hits, and Baez was donned the "Queen of Folk Music." She met Bob Dylan in Greenwich Village and convinced him to make guest appearances during her concerts. His songs gave her a vehicle for her emerging protest stance, and, in turn, she gave the rising star public exposure. As her successful career continued, protest took up more and more of her time. She founded the Institute for the Study of Nonviolence in Carmel, California, and spent time in jail for civil disobedience relating to Vietnam War protests. Baez has more than thirty albums, the latest being *Gone from Danger*. This excerpt is from her autobiography, *And a Voice to Sing With*.

Isabel Allende

Paula

"Listen, Paula. I am going to tell you a story so that when you wake up you will not feel so lost," Isabel Allende writes in the opening lines of Paula. Allende recalls her Chilean childhood and family history in an effort to chronicle her youth, adolescence, and womanhood for her daughter, Paula, who is in a coma. In this brief passage, Allende unfolds a period in her young life when she awakened to her creativity.

That same year, I was informed at school that babies are not brought by the stork but grow like melons in their mother's belly, and also that there was no such thing as good old Santa Claus, it was your parents who bought your Christmas presents. The first part of that revelation had little effect on me because I did not intend to have children just yet, but the second part was devastating. I planned to stay awake all Christmas Eve to discover the truth, but my best efforts failed, and I fell asleep. Tormented by doubts, I had written a letter, a kind of trap, asking for the impossible: another dog, a host of friends, and a list of toys. When I awoke on Christmas morning, I found a box containing bottles of tempera paint, brushes, and a clever note from that wretched Santa — whose writing looked suspiciously like my mother's — explaining that in order to teach me to be less greedy, he had not brought what I asked; instead, he was offering the walls of my room, where I could paint the dog, the friends, and the toys I had requested. I looked around and saw that several stern old portraits had been removed, along with a lamentable Sacred Heart of Jesus, and on the bare wall facing my bed was a color reproduction cut from an art book. My disenchantment immobilized me for a few minutes, but finally I pulled myself together sufficiently to examine the picture, which turned out to be a work by Marc Chagall. At first, all I could see were anarchical smudges, but soon I discovered on that small piece of paper an astounding universe of blue brides tumbling head over heels through the air and a pale musician floating amid a seven-armed candelabrum, a red nanny goat, and other mutable characters. There were so many different colors and objects that I was a long time taking in the marvelous disorder of the composition. That painting had music: a ticking clock, moaning violins, bleating goats, fluttering wings, and endless streams of words. It also had scents: lighted candles, wildflowers, an animal in heat, women's lotions and creams. The whole scene seemed bathed in the nebula of a happy dream; on one side the atmosphere was as warm as an afternoon siesta, and on the other you could feel the cool of a country night. I was too young to be able to analyze the artistry, but I remember my surprise and curiosity: that Chagall was an invitation to a game. I asked myself, fascinated, how it was possible to paint like that, without an ounce of respect for the norms of composition and perspective my art teacher was trying to instill. If this artist can do whatever he pleases, so can I, I concluded, opening the first bottle of tempera. For years I painted — freely, with unbounded pleasure — a complex mural in which were registered my desires, fears, rages, childhood doubts, and growing pains. In a place of honor, surrounded by delirious flora and impossible fauna, I drew the silhouette of a boy with his back turned as if looking at the mural. It was the portrait of Marc Chagall, with whom I had fallen in love as only children can. At the time I was furiously decorating the walls in my house in Santiago, Chile, the object of my love was sixty years older than I; he was famous throughout the world, he had just ended a long period of widowhood with a second marriage, and he lived in the heart of Paris . . . but distance and time are fragile conventions. I thought Chagall was a boy my own age and years later, in April 1985, when he died in the ninety-seventh year of his eternal youth, I found that in fact he had always been the boy I imagined. When we left that house and I had to bid my mural goodbye, my mother gave me a notebook in which to note down things I previously had painted: a notebook to record my life. "Here, write what's in your heart," she said. That is what I did then, and that is what I am doing now in these pages. What else can I do? I have time left over. I have the whole future ahead of me.

—ৎ৶১—

Isabel Allende (1942 –) grew up in Santiago, Chile, where she lived and worked as a journalist until 1973, when her uncle, President Salvador Allende, was assassinated in a military coup. Allende fled Chile and went into self-imposed exile in Venezuela, where she began writing her first highly acclaimed novel, *The House of the Spirits* (1985). Following its successful publication Allende published several other novels, including *Of Love and Shadows* (1987), *Eva Luna* (1987), and *The Infinite Plan* (1993), and her memoir, *Paula* (1995). Her latest book is *Aphrodite: A Memoir of the Senses* (1998).

Sally Fisher

News for the Cafeteria

News reached us in the high school cafeteria
that Darlene, the shapely one, who danced
to "The Breeze and I" in the sophomore show,
had eloped, on a school night, had climbed out
the window (left a note on the bed), and was gone.

How limber she must have been, in that one-
story ranch house, to roll through the narrow
horizontal window — up near the ceiling —
with a suitcase, and drop to the evergreen
shrubbery below. I never wondered then
why she hadn't used the door. To me,
perhaps to everyone in high school, out
the window was the only way to go.

The window had been my best hope for years:
when I lowered my dolls on ropes to see
the view, or coaxed a trembling squirrel over
the sill, me as still as Buddha with a
peanut. Or when I stared for hours into
the neighbor's guest room that never had a guest.
I was Rapunzel, longing for my great
release, impossible downstairs, through the door.

Even now I use the window when I can,
dropping down to city streets as if
it were water I moved in, and I lived
in a boat, and buildings and stores were coral reefs
waiting to be explored. I rise in the last
dark, press my palms through the yielding glass

and joining the predawn breeze I take my flight.
Sometimes, I turn back and see my room,
a charming little lamp-lit place, where one
could stage a play, or live an interesting life.

Sally Fisher (1939 –) grew up in Park Ridge, Illinois, a suburb of Chicago and the scene of Darlene's elopement. She now lives in New York City where she works as a freelance writer and editor. She is the author of two children's books, *The Tale of the Shining Princess* (1980) and *The Christmas Journey* (1993), and a book about art, *The Square Halo* (1995). Her poems have appeared in several magazines and anthologies.

Benazir Bhutto

Daughter of Destiny

Ghulam Murtaza Bhutto's son, my grandfather Sir Shah Nawaz, was the first to start breaking the Bhuttos away from the feudal ethos that was stifling a whole segment of society. Until his time, the Bhuttos had married only other Bhuttos, first cousins or, possibly, second. Islam entitled women to inherit property and the only way to keep the land within the family was through marriage. Such a "business" marriage had taken place between my father and his cousin Amir when he was only twelve and she eight or nine years older. He had resisted until my grandfather tempted him with a cricket set from England. After their marriage, Amir had returned to live with her family and my father had returned to school, leaving a lasting impression on him of the inequities, especially for the woman, of forced, family marriages.

At least Amir had married. When there was no suitable cousin in the family, the Bhutto women did not marry at all. For this reason my aunts, my grandfather's daughters from his first marriage, had remained single all their lives. Over great opposition from the family, my grandfather had allowed his daughters from his second marriage to marry outside the family, though they were not love matches, but strictly arranged affairs. A generation later, my sister, Sanam, would become the first Bhutto woman to make her own decision. Contrary to my expectations, I would follow the traditional path and have an arranged marriage myself.

Still, my grandfather was considered very progressive. He educated his children, even sending his daughters to school, an act that was considered scandalous by the other landowners. Many feudals did not even bother to educate their sons. "My sons have land. They have a guaranteed income, and will never become employees or work for anyone else. My daughters will inherit land, and be looked after by their husbands or their brothers. So why bother with education?" ran the feudal ethos.

My grandfather, however, had seen firsthand the advances being made by the educated Hindus and urban Muslims in Bombay, where he served in the government during the rule of the British raj. By educating his own children, Sir Shah Nawaz tried to set an example for the others Sindhi landowners so that after partition of India in 1947 and the establishment of independent Pakistan, our society would not stagnate. Despite the raised eyebrows of his peers, he sent my father abroad to study. My father had not disappointed him, graduating with honors from the University of California at Berkeley and then going on to read law at Christ Church, Oxford, and to be called to the bar at Lincoln's Inn before returning to Pakistan to practice law.

My mother, on the other hand, came from a new class of urban industrialists whose views were more cosmopolitan than those of the landowning class. While the Bhutto women still lived in *purdah*, rarely allowed to leave the four walls of their compounds and then completely covered in black *burqas*, my mother and her sisters went around Karachi without veils and drove their own cars. The daughters of an Iranian businessman, they had gone to college and after the birth of Pakistan had even served as officers in the National Guard, a paramilitary force of women. Such public exposure would have been impossible for the Bhutto women.

My mother became my father's second wife in 1951, Islam allowing a man to have up to four wives provided he treats them all fairly. After their marriage my mother entered *purdah* with the other Bhutto women, and at first was allowed to leave the compound only once a week to visit her family. But the old ways were getting tiresome to everyone. When my grandmother wanted to leave the family compound in Karachi and there was no driver available, she often asked my mother to drive her. When the family went to Al-Murtaza, my father insisted on staying with my mother in the women's wing instead of returning to the men's quarters. And when 70 Clifton was built there were no separate quarters provided for the women, though my grandfather bought a house opposite to meet his male visitors. A new and more enlightened generation was taking root in Pakistan.

In our male-dominated culture, boys had always been favored over girls and were not only more apt to be educated, but in extreme instances to be given food first while the mother and daughters waited. In our family, however, there was no discrimination at all. If anything, I received the most attention. The oldest of four, I was born in Karachi on June 21, 1953, my skin evidently so rosy that I was immediately nicknamed "Pinkie." My brother Mir Murtaza was born a year after me, Sanam in 1957, and the baby, Shah Nawaz, in 1958. As the firstborn, I held a special and sometimes lonely place in the family from the beginning.

I was only four and my father twenty-eight when he was first sent to the United Nations by the then president, Iskander Mirza. My father's subsequent government posts as commerce minister under President Ayub Khan, then as minister of energy, foreign minister, and leader of Pakistan's delegation to the United Nations off and on for seven years kept him and my mother away from home much of the time.

I saw my father as much on the front pages of newspapers as in person, arguing for Pakistan and other third world countries at the United Nations, negotiating a 1960 financial and technical assistance agreement with the Soviet Union, returning from forbidden Peking in 1963 with a border treaty peacefully ceding 750 square miles of disputed territory to Pakistan. My mother usually traveled with him, leaving the children at home with the household staff — and me. "Look after the other children," my parents would charge me. "You are the oldest."

I was only eight or so when I was left nominally in charge of the house when my parents were away. My mother would give me the money for food and household supplies, which I hid under my pillow. Though I was just learning my sums in school, every night in her absence I would climb on a stool in the kitchen and pretend to go over the accounts with Babu, our longtime and loyal majordomo. Whether the figures tallied, I have no recollection. Luckily very small sums were involved. At that time, ten rupees, about two dollars, bought food for the whole household.

In our house education was a top priority. Like his father before him, my father wanted to make examples of us, the next generation of educated and progressive Pakistanis. At three I was sent to Lady Jennings nursery school, then at five to one of the top schools in Karachi, the Covent of Jesus and Mary. Instruction at CJM was in English, the language we spoke at home more often than my parents' native languages of Sindhi and Persian or the national language, Urdu. And though the

Irish nuns who taught there divided the older students into houses with inspirational names like "Discipline," "Courtesy," "Endeavor," and "Service," they made no effort to convert us to Christianity. The school was too good a source of income for the missionaries who ran it to risk alienating the small numbers of Muslim families rich enough and far-sighted enough to educate their children.

"I ask only one thing of you, that you do well in your studies," my father told us over and over. As we grew older he hired tutors to instruct us in math and English in the afternoons after school and kept track of our school reports by phone from wherever he was in the world. Luckily I was a good student, for he had great plans for me to be the first woman in the Bhutto family to study abroad.

"You will pack your suitcases and I will take you to the airport to see you off" he started to say to the four of us as early as I can remember. "Pinkie will leave as a scruffy little kid and come back a beautiful young lady in a sari. Shah Nawaz will pack so many clothes his suitcase won't close. We will have to call Babu and ask him to sit on it."

There was no question in my family that my sister and I would be given the same opportunities in life as our brothers. Nor was there in Islam. We learned at an early age that it was men's interpretation of our religion that restricted women's opportunities, not our religion itself. Islam in fact had been quite progressive toward women from its inception, the Prophet Mohammed (PBUH)* forbidding the practice of killing female infants that was common among the Arabs of the time, and calling for women's education and their right to inherit long before these privileges were granted to them in the West.

Bibi Khadijah, the first convert to Islam, was a widow who ran her own business, employed the Prophet Mohammed (PBUH) when he was a young boy, and later married him. Umm e-Umara fought alongside the men in the Muslims' early battles against their enemies, her powerful sword arm saving the life of the Prophet (PBUH). Chand Bibi, the female ruler of the South Indian state of Ahmadnagar, defeated the mogul emperor Akbar and forced him to enter into a peace treaty with her.

---

* Peace Be Upon Him.

Noor-Jehan, the wife of Emperor Jehangir and the virtual ruler of India, was famous for her skill in the field of administration. Muslim history was full of women who had taken a public role and performed every bit as successfully as men. Nothing in Islam discouraged them, or me, from pursuing that course. "I have found a woman ruling over them. And she has been given abundance of all things and hers is a mighty throne," reads the sura of the Ant in the Holy Quran. "To men is allotted what they earn, and to women what they earn," reads the Women *sura*.

Every afternoon we read these and other *suras* from our Holy Book with the *maulvi* who came to the house after our academic tutoring to give us religious instruction. Reading the Holy Quran in Arabic and understanding its lessons was the most important subject of all. We spent hours struggling over the difficult Arabic, whose alphabet was similar to the one we used in Urdu but with totally different grammar and meanings, like the differences between English and French.

"Paradise lies at the feet of the mother," our *maulvi* taught us during those afternoons, citing the Quranic injunction to always be kind to one's parents and to obey them. Not surprisingly, it was an instruction my mother would often use to keep us in line. The *maulvi* taught us, too, that our actions on earth would determine our destiny in the afterlife. "You will have to cross above a valley of fire and the bridge will be a hair. Do you know how thin a hair is?" he said with great drama. "Those who have committed sin will fall into the fire of hell and burn, whereas those who have been good will cross into Paradise where milk and honey flow like water."

It was my mother, however, who taught me the rituals of prayer. She took her faith very seriously. No matter where she was in the world, or what she was doing, she prostrated herself five times a day in prayer. When I was nine years old, she began to include me, slipping into my bedroom to lead me in the morning prayer. Together we would perform the *wuzoo*, the washing of our hands, feet, and faces so that we would be pure before God, then prostrate ourselves facing west toward Mecca.

My mother is a Shiite Muslim, as are most Iranians, while the rest of the family was Sunni. But that was never a problem. Shiites and Sunnis had lived side by side and intermarried for over a thousand years and our differences were far fewer than our similarities. What was fundamental was that all Muslims, regardless of their sects, surrender to the will of God, and believe that there is no God but Allah and Mohammed is his last Prophet. That is the Quranic definition of a Muslim and, in our family, what mattered most.

During *muharram*, the month commemorating the massacre of the Prophet's grandson Imam Hussein at Karbala in Iraq, I would sometimes dress all in black and go with my mother to join other women in the Shiite rituals. "Follow closely," my mother would say to me, for the Shiite ceremonies were more elaborate than those of the Sunnis. I never took my eyes off the speaker, who dramatically recaptured the tragedy that befell Imam Hussein and his small band of followers at Karbala, where they were ambushed and brutally slaughtered by the troops of the usurper Yazid. No one was spared, not even the little children who fell under Yazid's knives. Imam Hussein was beheaded, and his sister Zeinab was made to walk bareheaded to Yazid's court, where she watched the tyrant play with the head of her brother. But instead of allowing her spirit to be broken, Bibi Zeinab became filled with resolve, as did the other followers of Imam Hussein. Their descendants, known today as the Shiites, never let themselves forget the tragedy at Karbala.

"Hear the little baby cry for water," the speaker called out, her voice filled with emotion. "Feel the heart of the mother, hearing the cry of her child. Look at the handsome man on his horse, going for the water. We see him bending. Look! Look! Men are attacking them with swords. . . ." As she spoke some of the women performed the *matam*, striking their chests in anguish. The vivid recounting was very moving, and I often cried.

My father determined to bring his country — and his children — into the twentieth century. "Will the children marry into the family?" I overheard my mother ask my father one day. I held my breath for his answer. "I don't want the boys to marry their cousins and leave them behind our compound walls any more than I want my daughters buried alive behind some other relative's compound walls," he said to my great relief. "Let them finish their educations first. Then they can decide what to do with their lives."

His reaction was just as welcome the day my mother covered me in a *burqa* the first time. We had been on the train from Karachi to Larkana when my mother took a black, gauzy cloth just like her own out of her pocketbook and draped it over me. "You are no longer a child," she told me with a tinge of regret. As she performed this age-old rite of passage for the daughters of conservative landowning families, I passed from childhood into the world of the adult. But what a disappointing world it turned out to be. The colors of the sky, the grass, the flowers were gone, muted and grayish. Everything was blurred by the pattern over my eyes. As I got off the train, the fabric which covered me from head to toe made it difficult to walk. Shut off from whatever breeze there might be, the sweat began to pour down my face.

"Pinkie wore her *burqa* for the first time today," my mother told my father when we reached Al-Murtaza. There was a long pause. "She doesn't need to wear it," my father finally said. "The Prophet himself said that the best veil is the veil behind the eyes. Let her be judged by her character and her mind, not by her clothing." And I became the first Bhutto woman to be released from a life spent in perpetual twilight.

— ৩৹ —

In 1988 at the age of thirty-five, *Benazir Bhutto* (1953 –) became the first woman leader of the Muslim world when she was democratically elected prime minister of Pakistan. Bhutto was ousted on corruption charges two years later but struggled back to power in 1993, when she was reelected prime minister, a position she held until 1996. During her two periods in office, the government of her Pakistan People's Party (PPP) greatly enhanced the standing of Pakistan both internally and internationally. Her government projected Islam as a religion of moderation, and her speeches at international conferences — on population planning in Cairo and on women's rights in Beijing — united women in the East and the West. However, during this period of political unrest, Bhutto was arrested on numerous occasions; in all she spent nearly six years either in prison or under detention for her dedicated leadership of the then opposition PPP and for her struggle to restore democracy to her country. Throughout the years in opposition, Bhutto pledged to transform Pakistani society by focusing attention on programs for health, social welfare, and education for the underprivileged. In 1996 Bhutto was removed from her post as prime minister on grounds of corruption and human rights violations. In the most recent series of cases leveled against her by the current regime, the Pakistan Muslim League, Bhutto faces prison and a ban from politics. This excerpt is from her autobiography, *Daughter of Destiny*.

Dr. Shirley Ann Jackson

Discovering Science in My Backyard

As a child, I was captivated with the idea that experimentation could unlock the secrets of the physical world around me, and I ran experiments of my own to help me understand how various parts of my world — creatures, objects, and forces — influenced each other. A good example was my extended fascination with bees. From the age of ten until I was thirteen or fourteen, as a matter of private investigation, I collected and experimented with various types of bees — bumblebees, yellow jackets, and wasps. I kept them in various habitats (including a large collection under my parents' back porch), adjusted their diets (using sugar, honey, or the nectar from various flowers), and altered their exposure to light, heat, and other stimuli. I also observed their interactions with each other, mixing the various populations and watching how variations in diet or other conditions would affect these interactions. Through the whole period, I kept a detailed log of my results. Needless to say, my parents were very indulgent, not only putting up with the buzzing subjects of my research, but even encouraging me to pursue my developing interest in science.

For a young African-American girl growing up in Washington, DC, in the 1950s, a budding enchantment with the experimental method was hardly the norm, but at the time I was barely aware that my pursuits were unusual. From my perspective, experimentation was like a good mystery novel: a tangible, unfolding chronicle of what made nature click. Best of all, in this docudrama, I was at the controls, in contact with the characters, changing the plot and scenery according to the direction of my own interests. My experience with bees not only solidified my fascination with the way the world worked, but also cemented my passion for experimentation as an approach to learning. Ironically, while I was focused on the behavior of the bees, my own behavior was being molded by the experiment itself.

As a further point of irony, while those early interests were in biological science, my later experimental training and career focused largely on physical science and physics research. I decided to study theoretical elementary particle physics at the Massachusetts Institute of Technology (MIT) and, after receiving my Ph.D. from MIT in 1973, went on to conduct extensive research in condensed matter theory at Bell Labs. Once again, these were hardly common disciplines for a young African-American woman in the early 1970s, but I have never regretted my choice of vocation or the course of my career. On the contrary, I am proud of any positive influence my choice, in taking "the road less traveled," has had on other young women who have followed.

In the broadest sense, even in my current position as chairperson of the Nuclear Regulatory Commission (NRC), I still am proceeding along the same lines of inquiry — interested in understanding the environmental interactions around me and taking responsible action based on that understanding. Certain NRC areas of focus bear directly on human interactions with the environment — such as our surveillance of radiological protection in the use of nuclear materials, our regulation of nuclear waste disposal and cleanup operations, or even, in a more benign way, our oversight of civilian uses of nuclear energy. Whether examining the world from a microscopic or macroscopic level, or whether studying biological systems or physical effects, my focus still is on asking perceptive questions, making keen observations, drawing insightful conclusions, and using this learning as the basis for making sound decisions. Looking backward, I find it remarkable how a childhood fascination can shape and foreshadow an adult passion. Remembering my childhood days fills me with gratitude for parents that were encouraging, for an environment rich with stimulation, and for the bees themselves — for teaching me the joy of an unanswered question and the value of the experimental method.

—❧—

The Honorable *Dr. Shirley Ann Jackson* (1946 –), chair of the U.S. Nuclear Regulatory Commission (NRC), has achieved several career firsts. She is the first African-American woman to receive a doctorate from MIT. She is the first

African American to become a commissioner of the NRC, and both the first woman and the first African American to serve as chair of the NRC. With the May 1997 formation of the International Nuclear Regulator's Association, Dr. Jackson was elected as the group's first chairperson. The association comprises the most senior nuclear regulatory officials from Canada, France, Germany, Japan, Spain, Sweden, the United Kingdom, and the United States. Dr. Jackson was inducted into the National Women's Hall of Fame for her profound contributions as a distinguished scientist and as an advocate for education, science, and public policy. Her achievements are of enduring value to the progress and freedom of women in this country.

Agate Nesaule

Learning America

In her memoir, Agate Nesaule chronicles her Latvian family's escape from a World War II-ravaged Europe to Indianapolis, Indiana, where they arrived penniless. Sponsored by a Lutheran church and then later accepted into a community of recently emigrated Latvians (of which Mrs. Cīgāns is a part), a twelve-year-old Nesaule comes to terms with the realities of living in America.

Mrs. Cīgāns takes me to the Indianapolis Public Library, an imposing gray building that spans an entire block. Our steps echo over the marble floors, through the cavernous rooms and long galleries.

She conducts the negotiations with the elderly blue-haired librarian who looks at me suspiciously. Finally the librarian sighs elaborately and starts typing. She pecks out a few letters, sighs again, types some more and hands me a yellow card.

"Thank you," I imagine saying to her. These are the first two words of English I learned in the camps from Mrs. Saulitis. Mrs. Cīgāns has listened to me on the bus and told me they are the right words. The *th* is hard to pronounce, there is no such sound in Latvian, but Mrs. Cīgāns assures me that I am pronouncing it almost right. Nevertheless I cannot bring myself to say anything now.

"With this you can take home any three books you want, any time you want. You just have to bring them back in two weeks, and then you can take three others. Don't let *her* tell you any differently," Mrs. Cīgāns whispers.

Alcoves, balconies, dim rooms, all full of books. One ceiling-high bookcase after another, rows and rows of them. I have never seen so many books in one place; I have held very few books that are not flimsily bound, printed on cheap yellow paper that crumbles easily. I will read these one by one, I will try to read them all, I will learn everything I need to know. If I read three every week, how long will it take to get through them all? I cannot wait to begin. But first I have to learn English. Is that possible?

Mrs. Cīgāns confers with the librarian once again. "Whoosh, whoosh" she says and waves her arms. The librarian stares at her. Mrs. Cīgāns cups her hands around her mouth and blows.

"Oh," says the librarian and clicks away over the white marble floor. She returns with several books. *Gone with the Wind* is on top of the pile.

Mrs. Cīgāns translates. I feel a smile of pure joy breaking out on my face, so that the librarian remembers why she became a librarian in the first place and smiles too. She stamps the books and hands them directly to me. My mouth is dry and my hands tremble, I can't wait to get home.

Gone with the Wind has been translated into Latvian and published in the camps in four separate paperback volumes. My mother owns only the first volume, which I have read three times already. Will Scarlett O'Hara get Ashley Wilkes to fall in love with her and marry her? Will she fall in love with Rhett Butler instead? Will she have to leave Tara? What will happen to her during the war? Will she survive? Will she ever be able to return to her home? I burn to know.

As soon as I get back to the Pastor's house I find the English/Latvian dictionary that my parents, nonsmokers both, have gotten by saving and trading their cigarette allocations. At the head of the stairs going up the attic is a door that opens onto a tiny balcony that no one ever uses. The railing is wobbly, the space is so small that it is suitable only for one person. It is a perfect place — light, silent and shady most of the day. Nobody ever sits there.

I have had a few English lessons in the camps. "This is a pen, this is a pencil," the children would recite from memory. One summer we were sent for a week to a derelict house by a canal, an attempt by the camp administrators to recreate the summer country holidays they remembered. We learned to sing "My Bonnie Lies Over the Ocean" and "Oh, My Darling Clementine," the girl who had to wear herring boxes for sandals. Once we sang *"Man cepurei tris stari,"* and the British woman officer laughed and joined in: "My hat it has three corners, Three corners has my hat." But I know there is a lot more to learn.

I begin by comparing words in the Latvian translation with words on the first page of English. I search the dictionary for those I do not know.

Some of them appear with puzzling variations and approximations, others are not listed at all. But most are. Line by line, painstakingly, I work through sentences, then paragraphs of the material already so familiar in Latvian. I am interested in Scarlett losing her temper so I find that passage. When a word or sentence refuses to yield, I go to another, worried that I will always understand just parts. But I continue.

Hours later the book falls open in the middle. "I'm never going to be hungry again," Scarlett promises herself. This is not a part that I have read before in Latvian. I look up each word, and then, keeping my fingers in different parts of the dictionary, I stare at the whole sentence. A miraculous intense knowledge, like light, fills me. I understand this, I understand it. "I'm never going to be hungry again." I realize I will be able to figure out the unknown parts of the book, I will teach myself English, I am elated. The sun setting over the maple tree in the backyard seems to confirm it.

I spend every hour I can on the balcony. I worry about the other two books that the librarian has given me, studies of air currents and weather patterns, but Mrs. Cīgāns assures me that the librarian will not care whether I have read them or not. I experience absolute despair but also great elation in my solitude. Only Mrs. Cīgāns asks me occasionally how I am doing.

"See," she says, "you'll speak English by the time school comes. You're smart like me. I learned in less than a year, but of course I could practice it every day, there were so many young American men in and out of the camp office every day." This prospect terrifies me, since school is only a few weeks away.

But Mrs. Cīgāns is quick to reassure me. "You've already learned how to look up the words you don't know and figure out how they fit. That's the hardest part. You've stepped over the dog, now all you have to do is step over the tail. . . ."

By now I can translate just about anything with the help of the dictionary, but understanding when others speak is more difficult. I can catch a few words or an occasional sentence on the radio. I then have to translate the words one by one into Latvian since I cannot yet understand them directly. Speaking English is even further away. I am afraid of making mistakes at school and of being punished for being stupid. The other children will certainly beat me on the way home.

School starts on a sunny September morning. My mother works in the kitchen at LaRue's Supper Club in the morning, and she also works there most nights.

"You're old enough to go alone," she says.

Since [my sister] Beate is going to Shortridge High School, we will be separated. Beate will have to go on the bus; she will have to have eleven cents or a token for each ride. She is worried that she may miss her stop and never find her way back home. I will have to walk the two-block gauntlet to Public School 45.

Mrs. Cīgāns cannot accompany me either. She has a job frying hamburgers at Hooks Drugstore, where she is also learning to make sodas and sundaes. The manager has told her that she is too old for this job, but since she catches on fast, he has promised her that he will eventually teach her how to be a cashier. Then she can wear a nice dress, stand behind the counter and take in money.

I am scared but relieved my mother cannot come along to school. She is also learning English from books and newspapers, but is no closer than I am to speaking it. I blush when I imagine my mother trying to make herself understood. Besides, what would my mother wear? Her one good Sunday dress of dark blue wool with the white lace collar, rows of tiny buttons and long sleeves is shiny and stretched out in the back. She wears black shoes that lace up. No one has clothes like that. I am ashamed of my mother, and even more ashamed of myself for my disloyalty.

Mrs. Cohen, the landlady, has offered to take me. I am waiting on the steps when she arrives later than she has promised. Mrs. Cohen is dressed the same as when she shows apartments to new Latvian families. The hem of her dress is ripped, several threads dangle over her sturdy bare legs, food stains spread over her copious bosom. The dress is cut differently than my mother's, but it too is dark blue and has tiny buttons. Mrs. Cohen's stringy hair is greasy and uncombed, her face is flushed. She is wearing a man's scuffed bedroom slippers with no backs, which flap as she walks. Her purse is bulging with keys, cigarettes, envelopes of rent receipts. One of its straps is broken and pinned with two safety pins. She is eating a donut, and the powdered sugar makes more spots on her dress.

She takes out another donut, breaks it in half and offers it to me. When I decline, Mrs. Cohen shakes her head sadly. She has done her best.

Groups and pairs of children are walking to school. They greet each other, hold hands, laugh with pleasure. There does not seem to be anyone walking alone. I hope they are not noticing me with Mrs. Cohen, but it is impossible that they would not. I believe I hear them laugh and whisper. They are probably making plans to ambush me later. When they do, I must not, must not cry or it will be worse.

Mrs. Cohen takes me to the principal's office. Miss Abbot, a tall elegant gray-haired lady, looks me over, points to Mrs. Cohen and asks, "Is this your mother?" She repeats the question slowly. Mrs. Cohen shakes her head and launches into a long explanation that I cannot understand.

I shake my head vigorously too. Miss Abbot nods her approval. She points to a piece of paper and asks me to fill in my name and address. Mrs. Cohen translates the questions into Yiddish for me. There are many spaces on the form, but Miss Abbot dismisses most with a regal wave of her hand. She takes me by the elbow and firmly guides me towards the stairs. Mrs. Cohen shuffles away, then turns and waves at me encouragingly.

The corridors are as wide as rooms; sunlight pours through the immense high windows in the stairwells at both ends of the building. The wood floors are polished, and there are dozens of gilt-framed pictures of men in old-fashioned frock coats and uniforms of wars gone by. Glass cases lining one side of the corridor are full of books, stuffed birds, globes, and charts. It is a beautiful school. I would like to be alone here, it should be easier to learn here than in the bare rooms in the camps. Maybe if I get all fives, I can help some of the other children and a few will accept me.

I glance at my freshly pressed gray wool skirt and gray wool blouse, which already feel too hot. On each pocket of the blouse are red strawberries embroidered by [my mother's mother] Ōmite in the camp. My braids are tied with small red ribbons, my black laced shoes are polished. The other girls are carrying purses and wearing seersucker and madras cotton blouses or printed cotton dresses and penny loafers. I am not hopeful about my future. I must not, must not cry.

Miss Abbot guides me into a room where other children are already in their seats and points to an empty desk in the front. She confers briefly with Miss Buechler, the seventh-grade homeroom teacher, then addresses the other children. War, camps, Latvia, Russia, Germany, America — I catch a few words. The eyes of the other children bore through me; I feel like a freak. I wish that Miss Abbot would stop. Presently she does. She gently pushes me down into the seat and walks out.

Miss Buechler leans over me and asks a questions, which I do not understand. She repeats. "Yes or no?" she offers. I drop my eyes in confusion. I do not know what will happen if I give the wrong answer or no answer at all. "Yes or no?" Miss Buechler waits.

When I do not answer, Miss Buechler reaches over and reassuringly pats my shoulder. This unexpected kindness brings tears to my eyes. I will them to disappear, but they do not. "There, there," she soothes. My tears spill out, I am powerless to stop them. Will Miss Buechler now make me stand in the corner for crying, send me out of the room until I have gained control of myself, tell me my mother must come to discuss my behavior?

"Oh, you poor thing," Miss Buechler says. She offers me a box of Kleenex, and when she sees me hesitate, she demonstrates by pulling out a few tissues and pressing them into my hand. She walks back to her desk, takes out a large yellow box of chocolates and passes them around the room. Everyone takes one, so do I. Miss Buechler sets an extra piece in front of me. If only Miss Buechler had not done that — I am too different already. Oh, if only I could go back to the moment before I cried. The eyes of the other children rake my back.

Miss Buechler gives directions, everyone takes out books. They turn quickly to the page she wants. She opens a book, hands it to me, points to a passage. I wish I had my dictionary, but I would not dream of bringing it or of asking if I may. I believe anything like that would be considered cheating and strictly punished.

In a few minutes the children open their desks. They all have brought pens, paper, pencils, notebooks, crayons, and other supplies. Miss Buechler looks at me and sighs.

There is so much to learn that it seems hopeless. When must I stand

and sit? Where is the bathroom and when may I use it? What time can I go home for lunch and what time must I be back? What are all the supplies I need, where am I to get them, how am I to pay for them? What will happen if I return without the things on the list that Miss Buechler gives me? What if someone expects me to speak again? What if I cry?

The morning passes slowly. The teachers smile at me, the other children ignore me. When the bell finally rings and I understand that we can all go home for lunch, I get up quickly. I walk out of the building tensing myself for the ambush. I must try to protect my eyes and my face when the children start to push, hit, and kick me as soon as we are out of sight of the teachers.

I walk the two blocks ready for blows, but nothing happens. The other children are behind me, whispering and laughing together, but they do not jump me. They watch as I go into the dilapidated building, relieved to shut the door behind me.

I hope they do not think that I will live here forever, I hope even more that they do not assume Mrs. Cohen is my mother. Most of all I hope that I can learn to speak English. Maybe that will make some difference, maybe I will be able to make a friend. It seems unlikely, but that is all there is to hope for.

And I do learn English in the months that follow. Math is the most useful for understanding what is being said. Miss Pinkerton, the math teacher, writes problems and equations on the board, and I listen intently to her explanations. The problems are easy, they are like those I had to solve two years ago in the camps, so I can concentrate fully on the words.

The air-raid drills for nuclear war are also familiar. Every week we practice leaving our desks quickly, crossing our arms over our heads, lying still on the classroom floor. The shades are drawn over the vast windows. In a few minutes, Miss Buechler rings a hand bell. "All clear," she says.

At other times, we are told to lie face down in the hallways, and the doors of the classroom are shut. We have to lie still for five minutes, while the teachers whisper to each other as they mark time. The girls wrinkle their noses at having to get down on the floor. Later yet we are herded down to the basement, told to crouch and to cover our heads with our arms. Many wiggle and complain under their breaths that this is uncomfortable and boring.

At times like this I feel vastly superior to the American children. They seem to have no idea that they could be bombed at any time. How grateful they would be then for a safe place to hide. I want to tell the teachers that the basement is really the best spot but that no one could ever crouch like that through a whole air raid. It would be so much better to have cots down there, so that we could lie quietly while the planes passed. The others seem childish for complaining and wiggling. In my imagination I repeatedly furnish the basement with comfortable chairs, warm blankets, working radios and batteries, vast stores of food. This is my favorite fantasy during recess while I stand alone, feeling exposed and awkward, and watch others play.

Thanksgiving is approaching, another unfamiliar holiday. Like Halloween, this holiday seems to be celebrated a lot at school. Cardboard pilgrims, turkeys, and pumpkins decorate the walls. The skies are overcast, it is chilly and damp, the two-block walk to school is faster. I still walk by myself. A few times — I can count them on my fingers — the boys on the Safety Patrol have said "Hi" to me, but mostly no one speaks to me. I hurry home, do my homework, listen to the radio and read. Two nights a week I wash dishes at LaRue's Supper Club.

I am watching the clock, counting the minutes till the last period of the morning is over. At home I have *Little Women* waiting for me. I love the sisters confiding in their mother, getting to know Laurie, putting on plays, sitting in their cozy parlor. I can't wait to get home to read while I eat lunch, with the book propped up behind my soup bowl. Miss Buechler is talking about the pilgrims coming to a rocky shore to spend a winter of hardship in the new land.

And then it happens.

I suddenly understand everything Miss Buechler is saying — everything! I am not understanding just separate words, I do not have to translate sentences back into Latvian. I understand exactly what Miss Buechler is saying at the very moment she says it.

It's miraculous! My heart races with excitement, pure joy washes over me. I want to tell someone, everyone, what has happened. I under-stand English!

I look around the room. I cannot believe that others are not aware of the miracle, but they seem not to be. I wish I could tell them so they could be happy with me. But the gloomy skies seem brighter. Thanksgiving doesn't seem to be such an odd holiday.

I run home, skipping and humming to myself. I hope that someone will be around on Park Avenue I can tell, but there isn't. Everyone is at work. I get my book, prop it up and start heating the soup.

"I can understand English, I can understand English," I chant.

As if to celebrate my accomplishment, a letter from Ōmite arrives that afternoon. She has passed all the tests and examinations and has been cleared to come to the United States to join my Uncle Jaša's fam-ily. She will come to Indianapolis later, as soon as there is money enough to pay for bus fare.

That day is by no means the end of learning English, but it encour-ages me to continue. It is well after New Year's when I finally have the courage to actually try to speak it.

Miss Buechler is in front of the room, asking questions about a story we have just read. I cautiously raise my hand. At first she looks past me, then she notices me and beams.

"He rode to warn that the British were coming," I say. My voice trembles. I can feel myself blushing and red blotches appearing on my neck, but there, I have said it.

"Why yes, that's right, that's very good," Miss Buechler smiles. "You said it," she adds. The other children behind me burst into applause.

"She talked," someone says, "she said something."

"Good for you," says John Stafne, the boy sitting next to me. I am embarrassed and totally gratified. I have learned English, I have done it. And I have done it by myself.

This event does not magically change my life in school, but slowly the children start speaking to me. A few of the girls walk home with me occasionally, most of the others say "Hi." I am still not invited to play after school or to go to any of the birthday parties that are passionately discussed during recess, but I do not always walk the long blocks home alone. During the next gym class I am not the very last one chosen for the volleyball team.

"You are making friends," Mrs. Cīgāns says. "I saw you walking with two young American ladies."

"I guess so," I say, but I know no one is my friend. Friends meet each other's mothers, visit each other's houses, talk on the phone. My family does not have a telephone, and I do not want anyone to enter our rooms on Park Avenue. I could not bear someone seeing the crowded rooms or asking to look in our closet to try on my clothes. I have neither a dresser nor a makeup kit, items I believe to be essential, to practice painting eyebrows and cheeks. That is what other girls do after school.

Book reports are another way to learn. Some of the books, like *Little Women*, are suggested by the teachers, but most Beate and I find in the library ourselves. Beate cleans houses most nights after school, and some nights I wash dishes at LaRue's but on Friday evenings we are both free. If we have enough money we go to the main library downtown. Sometimes we go to a movie, though usually the only theater we can afford is on Ohio Street, and costs a quarter. The theater is next to burlesque houses and bars, so we have to be careful. It is filled with boys in army uniforms from Fort Benjamin Harrison and with seedy old men who touch our backs and legs. We have to move innumerable times to find a place where we can watch in peace. Usually we walk the twelve blocks to the library branch on 30th and Meridian. We spend the entire evening there, choosing books and reading in the comfortable leather chairs in front of the fireplace until an adult comes in and we give up our seats.

We read everything teachers have told us is important. Miss Buechler tells me to read *I Remember Mama*, which makes me gloomy instead of pleasing me as she has obviously intended. The story of another girl isolated at school because she is from a foreign country is at first comforting, then unbelievable. I cannot imagine my mother winning over the other children by inviting them in to a lovely sparkling kitchen, laughing, cooking them a meal, getting them to value her. To Miss Buechler's astonishment, I announce I have read *Anna Karenina* for one of my book reports.

"Did you understand it?" she asks.

"Yes, of course, I loved it." My mother read it too when she was twelve. I announce that I am going to read *War and Peace* for the next book report, but at this Miss Buechler draws the line.

"That's too old for you. Besides, you should not keep thinking about war. You should develop some normal interests."

I do not tell her that I have also read, with only partial understanding but passionate interest, *Farewell to Arms* and *For Whom the Bell Tolls*; that would make me even less normal. By accident I find a book that seems written for me, *A Tree Grows in Brooklyn*. It is about a girl living in poverty, who also has to walk alone on deserted dangerous streets, whose parents are seldom around. I have never read a story about someone in a situation that seems so real, someone like myself, in a city in America, rather than centuries ago or continents away. I tell Miss Buechler that it is the very best book I ever read.

———— ৣ৹ ————

Writer/scholar *Agate Nesaule* (1938 –) graduated from Indiana University and received her doctorate from the University of Wisconsin at Madison. For thirty-three years she taught as a professor of English and women's studies at the University of Wisconsin at Whitewater. Currently, she is writing full-time and at work on a novel. This excerpt is from her first book, *A Woman in Amber: Healing the Trauma of War and Exile*, which received a 1996 American Book Award.

Karen Mitchell

Black Patent Leather Shoes

Slipping in my black patent leather shoes
Papa would make sure they reflected
Me
Not caring how many times they were
Used
He would make me put them on
With laced stockings
I never danced in those black leather
Shoes
Only studied their simple details:
Black
As black as my hair they surely were
With three straps, that held me there, and heels
Stacked
And I could not wear my black leather
Shoes
Every day, but only once or twice a
Week
And he would make sure black polish was
Used
Papa would make sure those shoes
Reflected me

Karen Mitchell (1955 –) grew up in Holly Springs, Mississippi. Her greatest ambition as a child was to be a writer and publish a book of poetry. She began writing poetry at age twelve, and won her first literary contest — the 1973

Mississippi Arts Festival Literary Competition — while she was in high school. She has worked in a variety of jobs: for libraries, for a historical society, and for a literary magazine. Her first book, *The Eating Hill,* from which this poem is taken, was published in 1989. Mitchell is currently at work on her second poetry collection.

Jane Wagner and Tina DiFeliciantonio

Girls Like Us

My path of self-discovery.

Step 1: I was having fun running around bullying the boys and being the class clown. My grades were rapidly falling and my parents were dismayed.

I came from a family of high-achieving intellectuals. My parents were both doctors. My grandmother was a mathematician and my grandfather a geologist. My parents believed in the fundamental importance of a solid scientific education. At the age of nine they sent me to a very traditional all-girls prep school. I was totally unprepared. Being hit over the head with a sledge hammer might have been less painful.

I spent my time at prep school in a state of high anxiety. Food became my solace. As the next door neighbor remarked to my mother, "My, Jane has become quite a . . . ," pause, deep breath, "a bonny child."

Step 2: As my mother and older sister silently drove off without a backward glance, I was left at the imposing entrance of an all-girls boarding school in England. Backlit by a full moon, I can still picture myself standing there, tears streaming down my plump cheeks, muttering, "But I don't have any friends." I had just turned twelve.

My very first outing with my classmates was on a warm September day, and I decided to buy ice cream. "Goodness, Jane, what are you doing?" said Mrs. Goddard, the housemistress. "Throw that away at once! One doesn't eat in the street. Does one?" The other girls began to snicker, and I began to understand the inner workings of boarding school life — the game of power play: currying favor with the "in-crowd" while simultaneously positioning oneself against "the outsider." It was a period of exponential learning, of absorbing all the social skills necessary to blend in and then adapting them to find my identity.

When I was fitted for my boarding school uniform the very staid sales ladies had to find bigger and bigger sizes, tut-tutting all the time. From the age of twelve to eighteen I never grew out of my skirts because at some point in my first term the school doctor suggested that I lose a few pounds. This seemed like an achievable goal, and my weight began its pendulous swings. I became very adept at pretending to eat all the requisite meals, while actually sticking to my five-hundred-calorie-a-day diet, or my two-week-carrots-only special. As my weight fluctuated, so did my position on the swimming team. After a two week fast — drinking only a can of one-calorie orange soda a day — it was rather hard to finish even a lap.

Step 3: My friend Gillian Moody returned from the summer holiday with Jesus. She had become a born-again Christian and could speak in tongues. Gillian was an intense, tough, straightforward gal who was good at games. I liked her and wanted to speak in tongues, too.

Jesus was good to me. The year was 1976. There were elaborate bicentennial celebrations in England. I was in the choir and we went on tour. I had never been so thin, or so focused. My grades were soaring. I was on top of the world. I did fantastically well on my "O" level exams, much to the surprise of my teachers who, henceforth, described me as a "late developer." I was all set for my "A" levels of physics, chemistry, and biology, and on the path to medical school.

In my Sunday letter home, I told my parents that I had found God, that I didn't swear anymore, and that because the poor and needy were calling I may not be home for the Christmas holidays. I also wrote that I no longer believed in abortion. My mother went ballistic. Forget swearing and Christmas, but abortion?? "If you had seen what I saw as a medical student. The desperate lengths women go to . . ." Religion began to lose its appeal.

Step 4: By the age of sixteen, I had done Jesus, David Essex, the Bay City Rollers. Nothing was quite satisfying. And then I became a punk. It was a fabulous time before the commodification of punk and before Thatcher was elected. It was a time of pure rebellion. I was the only punk in my school, not that it mattered. On Sunday I created quite a stir walking down the church aisle with the choir wearing my new school uniform: skirt, shirt and tie, shaved head, and army boots.

While everyone else was gearing up to graduate, getting ready to become the next generation of leaders, I was working on my downward mobility. I told my headmistress that the school was merely a profit-making venture. I recommended that she read Martin Amis. My mantra became Philip Larken's poem: "They *&!# you up your mum and dad/They don't mean to but they do/They fill you with the faults they had and add some extra just for you." I had visions of standing in front of the school assembly, parents visiting, reciting the poem and reenacting the bloody ending to the movie *If*.

During my time of punk rebellion, I had very little time to study. My biology teacher suggested that unless I pulled my finger out I was more suited to becoming a lab technician than a doctor. I walked into my final "A" level exams knowing nothing. I sat at the desk, palms sweating, not even understanding the words. Yet I stayed in the room for the duration of the exam, making up answers. It was an indescribable state of being. A painful act of rebellion that still haunts my nightmares.

My parents, understanding that something was going disastrously wrong, were silently arranging for me to retake my "A" levels at a small finishing school in Oxford. My mother had not given up her dream of my studying medicine or of attending Oxford University. In a numb state of absolute dejection, I managed to see through the haze and discovered that I was not a scientist. It took me another ten years to discover what I wanted to be.

— Jane Wagner

Bottom left:
Jane Wagner

—

Age 13. My eighth-grade class had a reputation for being the worst group of students in the history of the school. Richie had unsuccessfully tried to rob the neighborhood bank. Robby set off stink bombs that forced the evacuation of the entire school. The girls were sassy, smart-mouthed, and sexy. No faculty members wanted us, so we had the same teachers two years in a row.

Mrs. LaMorgia's jet black hair was styled into a tight little bun. She was thin, wore tailored clothes, and was sharp, stern, and intelligent. As my unruly class knew from the previous year, she wielded control by challenging us. In the two years under her tutelage we never saw her sweat. Our parents loved her. We didn't share the same sentiment.

Sister Rafael had a pasty-white complexion that we presumed was the byproduct of her close proximity to God. She had a calm demeanor, but was known for her portentous eraser throwing, hitting targets (badly behaved students) with unrelenting precision. Upon reaching the point of full exasperation, she'd resort to pulling girls' hair with a jolt and twisting boys' ears until they turned red and remained so for the rest of the day.

By the eighth grade I had become adept at remaining off the teachers' radar screen. Despite a rocky start during my first few years of school, I learned to do well academically. And as the middle child of Italian immigrants who valued assimilation, fitting in was deeply instilled.

Sister Rafael trusted me enough to take attendance. It took me weeks to recognize that the boy across the aisle wasn't just teasing when he'd poke or pinch me to make sure I knew he was present. Let's just say that flirting never came naturally. Sister Rafael knew that at some level I was going through the motions when it came to boys. One afternoon after helping to clean the church (I can still smell the lemon scent of Pledge), she confided that she thought the boy I was "dating" didn't seem my type. Mrs. LaMorgia would never have uttered anything that personal, or so I thought.

As part of our graduation ritual, the students and teachers signed momento books. The boys wrote funny, rude little notes. The girls scribed cutesy well-wishes for the high school years ahead. I don't know where that book is now, but I do remember one particular note. It was from Mrs. LaMorgia. And it went something like, "You have a good head on your shoulders. Use it! You have the potential. Live up to it!"

I was mystified, confused. My academic average was around 95 and I was graded with A's in conduct. Mrs. LaMorgia's note burned like a fire in my belly and smoldered over the course of the summer.

The following fall I left the familiarity of my predominately working-class Italian-American neighborhood and commuted across the city to an all-girls academic high school. For the first time in my life, I didn't automatically fit in. Unlike the homogeneity at my elementary school, this student body was diverse. And unlike many kids in grade school, the students here were fiercely ambitious.

It was in high school that Mrs. LaMorgia's words seemed to ignite — I became class president, graduated among the top of the class, and went on to college. While my parents had always encouraged my sisters and me to work hard and try our best, we were also urged not to venture too far. A practical degree in business would help assure that I'd successfully assimilate, get a decent job, find an appropriate husband, and be realistic about my expectations of life. I began to feel deadened by the prospect of what lay ahead.

And so I ran. I moved three thousand miles away and entered Stanford's graduate film program. I didn't know exactly where I was going, but was comforted by the fact that I was following my bliss. As a filmmaker I've discovered the power of taking risks . . . the rewards that can come from rocking the boat and appearing on the radar screen. It's been about two dozen years since I left the halls of Holy Spirit Elementary. That graduation note still lingers — an enduring challenge from the past and an immutable beacon of hope that propels me into the future.

— Tina DiFeliciantonio

Tina DiFeliciantonio

⚬⚭⚬

Jane Wagner (1961 –) and *Tina DiFeliciantonio* (1961 –) began collaborating while at film school, where Wagner made her directing debut with the award-winning film *Hearts & Quarks,* and DiFeliciantonio with the National Emmy Award-winning *Living With AIDS.* In 1991 they embarked on a six-year project under their newly formed production company, Naked Eye Productions, entitled *Girls Like Us,* a film that examines a turning point in women's lives — adolescence — when teens struggle to define their burgeoning sexual and gender identity. The film was screened and broadcast throughout the world, garnering several top honors including the 1997 Sundance Grand Jury Prize for Best Documentary and a National Emmy. (*Girls Like Us* is distributed by Girls Make Movies, 462 Broadway, #500K, New York, New York 10013.) Other award-winning films include *Two or Three Things But Nothing for Sure,* an impressionistic film about author Dorothy Allison; *Walk This Way,* a documentary special about understanding diversity; *Tom's Flesh,* winner of the 1995 Sundance Film Festival Award for Short Filmmaking; *Culture Wars,* a program in the series *The Question of Equality;* and *Una Donna,* which aired as part of National Public Radio's multicultural series *Legacies: Tales from America.* Their upcoming film, *Silent Voices,* a historical documentary on the marginalization of women filmmakers during cinema's silent era, was recently awarded a Rockefeller Fellowship.

Gish Jen

What Means Switch

In this short story excerpt, Gish Jen depicts the tribulations of Mona Chang, a Chinese-American newcomer to a Scarsdale, New York, junior high school. The acclaimed story explores the sometimes tense relations between Japanese and Chinese Americans, and youth's ability to dismantle them in the midst of a first crush.

"Are you just friends, or more than just friends," Barbara Gugelstein is giving me the cross-ex.

"Maybe," I say.

"Come on," she says, "I told you everything about me and Andy."

I actually am trying to tell Barbara everything about Sherman, but everything turns out to be nothing. Meaning, I can't locate the conversation in what I have to say. Sherman and I go places, we talk, one time my mother threw him out of the house because of World War II.

"I think we're just friends," I say.

"You think or you're sure?"

Now that I do less of the talking at lunch, I notice more what other people talk about — cheerleading, who likes who, this place in White Plains to get earrings. On none of these topics am I an expert. Of course, I'm still friends with Barbara Gugelstein, but I notice Danielle Meyers has spun away to other groups.

Barbara's analysis goes this way: To be popular, you have to have big boobs, a note from your mother that lets you use her Lord & Taylor credit card, and a boyfriend. On the other hand, what's so wrong with being unpopular? "We'll get them in the end," she says. It's what her dad tells her. "Like they'll turn out too dumb to do their own investing, and then they'll get killed in fees and then they'll have to move to towns where the schools stink. And my dad should know," she winds up. "He's a broker."

"I guess," I say.

But the next thing I know, I have a true crush on Sherman

Matsumoto. Mister Judo, the guys call him now, with real respect; and the more they call him that, the more I don't care that he carries a notebook with a cat on it.

I sigh. "Sherman."

"I thought you were just friends," says Barbara Gugelstein.

"We were," I say mysteriously. This, I've noticed, is how Danielle Meyers talks; everything's secret, she only lets out so much, it's like she didn't grow up with everybody telling her she had to share.

And here's the funny thing: The more I intimate that Sherman and I are more than just friends, the more it seems we actually are. It's the old imagination giving reality a nudge. When I start to blush; he starts to blush; we reach a point where we can hardly talk at all.

"Well, there's first base with tongue, and first base without," I tell Barbara Gugelstein.

In fact, Sherman and I have brushed shoulders, which was equivalent to first base I was sure, maybe even second. I felt as though I'd turned into one huge shoulder; that's all I was, one huge shoulder. We not only didn't talk, we didn't breathe. But how can I tell Barbara Gugelstein that? So instead I say, "Well, there's second base and second base."

Danielle Meyers is my friend again. She says, "I know exactly what you mean," just to make Barbara Gugelstein feel bad.

"Like *what* do I mean?" I say.

Danielle Meyers can't answer.

"You know what I think?" I tell Barbara the next day. "I think Danielle's giving us a line."

Barbara pulls thoughtfully on one of her pigtails.

If Sherman Matsumoto is never going to give me an ID to wear, he should at least get up the nerve to hold my hand. I don't think he sees this. I think of the story he told me about his parents, and in a synaptic firestorm realize we don't see the same things at all.

So one day, when we happen to brush shoulders again, I don't move away. He doesn't move away either. There we are. Like a pair of bleachers, pushed together but not quite matched up. After a while, I have to breathe, I can't help it. I breathe in such a way that our elbows start to touch too. We are in a crowd, waiting for a bus. I crane my neck to look at the sign that says where the bus is going; now our wrists are touching. Then it happens: He links his pinky around mine.

Is that holding hands? Later, in bed, I wonder all night. One finger, and not even the biggest one.

Sherman is leaving in a month. Already! I think, well, I suppose he will leave and we'll never even kiss. I guess that's all right. Just when I've resigned myself to it, though, we hold hands, all five fingers. Once when we are at the bagel shop, then again in my parents' kitchen. Then, when we are at the playground, he kisses the back of my hand.

He does it again not too long after that, in White Plains.

I invest in a bottle of mouthwash.

Instead of moving on, though, he kisses the back of my hand again. And again. I try raising my hand, hoping he'll make the jump from my hand to my cheek. It's like trying to wheedle an inchworm out the window. You know, *This way, this way.*

All over the world, people have their own cultures. That's what we learned in social studies.

If we never kiss, I'm not going to take it personally.

It's the end of the school year. We've had parties. We've turned in our textbooks. Hooray! Outside the asphalt already steams if you spit on it. Sherman isn't leaving for another couple of days, though, as he comes to visit every morning, staying until the afternoon, when [my sister] Callie comes home from her big-deal job as a bank teller. We drink Kool-Aid in the backyard and hold hands until they are sweaty and make smacking noises coming apart. He tells me how busy his parents are, getting ready for the move. His mother, particularly, is very tired. Mostly we are mournful.

The very last day we hold hands and do not let go. Our palms fill up with water like a blister. We do not care. We talk more than usual. How much airmail is to Japan, that kind of thing. Then suddenly he asks, will I marry him?

I'm only thirteen.

But when old? Sixteen?

If you come back to get me.

I come. Or you can come to Japan, be Japanese.

How can I be Japanese?

Like you become American. Switch.

He kisses me on the cheek, again and again and again.

His mother calls to say she's coming to get him. I cry. I tell him how I've saved every present he's ever given me — the ruler, the pencils, the bags from the bagels, all the flower petals. I even have the orange peels from the oranges.

All?

I put them in a jar.

I'd show him, except that we're not allowed to go upstairs to my room. Anyway, something about the orange peels seems to choke him up too. Mister Judo, but I've gotten him in a soft spot. We are going together to the bathroom to get some toilet paper to wipe our eyes when poor tired Mrs. Matsumoto, driving a shiny new station wagon, skids up onto our lawn.

"Very sorry!"

We race outside.

"Very sorry!"

Mrs. Matsumoto is so short that about all we can see of her is a green cotton sun hat, with a big brim. It's tied on. The brim is trembling.

I hope my mom's not going to start yelling about World War II.

"Is all right, no trouble," she says, materializing on the steps behind me and Sherman. She propped the screen door wide open; when I turn I see she's waving. "No trouble, no trouble!"

"No trouble, no trouble!" I echo, twirling a few times with relief.

Mrs. Matsumoto keeps apologizing; my mom keeps insisting she shouldn't feel bad, it was only some grass and a small tree. Crossing the lawn, she insists Mrs. Matsumoto get out of the car, even though it means trampling some lilies-of-the-valley. She insists that Mrs. Matsumoto come in for a cup of tea. Then she will not talk about anything unless Mrs. Matsumoto sits down, and unless she lets my mom prepare her a small snack. The coming in and the tea and the sitting down are settled pretty quickly, but they negotiate ferociously over the small snack, which Mrs. Matsumoto will not eat unless she can call Mr. Matsumoto. She makes the mistake of linking Mr. Matsumoto with a reparation of some sort, which my mom will not hear of.

"Please!"

"No no no no."

Back and forth it goes: "No no no no." "No no no no." "No no no no." What kind of conversation is that? I look at Sherman, who shrugs. Finally Mr. Matsumoto calls on his own, wondering where his wife is. He comes over in a taxi. He's a heavy-browed businessman, friendly but brisk — not at all a type you could imagine bowing to a lady with a taste for tie-on sun hats. My mom invites him in as if it's an idea she just this moment thought of. And would he maybe have some tea and a small snack?

Sherman and I sneak back outside for another farewell, by the side of the house, behind the forsythia bushes. We hold hands. He kisses me on the cheek again, and then — just when I think he's finally going to kiss me on the lips — he kisses me on the neck.

Is this first base?

He does it more. Up and down, up and down. First it tickles, and then it doesn't. He has his eyes closed. I close my eyes too. He's hugging me. Up and down. Then down.

He's at my collarbone.

Still at my collarbone. Now his hand's on my ribs. So much for first base. More ribs. The idea of second base would probably make me nervous if he weren't on his way to Japan and if I really thought we were going to get there. As it is, though, I'm not in much danger of wrecking my life on the shoals of passion; his unmoving hand feels more like a growth than a boyfriend. He has his whole face pressed to my neck skin so I can't tell his mouth from his nose. I think he may be licking me.

From indoors, a burst of adult laughter. My eyelids flutter. I start to try and wiggle such that his hand will maybe budge upward.

Do I mean for my top blouse button to come accidentally undone?

He clenches his jaw, and when he opens his eyes, they're fixed on that button like it's a gnat that's been bothering him for far too long. He mutters in Japanese. If later in life he were to describe this as a pivotal moment in his youth, I would not be surprised. Holding the material as far from my body as possible, he buttons the button. Somehow we've landed up too close to the bushes.

What to tell Barbara Gugelstein? She says, "Tell me what were his last words. He must have said something last."

"I don't want to talk about it."

"Maybe he said, Good-bye?" she suggests. "Sayonara?" She means well.

"I don't want to talk about it."

"Aw, come on, I told you everything about —"

I say, "Because it's private, excuse me."

She stops, squints at me as though at a far-off face she's trying to make out. Then she nods and very lightly places her hand on my forearm.

The forsythia seemed to be stabbing us in the eyes. Sherman said, more or less, *You will need to study how to switch.*

And I said, *I think you should switch. The way you do everything is weird.*

And he said, *You just want to tell everything to your friends. You just want to have boyfriend to become popular.*

Then he flipped me. Two swift moves, and I went sprawling through the air, a flailing confusion of soft human parts such as had no idea where the ground was, much less how hard it could be.

―∽∾―

Gish Jen (1955 –) grew up in New York City with parents who immigrated from Shanghai to the United States in the 1940s. "Our family was always a one-of-a-kind family living in a white neighborhood," she recalls. "It didn't occur to me until I was in college that writers like me were left out of the books I read." After graduating from Harvard, Jen still didn't turn to writing full-time. Instead, she worked briefly for a publisher, attended the business school at Stanford University for a year, taught English in China for a year, and then completed her master of fine arts degree at the University of Iowa. The author of two critically acclaimed novels, *Typical American* (1991) and *Mona in the Promised Land* (1996), Jen's work has appeared in *The Atlantic Monthly*, *The New Yorker*, and the *New York Times*, as well as in an array of textbooks and anthologies. Her first collection of stories, *Who's Irish?*, will be published in 1999.

Rita Quillen

Sugar-n-Spice, etc.

All us girls knew about sin
sought after it.
Torn pieces of brown paper bags
wrapped around dried corn silks
secretly cured in the toolshed
supplied cigarettes to wave around
like those women on the soap operas.
In my friend's playhouse
we practiced kissing,
furtive and ashamed.
A high-powered telescope
Santa Claus brought
opened up the mysteries
of neighborhood bedrooms.

Once we sneaked out of a slumber party
tiptoed onto an icy bridge
still in our baby-doll pajamas,
froze our prissy asses off
to watch the sun stick out its tongue
at the gray world.
Then there was that Halloween
we rolled a septic tank
into the middle of the highway
and set it afire.
It took about 20 state troopers
two tow trucks and a tractor
to move that white-hot donut.
We were fairly disappointed

when nobody got arrested.
Our reputations weren't the best,

but at least what we were made of
wouldn't melt in your mouth.

⁓ ·ᴑ·ᴑ ⁓

Rita Quillen (1954 –   ) is an accomplished poet whose collections include *October Dusk* (1987) and *Counting the Sums* (1995). She also published a book of critical essays entitled *Looking for Native Ground: Contemporary Appalachian Poetry* (1989). Quillen's work has been featured in many periodicals and anthologies, and her personal essay is included in the award-winning *Bloodroot: Appalachian Women Writers* (1998). Quillen is the fifth generation of her father's family to be born and raised in Scott County in southwest Virginia. Of "Sugar-n-Spice, etc." she says, "Much to my mother's chagrin, the poem is 100 percent autobiographical!" Currently, she is an associate professor of English at Northeast State Technical Community College in Tennessee.

Family

God sent children for another purpose than merely to keep up the race — to enlarge our hearts; and to make us unselfish and full of kind sympathies and affections; to give our souls higher aims; to call out all our faculties to extended enterprise and exertion; and to bring round our firesides bright faces, happy smiles, and loving, tender hearts.

— Mary Botham Howitt

Joan Baez

Honest Lullaby

Early early in the game
I taught myself to sing and play
And use a little trickery
On kids who never favored me
Those were years of crinoline slips
And cotton skirts and swinging hips
And dangerously painted lips
And stars of stage and screen
Pedal pushers, ankle socks
Padded bras and campus jocks
Who hid their vernal equinox
In pairs of faded jeans
And slept at home resentfully
Coveting their dreams

And often I have wondered
How the years and I survived
I had a mother who sang to me
An honest lullaby

Yellow, brown, and black and white
Our Father bless us all tonight
I bowed my head at football games
And closed the prayer in Jesus' name
Lusting after football heroes
Tough Pachuco, little Neroes
Forfeiting my A's for zeroes
Futures unforeseen
Spending all my energy

In keeping my virginity
And living in a fantasy
In love with Jimmy Dean
If you will be my king, Jimmy, Jimmy,
I will be your queen

And often I have wondered
How the years and I survived
I had a mother who sang to me
An honest lullaby

I traveled all around the world
And knew more than the other girls
Of foreign languages and schools
Paris, Rome and Istanbul
But those things never worked for me
The town was much too small you see
And people have a way of being
Even smaller yet
But all the same though life is hard
And no one promised me a garden
Of roses, so I did okay
I took what I could get
And did the things that I might do
For those less fortunate

And often I have wondered
How the years and I survived
I had a mother who sang to me
An honest lullaby

Now look at you, you must be growing
A quarter of an inch a day
You've already lived near half the years

You'll be when you go away
With your teddy bears and alligators
Enterprise communicators
All the tiny aviators head into the sky
And while the others play with you
I hope to find a way with you
And sometimes spend a day with you
I'll catch you as you fly
Or if I'm worth a mother's salt
I'll wave as you go by

And if you should ever wonder
How the years and you'll survive
Honey, you've got a mother who sings to you
Dances on the strings for you
Opens her heart and brings to you
An honest lullaby

―⁂―

This song appears on the album *Honest Lullaby*.

Bebe Moore Campbell

Sweet Summer

In telling her everyday life, Bebe Moore Campbell describes the mother and grandmother who raised her during the school year, a pair of women she calls "the Bosoms" for their protective yet powerful presence in her life. Although Campbell's story is infused with experiences unique to African-American culture, it speaks to the universal truths of girlhood, including the inevitable disillusionment that children face when confronted with their parents' humanness and fallibility.

The red bricks of 2239 North 16th Street melded into the uniformity of look-alike doors, windows, and brownstone-steps. From the outside our rowhouse looked the same as any other. When I was a toddler, the similarity was unsettling. The family story was that my mother and I were out walking on the street one day when panic rumbled through me. "Where's our house? Where's our house?" I cried, grabbing my mother's hand.

My mother walked me to our house, pointed to the numbers painted next to the door. "Twenty-two thirty-nine," she said, slapping the wall. "This is our house."

Much later I learned that the real difference was inside.

In my house there was no morning stubble, no long johns or Fruit of the Loom on the clothesline, no baritone hollering for keys that were sitting on the table. There was no beer in the refrigerator, no ball game on TV, no loud cussing. After dark the snores that emanated from the bedrooms were subtle, ladylike, little moans really.

Growing up, I could have died from overexposure to femininity. Women ruled at 2239. A grandmother, a mother, occasionally an aunt, grown-up girlfriends from at least two generations, all the time rubbing up against me, fixing my food, running my bathwater, telling me to sit still and be good in those grown-up, girly-girl voices. Chanel and Prince Matchabelli wafting through the bathrooms. Bubble bath and Jergens came from the bathroom, scents unbroken by aftershave, macho beer breath, a good he-man funk. I remember a house full of 'do rags and rollers, the soft sweet allure of Dixie peach and bergamot; brown-skinned queens wearing pastel housecoats and worn-out size six-and-a-half flip-flops that slapped softly against the wood as the royal women climbed the stairs at night carrying their paperbacks to bed.

The outside world offered no retreat. School was taught by stern, old-maid white women with age spots and merciless gray eyes; ballets lessons, piano lessons, Sunday school, and choir were all led by colored sisters with a hands-on-their hips attitude who cajoled and screeched in distaff tongues.

And what did they want from me, these Bosoms? Achievement! This desire had nothing to do with the pittance they collected from the Philadelphia Board of Education or the few dollars my mother paid them. Pushing little colored girls forward was in their blood. They made it clear: a life of white picket fences and teas was for other girls to aspire to. I was to *do* something. And if I didn't climb willingly up their ladder, they'd drag me to the top. Rap my knuckles hard for not practicing. Make me lift my leg until I wanted to die. Stay after school and write "I will listen to the teacher" five hundred times. They were not playing. "Obey them," my mother commanded.

When I entered 2B — the Philadelphia school system divided grades into A and B — in September 1957, I sensed immediately that Miss Bradley was not a woman to be challenged. She looked like one of those evil old spinsters Shirley Temple was always getting shipped off to live with; she was kind of hefty, but so tightly corseted that if she happened to grab you or if you fell against her during recess, it felt as if you were bouncing into a steel wall. In reality she was a sweet lady who was probably a good five years past her retirement age when I wound up in her class. Miss Bradley remained at Logan for one reason and one reason only: she was dedicated. She wanted her students to learn! learn! learn! Miss Bradley was halfway sick, hacking and coughing her lungs out through every lesson, spitting the phlegm into fluffy white tissues from the box on her desk, but she was never absent. Each day at three o'clock she kissed each one of her "little pupils" on the cheek, sending a faint scent of Emeraude home with us. Her rules for teaching children seemed to be: Love them; discipline them; reward them; and make sure they are clean. . . .

. . . I sat in Miss Bradley's classroom on a rainy Monday watching her write spelling words on the blackboard. The harsh sccurr, sccurr of Miss Bradley's chalk and the tinny sound the rain made against the window took my mind to faraway places. I couldn't get as far away as I wanted. Wallace, the bane of the whole class, had only moments earlier laid the most gigunda fart in history, one in a never-ending series, and the air was just clearing. His farts were silent wonders. Not a hint, not the slightest sound. You could be in the middle of a sentence and then wham! bam! Mystery Funk would knock you down.

Two seats ahead of me was Leonard, a lean colored boy from West Philly who always wore suits and ties to school, waving his hand like a crazy man. A showoff if ever there was one.

I was bored that day. I looked around at the walls. Miss Bradley had decorated the room with pictures of the ABCs in cursive. Portraits of the presidents were hanging in a row on one wall above the blackboard. On the bulletin board there was a display of the Russian satellite, *Sputnick I*, and the American satellite, *Explorer I*. Miss Bradley was satellite-crazy. She thought it was just wonderful that America was in the "space race" and she constantly filled our heads with space fantasies. "Boys and girls," she told us, "one day man will walk on the moon." In the far corner on another bulletin board there was a Thanksgiving scene of turkeys and pilgrims. And stuck in the corner was a picture of Sacajawea. Sacajawea, Indian Woman Guide. I preferred looking at Sacajawea over satellites any day.

Thinking about the bubble gum that lay in my pocket, I decided to sneak a piece, even though chewing gum was strictly forbidden. I rarely broke the rules. Could anyone hear the loud drumming of my heart, I wondered, as I slid my hand into my skirt pocket and felt for the Double Bubble? I peeked cautiously to either side of me. Then I managed to unwrap it without even rustling the paper; I drew my hand to my lips, coughed and popped the gum in my mouth. Ahhh! Miss Bradley's back was to the class. I chomped down hard on the Double Bubble. Miss

Bradley turned around. I quickly packed the gum under my tongue. My hands were folded on top of my desk. "Who can give me a sentence for 'birthday'?" Leonard just about went nuts. Miss Bradley ignored him, which she did a lot. "Sandra," Miss Bradley called.

A petite white girl rose obediently. I liked Sandra. She had shared her crayons with me once when I left mine at home. I remember her drawing: a white house with smoke coming out of the chimney, a little girl with yellow hair like hers, a mommy, a daddy, a little boy and a dog standing in front of the house in a yard full of flowers. Her voice was crystal clear when he spoke. There were smiles in that voice. She said, "My father made me a beautiful dollhouse for my birthday."

The lump under my tongue was suddenly a stone and when I swallowed, the taste was bitter. I coughed into a piece of tablet paper, spit out the bubble gum, and crumpled up the wad and pushed it inside the desk. The center of my chest was burning. I breathed deeply and slowly. Sandra sat down as demurely as a princess. She crossed her ankles. Her words came back to me in a rush. "Muuuy fatha made me a bee-yoo-tee-ful dollhouse." Miss Bradley said, "Very good," and moved on to the next word. Around me hands were waving, waving. Pick me! Pick me! Behind me I could hear David softly crooning, "You ain't nothin' but a hound dog, cryin' all the time." Sometimes he would stick his head inside his desk, sing Elvis songs and pick his boogies at the same time. Somebody was jabbing pins in my chest. Ping! Ping! Ping! I wanted to holler, "Yowee! Stop!" as loud as I could, but I pressed my lips together hard.

"Now who can give me a sentence?" Miss Bradley asked. I put my head down on my desk and when Miss Bradley asked me what was wrong I told her that I didn't feel well and that I didn't want to be chosen. When Leonard collected the homework, I shoved mine at him so hard all the papers he was carrying fell on the floor.

Bile was still clogging my throat when Miss Bradley sent me into the cloakroom to get my lunchbox. The rule was, only one student in the cloakroom at a time. When the second one came in, the first one had to leave. I was still rummaging around in my bookbag when I saw Sandra.

"Miss Bradley said for you to come out," she said. She was smiling. That dollhouse girl was always smiling. I glared at her.

"Leave when I get ready to," I said, my words full of venom.

Sandra's eyes darted around in confusion. "Miss Bradley said . . ." she began again, still trying to smile as if she expected somebody to crown her Miss America or something and come take her picture any minute.

In my head a dam broke. Terrible waters rushed out. "I don't care about any Miss Bradley. If she messes with me I'll, I'll . . . I'll take my butcher knife and stab her until she bleeds." What I lacked in props I made up for in drama. My balled-up hand swung menacingly in the air. I aimed the invisible dagger toward Sandra. Her Miss America smile faded instantly. Her eyes grew round and frightened as she blinked rapidly. "Think I won't, huh? Huh?" I whispered, enjoying my meanness, liking the scared look on Sandra's face. Scaredy cat! Scaredy cat! Muuuy fatha made me a bee-yoo-tee-ful dollhouse. "What do you think about that?" I added viciously, looking into her eyes to see the total effect of my daring words.

But Sandra wasn't looking at me. Upon closer inspection, I realized that she was looking over me with sudden relief in her face. I turned to see what was so interesting, and my chin jammed smack into the Emeraude-scented iron bosom of Miss Bradley. Even as my mind scrambled for an excuse, I knew I was lost.

Miss Bradley had a look of horror on her face. For a minute she didn't say anything, just stood there looking as though someone had slapped her across the face. Sandra didn't say anything. I didn't move. Finally, "Would you mind repeating what you just said, Bebe."

"I didn't say anything, Miss Bradley." I could feel my dress sticking to my body.

"Sandra, what did Bebe say?"

Sandra was crying softly, little delicate tears streaming down her face. For just a second she paused, giving a tiny shudder. I rubbed my ear vigorously, thinking, "Oh, please . . ."

"She said, she said, if you bothered with her she would cut you with her knife."

"Unh unh, Miss Bradley, I didn't say that. I didn't. I didn't say anything like that."

Miss Bradley's gray eyes penetrated me. She locked me into her gaze until I looked down at the floor. Then she looked at Sandra.

"Bebe, you and I had better go see the principal."

The floor blurred. The principal!! Jennie G., the students called her with awe and fear. As Miss Bradley wrapped her thick knuckles around my forearm and dutifully steered me from the cloakroom and out the classroom door, I completely lost what little cool I had left. I began to cry, a jerky, hiccuping, snot-filled cry for mercy. "I didn't say it. I didn't say it," I moaned.

Miss Bradley was nonplussed. Dedication and duty overruled compassion. Always. "Too late for that now," she said grimly.

Jennie G.'s office was small, neat and dim. The principal was dwarfed by the large brown desk she sat behind, and when she stood up she wasn't much bigger than I. But she was big enough to make me tremble as I stood in front of her, listening to Miss Bradley recount the sordid details of my downfall. Jennie G. was one of those pale, pale vein-showing white women. She had a vocabulary of about six horrible phrases, designed to send chills of despair down the spine of any young transgressor. Phrases like "We'll just see about that" or "Come with me, young lady," spoken ominously. Her face was impassive as she listened to Miss Bradley. I'd been told she had a six-foot paddle in her office used solely to beat young transgressors. Suppose she tried to beat me? My heart gave a lurch. I tugged rapidly at my ears. I longed to suck my thumb.

"Well, Bebe, I think we'll have to call your mother."

My mother! I wanted the floor to swallow me up and take me whole. My mother! As Jennie G. dialed the number, I envisioned my mother's face, clouded with disappointment and shame. I started crying again as I listened to the principal telling my mother what had happened. They talked for a pretty long time. When she hung up, ole Jennie G. flipped through some papers on her desk before looking at me sternly.

"You go back to class and watch your mouth, young lady."

As I was closing the door to her office I heard her say to Miss Bradley, "What can you expect?"

"Ooooh, you're gonna get it girl," is how [my cousin] Michael greeted me after school. Logan's colored world was small, and news of my demise had blazed its way through hallways and classrooms, via the brown-skinned grapevine. Everyone from North Philly, West Philly, and Germantown knew about my crime. The subway ride home was depressing. My fellow commuters kept coming up to me and asking, "Are you gonna get in trouble?" Did they think my mother would give me a reward or something? I stared at the floor for most of the ride, looking up only when the train came to a stop and the doors hissed open. Logan. Wyoming. Hunting Park. Each station grew me closer to my doom, whatever that was going to be. "What can you expect?" I mulled over those words. What did she mean? My mother rarely spanked, although Nana would give Michael or me, usually Michael, a whack across the butt from time to time. My mother's social-worker instincts were too strong for such undignified displays; Doris believed in talking things out, which was sometimes worse than a thousand beatings. As the train drew closer to Susquehanna and Dauphin I thought of how much I hated for my mother to be disappointed in me. And now she would be. "What can you expect?"

Of me? Didn't Jennie G. know that I was riding a subway halfway across town as opposed to walking around the corner to Carver Elementary School, for a reason: the same reason I was dragged away from Saturday cartoons and pulled from museum to museum, to Judimar School of Dance for ballet (art class for Michael), to Mrs. Clark for piano. The Bosoms wanted me to Be Somebody, to be the second generation to live out my life as far away from a mop and scrub brush and Miss Ann's floors as possible.

My mother had won a full scholarship to the University of Pennsylvania. The story of that miracle was a treasured family heirloom. Sometimes Nana told the tale and sometimes my mother described how the old Jewish counselor at William Penn High School approached her and asked her why a girl with straight Es (for "excellent") was taking the commercial course. My mother replied that Nana couldn't afford to send her to college, that she planned to become a secretary. "Sweetheart, you switch to academic," the woman told her. "You'll get to college." When her graduation day approached, the counselor pulled her aside. "I have two scholarships for you. One to Cheyney State Teacher's College and the other to the University of Pennsylvania." Cheyney was a small black school outside of Philadelphia. My mother chose Penn. I had been born to a family of hopeful women. One miracle had already taken place. They expected more. And now I'd thrown away my chance. Michael, who was seated next to me on the subway and whose generosity of spirit had lasted a record five subway stops, poked me in the arm. "Bebe," he told me gleefully, "your ass is grass."

Nana took one look at my guilty face, scowled at me and sucked her teeth until they whistled. My mother had called her and told her what happened and now she was possessed by a legion of demons. I had barely entered the room when she exploded. "Don't. Come. In. Here. Crying," Nana said, her voice booming, her lips quivering and puffy with anger. When Nana talked in staccato language she was beyond pissed off. Waaaay beyond. "What. Could. Possess. You. To. Say. Such. A. Thing? Embarrassingyourmotherlikethatinfrontof *those people!*" Before I could answer she started singing some Dinah Washington song, real loud. Volume all the way up. With every word she sang I sank deeper and deeper into gloom.

Later that evening, when my mother got home and Aunt Ruth, Michael's mother, came to visit, the three women lectured me in unison. The room was full of flying feathers. Three hens clucking away at me, their breasts heaving with emotion. Cluck! Cluck! Cluck! How could I have said such a thing? What on earth was I thinking about? Cluck! Cluck! Cluck! A knife, such a, a colored weapon.

"But I didn't do anything," I wailed, the tears that had been trickling all day now falling in full force.

"Umph, umph, umph," Nana said, and started singing. Billie Holiday this time.

"You call threatening somebody with a knife nothing?" Aunt Ruth asked. Ruth was Nana's middle girl. She was the family beauty, as pretty as Dorothy Dandridge or Lena Horne. Now her coral lips were curled up in disdain and her Maybelline eyebrows were raised in judgment against me. "They expect us to act like animals and you have to go and say that. My God."

Animals. Oh. Oh. Oh.

My mother glared at her sister, but I looked at Aunt Ruth in momentary wonder and appreciation. Now I understood. The unspoken rule that I had sensed all of my life was that a colored child had to be on her best behavior whenever she visited the white world. Otherwise, whatever opportunity was being presented would be snatched away. I had broken the rule. I had committed the unpardonable sin of embarrassing my family in front of *them*. Sensing my remorse and shame, Mommy led me out of the kitchen. We sat down on the living room sofa; my mother took my hand. "Bebe, I want you to go to your room and think about what you've done. I don't understand your behavior. It was very hard for me to get you in Logan." She drew a breath. I drew a breath and looked into the eyes of a social worker. "I'm extremely disappointed in you. . . ."

The Bosoms decided to forgive me. My mother woke me up with a kiss and a snuggle and then a crisp, "All right, Bebe. It's a brand-new day. Forget about yesterday." When I went to get a bowl of cereal that morning, my Aunt Ruth was sitting in the kitchen drinking coffee and reading the newspaper. She had spent the night. "Did you comb your hair?" she asked me.

I nodded.

"That's not what I call combed. Go get me the comb and the brush."

She combed out my hair and braided it all over again. This time there were no wispy little ends sticking out. "Now you look nice," she said. "Now you look like a pretty girl, and when you go to school today, act like a pretty girl. All right?"

I nodded.

Last night Nana had hissed at me between her teeth. "If you want to behave like a little *heathen*, if you want go up there acting like a, a . . . *monkey on a stick . . . well*, thenyoucangotoschoolrightaroundthecornerandI'llwalkyouthereandI'llwalkyoubackhomeandI'llcomeandgetyouforlunchnowyou*behave*yourself!" But today was sanguine, even jovial, as she fixed my lunch. She kissed me when I left for school.

On my way out the door my mother handed me two elegant letters, one to Miss Bradley and the other to Jennie G., assuring them that I had an overactive imagination, that I had no access to butcher knives or weapons of any kind, that she had spoken to me at length about my unfortunate outburst and that henceforth my behavior would be exemplary. These letters were written on the very best personalized stationery. The paper was light pink and had "D.C.M." in embossed letters across the top. Doris C. knew lots of big words and she had used every single one of them in those letters. I knew that all of her i's were dotted and all of her t's were crossed. I knew the letters were extremely dignified. My mother was very big on personal dignity. Anyone who messed with her dignity was in serious trouble. . . .

So I knew my mother's letters would not only impress Miss Bradley and Jennie G. but would also go a long way toward redeeming me. After Miss Bradley read the note she told me I had a very nice mother and let me know that if I was willing to be exemplary she would let bygones be bygones and I could get back into her good graces. She was, after all, a dedicated teacher. And I had learned my lesson.

My mother wrote my father about the knife incident. I waited anxiously to hear from him. Would he suddenly appear? I searched the street in front of the school every afternoon. At home I jumped up nervously whenever I heard a horn beep. Finally, a letter from my dad arrived — one page of southpaw scribble.

> *Dear Bebe,*
> *Your mother told me what happened in school about the knife. That wasn't a good thing to say. I think maybe you were joking. Remember, a lot of times white people don't understand how colored people joke, so you have to be careful what you say around them. Be a good girl.*
>
> > *Lots of love,*
> > *Daddy*

The crumpled letter hit the edge of the wastepaper basket in my mother's room and landed in front of her bureau. I picked it up and slammed it into the basket, hitting my hand in the process. I flung myself across the bed, buried my face into my pillow and howled with pain, rage, and sadness. "It's not fair," I wailed. Ole Blondie had her dollhouse-making daddy whenever she wanted him. "Muuuy fatha . . ." Jackie, Jane, and Adam had their wild, ass-whipping daddy. All they had to do was walk outside their house, look under a car, and there he was, tinkering away. Ole ugly grease-monkey man. Why couldn't I have my daddy all the time too? I didn't want a letter signed "Lots of love," I wanted my father to come and yell at me for acting like a monkey on a stick. I wanted him to come and beat my butt or shake his finger in my face, or tell me that what I did wasn't so bad after all. Anything. I just wanted him to come.

—◦◦◦—

Bebe Moore Campbell (1950 –) grew up influenced by the civil rights battles of the 1950s and 1960s. She turned to journalism in 1976 as a means of expressing her own frustrations and describing her discoveries, and within a few years was a regular contributor to *Ebony, Essence, Ms., Black Enterprise*, the *New York Times*, and the *Washington Post*. She is the author of the novels *Your Blues Ain't Like Mine* (1993), *Brothers and Sisters* (1995), and *Singing in the Comeback Choir* (1998). She is a recipient of numerous awards including the National Endowment for the Arts Literature Grant and the 1994 NAACP Image Award. Campbell is a regular commentator for "Morning Edition," on National Public Radio. This excerpt is from her memoir, *Sweet Summer: Growing Up with and without My Dad* (1990).

Amy Tan

The Voice from the Wall

With my bed against the wall, the nighttime life of my imagination changed. Instead of street sounds, I began to hear voices coming from the wall, from the apartment next door. The frontdoor buzzer said a family called the Sorcis lived there.

That first night I heard the muffled sound of someone shouting. A woman? A girl? I flattened my ear against the wall and heard a woman's angry voice, then another, the higher voice of a girl shouting back. And now, the voices turned toward me, like fire sirens turning onto our street, and I could hear the accusations fading in and out: *Who am I to say! . . . Why do you keep buggin' me? . . . Then get out and stay out! . . . rather die rather be dead! . . . Why doncha then!*

Then I head scraping sounds, slamming, pushing and shouts and then *whack! whack! whack!* Someone was killing. Someone was being killed. Screams and shouts, a mother had a sword high above a girl's head and was starting to slice her life away, first a braid, then her scalp, an eyebrow, a toe, a thumb, the point of her cheek, the slant of her nose, until there was nothing left, no sounds.

I lay back against my pillow, my heart pounding at what I had just witnessed with my ears and my imagination. A girl had just been killed. I hadn't been able to stop myself from listening. I wasn't able to stop what happened. The horror of it all.

But the next night, the girl came back to life with more screams, more beating, her life once more in peril. And so it continued, night after night, a voice pressing against my wall telling me that this was the worst possible thing that could happen: the terror of not knowing when it would ever stop.

Sometimes I heard this loud family across the hallway that separated our two apartment doors. Their apartment was by the stairs going up to the third floor. Ours was by the stairs going down to the lobby.

"You break your legs sliding down that banister, I'm gonna break your neck," a woman shouted. Her warnings were followed by the sounds of feet stomping on the stairs. "And don't forget to pick up Pop's suits!"

I knew this terrible life so intimately that I was startled by the immediacy of seeing her in person for the first time. I was pulling the front door shut while balancing an armload of books. And when I turned around, I saw her coming toward me just a few feet away and I shrieked and dropped everything. She snickered and I knew who she was, this tall girl whom I guessed to be about twelve, two years older than I was. Then she bolted down the stairs and I quickly gathered up my books and followed her, careful to walk on the other side of the street.

She didn't seem like a girl who had been killed a hundred times. I saw no traces of blood-stained clothes; she wore a crisp white blouse, a blue cardigan sweater, and a blue-green pleated skirt. In fact, as I watched her, she seemed quite happy, her two brown braids bouncing jauntily in rhythm to her walk. And then, as if she knew that I was thinking about her, she turned her head. She gave me a scowl and quickly ducked down a side street and walked out of my sight.

Every time I saw her after that, I would pretend to look down, busy rearranging my books or the buttons on my sweater, guilty that I knew everything about her.

My parents' friends Auntie Su and Uncle Canning picked me up at school one day and took me to the hospital to see my mother. I knew this was serious because everything they said was unnecessary but spoken with solemn importance.

"It is now four o'clock," said Uncle Canning, looking at his watch.

"The bus is never on time," said Auntie Su.

When I visited my mother in the hospital, she seemed half asleep, tossing back and forth. And then her eyes popped open, staring at the ceiling.

"My fault, my fault. I knew this before it happened," she babbled. "I did nothing to prevent it."

"Betty darling, Betty darling," said my father frantically. But my mother kept shouting these accusations to herself. She grabbed my hand and I realized her whole body was shaking. And then she looked at me, in a strange way, as if she were begging me for her life, as if I could pardon her. She was mumbling in Chinese.

"Lena, what's she saying?" cried my father. For once, he had no words to put in my mother's mouth.

And for once, I had no ready answer. It struck me that the worst possible thing had happened. That what she had been fearing had come true. They were no longer warnings. And so I listened.

"When the baby was ready to be born," she murmured, "I could already hear him screaming inside my womb. His little fingers, they were clinging to stay inside. But the nurses, the doctor, they said to push him out, make him come. And when his head popped out, the nurses cried, His eyes are wide open! He sees everything! Then his body slipped out and he lay on the table, steaming with life.

"When I looked at him, I saw right away. His tiny legs, his small arms, his thin neck, and then a large head so terrible I could not stop looking at it. The baby's eyes were open and his head — it was open too! I could see all the way back, to where his thoughts were supposed to be, and there was nothing there. No brain, the doctor shouted! His head is just an empty eggshell!

"And then this baby, maybe he heard us, his large head seemed to fill with hot air and rise up from the table. The head turned to one side, then to the other. It looked right through me, I knew he could see everything inside me. How I had given no thought to killing my other son! How I had given no thought to having this baby!"

I could not tell my father what she had said. He was so sad already with this empty crib in his mind. How could I tell him she was crazy?

So this is what I translated for him: "She says we must all think very hard about having another baby. She said she hopes this baby is very happy on the other side. And she thinks we should leave now and go have dinner."

After the baby died, my mother fell apart, not all at once, but piece by piece, like plates falling off a shelf one by one. I never knew when it would happen, so I became nervous all the time, waiting.

Sometimes she would start to make dinner, but would stop halfway, the water running full steam in the sink, her knife poised in the air over half-chopped vegetables, silent, tears flowing. And sometimes we'd be eating and we would have to stop and put our forks down because she had dropped her face into her hands and was saying, *"Mei gwansyi"* — It doesn't matter. My father would just sit there, trying to figure out what it was that didn't matter this much. And I would leave the table, knowing it would happen again, always a next time.

My father seemed to fall apart in a different way. He tried to make things better. But it was as if he were running to catch things before they fell, only he would fall before he could catch anything.

"She's just tired," he explained to me when we were eating dinner at the Gold Spike, just the two of us, because my mother was lying like a statue on her bed. I knew he was thinking about her because he had this worried face, staring at his dinner plate as if it were filled with worms instead of spaghetti.

At home, my mother looked at everything around her with empty eyes. My father would come home from work, patting my head, saying, "How's my big girl," but always looking past me, toward my mother. I had such fears inside, not in my head but in my stomach. I could no longer see what was so scary, but I could feel it. I could feel every little movement in our silent house. And at night, I could feel the crashing loud fights on the other side of my bedroom wall, this girl being beaten to death. In bed, with the blanket edge lying across my neck, I used to wonder which was worse, our side or theirs? And after thinking about this for a while, after feeling sorry for myself, it comforted me somewhat to think that this girl next door had a more unhappy life.

But one night after dinner our doorbell rang. This was curious, because usually people rang the buzzer downstairs first.

"Lena, could you see who it is?" called my father from the kitchen. He was doing the dishes. My mother was lying in bed. My mother was now always "resting" and it was as if she had died and become a living ghost.

I opened the door cautiously, then swung it wide open with surprise. It was the girl from next door. I stared at her with undisguised amazement. She was smiling back at me, and she looked ruffled, as if she had fallen out of bed with her clothes on.

"Who is it?" called my father.

"It's next door!" I shouted to my father. "It's . . ."

"Teresa," she offered quickly.

"It's Teresa!" I yelled back to my father.

"Invite her in," my father said at almost the same moment that Teresa squeezed past me and into our apartment. Without being invited, she started walking toward my bedroom. I closed the front door and followed her two brown braids that were bouncing like whips beating the back of a horse.

She walked right over to my window and began to open it. "What are you doing?" I cried. She sat on the window ledge, looked out on the street. And then she looked at me and started to giggle. I sat down on my bed watching her, waiting for her to stop, feeling the cold air blow in from the dark opening.

"What's so funny?" I finally said. It occurred to me that perhaps she was laughing at me, at my life. Maybe she had listened through the wall and heard nothing, the stagnant silence of our unhappy house.

"Why are you laughing?" I demanded.

"My mother kicked me out," she finally said. She talked with a swagger, seeming to be proud of this fact. And then she snickered a little and said, "We had this fight and she pushed me out the door and locked it. So now she thinks I'm going to wait outside the door until I'm sorry enough to apologize. But I'm not going to."

"Then what are you going to do?" I asked breathlessly, certain that her mother would kill her for good this time.

"I'm going to use your fire escape to climb back into my bedroom," she whispered back. "And she's going to wait. And when she gets worried, she'll open the front door. Only I won't be there! I'll be in my bedroom, in bed." She giggled again.

"Won't she be mad when she finds you?"

"Nah, she'll just be glad I'm not dead or something. Oh, she'll pretend to be mad, sort of. We do this kind of stuff all the time." And then she slipped through my window and soundlessly made her way back home.

I stared at the open window for a long time, wondering about her. How could she go back? Didn't she see how terrible her life was? Didn't she recognize it would never stop?

I lay down on my bed waiting to hear the screams and shouts. And late at night I was still awake when I heard the loud voices next door. Mrs. Sorci was shouting and crying, *You stupida girl. You almost gave me a heart attack.* And Teresa was yelling back, *I coulda been killed. I almost fell and broke my neck.* And then I heard them laughing and crying, crying and laughing, shouting with love.

I was stunned. I could almost see them hugging and kissing one another. I was crying for joy with them, because I had been wrong.

And in my memory I can still feel the hope that beat in me that night. I clung to this hope, day after day, night after night, year after year. I would watch my mother lying in her bed, babbling to herself as she sat on the sofa. And yet I knew that this, the worst possible thing, would one day stop. I still saw bad things in my mind, but now I found ways to change them. I still heard Mrs. Sorci and Teresa having terrible fights, but I saw something else.

I saw a girl complaining that the pain of not being seen was unbearable. I saw the mother lying in bed in her long flowing robes. Then the girl pulled out a sharp sword and told her mother, "Then you must die the death of a thousand cuts. It is the only way to save you."

The mother accepted this and closed her eyes. The sword came down and sliced back and forth, up and down, *whish! whish! whish!* And the mother screamed and shouted, cried out in terror and pain. But when she opened her eyes, she saw no blood, no shredded flesh.

The girl said, "Do you see now?"

The mother nodded: "Now I have perfect understanding. I have already experienced the worst. After this, there is no worst possible thing."

And the daughter said, "Now you must come back, to the other side. Then you can see why you were wrong."

And the girl grabbed her mother's hand and pulled her through the wall.

—◌·◌—

Born in California, *Amy Tan* (1952 –) grew up surrounded by influences from both Chinese and American cultures. She has written about trying to assimilate into the mainstream American world as a child. Tan's father and brother died of brain tumors when she was fourteen years old. At that time she also learned her mother had been married to a different man while in China and had three daughters from that marriage, a situation not unlike June's in *The Joy Luck Club* (1989), from which this excerpt was taken. Aside from winning numerous awards, *The Joy Luck Club* was a fixture on the bestseller list and later made into a feature film, for which Tan helped write the screenplay. Tan is also the author of *The Kitchen God's Wife* (1991), *The Moon Lady* (1992), *The Chinese Siamese Cat* (1994), and *The Hundred Secret Senses* (1995).

Marian Wright Edelman

A Family Legacy

South Carolina is my home state and I am the aunt, granddaughter, daughter, and sister of Baptist ministers. Service was as essential a part of my upbringing as eating and sleeping and going to school. The church was a hub of Black children's social existence, and caring Black adults were buffers against the segregated and hostile outside world that told us we weren't important. But our parents said it wasn't so, our teachers said it wasn't so, and our preachers said it wasn't so. The message of my racially segregated childhood was clear: let no man or woman look down on you, and look down on no man or woman.

We couldn't play in public playgrounds or sit at drugstore lunch counters and order a Coke, so Daddy built a playground and canteen behind the church. In fact, whenever he saw a need, he tried to respond. There were no Black homes for the aged in Bennettsville, so he began one across the street for which he and Mama and we children cooked and served and cleaned. And we children learned that it was our responsibility to take care of elderly family members and neighbors, and that everyone was our neighbor. My mother carried on the home after Daddy died, and my brother Julian has carried it on to this day behind our church since our mother's death in 1984.

Finding another child in my room or a pair of shoes gone was far from unusual, and twelve foster children followed my sister and me and three brothers as we left home.

Child-rearing and parental work were inseparable. I went everywhere with my parents and was under the watchful eye of members of the congregation and community who were my extended parents. They kept me when my parents went out of town, they reported on and chided me when I strayed from the straight and narrow of community expectations, and they basked in and supported my achievements when I did well. Doing well, they made clear, meant high academic achievement, playing piano in Sunday school or singing or participating in other church activities, being helpful to somebody, displaying good manners (which is nothing more than consideration to others), and reading. My sister Olive reminded me recently that the only time our father would not give us a chore ("Can't you find something constructive to do?" was his common refrain) was when we were reading. So we all read a lot! We learned early what our parents and extended community "parents" valued. Children were taught — not by sermonizing, but by personal example — that nothing was too lowly to do. I remember a debate my parents had when I was eight or nine as to whether I was too young to go with my older brother, Harry, to help clean the bed and bedsores of a very sick, poor woman. I went and learned just how much the smallest helping hands and kindness can mean to a person in need.

The ugly external voices of my small-town segregated childhood (as a very young child I remember standing and hearing former South Carolina Senator James Byrnes railing on the local courthouse lawn about how Black children would never go to school with whites) were tempered by the internal voices of parental and community expectation and pride. My father and I waited anxiously for the *Brown v. Board of Education* decision in 1954. We talked about it and what it would mean for my future and for the future of millions of other Black children. He died the week before *Brown* was decided. But I and other children lucky enough to have caring and courageous parents and other adult role models were able, in later years, to walk through the new and heavy doors that *Brown* slowly and painfully opened — doors that some are trying to close again today.

The adults in our churches and community made children feel valued and important. They took time and paid attention to us. They struggled to find ways to keep us busy. And while life was often hard and resources scarce, we always knew who we were and that the measure of our worth was inside our heads and hearts and not outside in our possessions or on our backs. We were told that the world had a lot of problems; that Black people had an extra lot of problems, but that we were able and obligated to struggle and change them; that being poor was no excuse for not achieving; and that extra intellectual and material gifts brought with them the privilege and responsibility of sharing with others less fortunate. In sum, we learned that service is the rent we pay for living. It is the very purpose of life and not something you do in your spare time.

When my mother died, an old white man in my hometown of Bennettsville asked me what I do. In a flash I realized that in my work at the Children's Defense Fund I do exactly what my parents did — just on a different scale. My brother preached a wonderful sermon at Mama's funeral, but the best tribute was the presence in the back pew of the town drunk, whom an observer said he could not remember coming to church in many years.

The legacies that parents and church and teachers left to my generation of Black children were priceless but not material: a living faith reflected in daily service, the discipline of hard work and stick-to-it-ness, and a capacity to struggle in the face of adversity. Giving up and "burnout" were not part of the language of my elders — you got up every morning and you did what you had to do and you got up every time you fell down and tried as many times as you had to to get it done right. They had grit. They valued family life, family rituals, and tried to be and to expose us to good role models. Role models were of two kinds: those who achieved in the outside world (like Marian Anderson, my namesake) and those who didn't have a whole lot of education or fancy clothes but who taught us by the special grace of their lives the message of Christ and Tolstoy and Gandhi and Heschel and Dorothy Day and King and that the Kingdom of God was within — in what you are, not what you have. I still hope I can be half as good as Black church and community elders like Miz Lucy McQueen, Miz Tee Kelly, and Miz Kate Winston, extraordinary women who were kind and patient and loving with children and others and who, when I went to Spelman College, sent me shoeboxes with chicken and biscuits and greasy dollar bills.

It never occurred to any Wright child that we were not going to college or were not expected to share what we learned and earned with the less fortunate. I was forty years old before I figured out, thanks to my brother Harry's superior insight, that my Daddy often responded to our requests for money by saying he didn't have any change because he *really* didn't have any rather than because he had nothing smaller than a twenty dollar bill.

I was fourteen years old the night my Daddy died. He had holes in his shoes but two children out of college, one in college, another in divinity school, and a vision he was able to convey to me as he lay dying in an ambulance that I, a young Black girl, could be and do anything; that race and gender are shadows; and that character, self-discipline, determination, attitude, and service are the substance of life.

I have always believed that I could help change the world because I have been lucky to have adults around me who did — in small and large ways. Most were people of simple grace who understood what Walker Percy wrote: You can get all As and still flunk life. . . .

I have always felt extraordinarily blessed to live in the times I have. As a child and as an adult — as a Black woman — I have had to struggle to understand the world around me. Most Americans remember Dr. King as a great leader. I do too. But I also remember him as someone able to admit how often he was afraid and unsure about his next step. But faith prevailed over fear and uncertainty and fatigue and depression. It was his human vulnerability and his ability to rise above it that I most remember. In this, he was not different from many Black adults whose credo has been to make "a way out of no way."

The Children's Defense Fund was conceived in the cauldron of Mississippi's summer project of 1964 and in the Head Start battles of 1965, where both the great need for and limits of local action were apparent. As a private civil rights lawyer, I learned that I could have only limited, albeit important, impact on meeting epidemic family and child needs in that poor state without coherent national policy and investment strategies to complement community empowerment strategies. I also learned that critical civil and political rights would not mean much to a hungry, homeless, illiterate child and family if they lacked the social and economic means to exercise them. And so children — my own and other people's — became the passion of my personal and professional life. For it is they who are God's presence, promise, and hope for humankind.

⸺◦◦⸺

Marian Wright Edelman (1939 –), founder and president of the Children's Defense Fund (CDF), has been an advocate for disadvantaged Americans for her entire professional career. Under her leadership the Washington-based CDF has become a strong national voice for children and families. It seeks to ensure that every child has a healthy start, a head start, a fair start, a safe start, and a moral start in life and successful passage into adulthood. A graduate of Spelman College and Yale Law School, Edelman, as the first black woman admitted to the Mississippi Bar, directed the NAACP Legal Defense and Educational Fund office in Jackson, Mississippi. She founded the Washington Research Project, a public interest law firm and the parent body of the Children's Defense Fund. She is the author of several books, including *Guide My Feet: Prayers and Meditations on Loving and Working for Children* (1995), *Families in Peril* (1987), and the highly acclaimed children's book, *Stand for Children* (1987). This excerpt is from *The Measure of Our Success: A Letter to My Children and Yours* (1992).

Front row, second from right:
Marian Wright Edelman

Rita Levi-Montalcini

In Praise of Imperfection

When I was still only a very small child, I developed an aversion to mustaches, and justified my reluctance to kiss my father by adducing the reason, in large part true, that they pricked me. "Rita," my father would note, with poorly concealed disappointment, "doesn't know how to kiss. She would rather kiss the air than her father." I had, in fact, developed the habit, when approaching him for the good-night kiss, of turning my head away upon contact with his face and sending the kiss into the air. A person with such a sharp eye as my father certainly could not have missed that I had no difficulty at all in kissing Mother; but in her case not only the fondness I felt but also the pleasant contact with her soft and fragrant face were reason enough for me to overcome my natural reluctance to engage in physical contact. The question of aerial kisses, however, had also presented itself in her regard, though in a different way. In an essay in which our second-grade teacher had asked us to explain what fingers were for, I wrote — to the great amusement of my brother Gino and those who knew the story — that they were "for sending kisses to Mother." Those, too, were a form of aerial kiss but had, in her case, a well-defined target. They revealed my lack of practical sense which was to persist in the future. This habit of blowing kisses, which lasted — not only in my father's regard, and even in the absence of mustaches — into adolescence, ought to have revealed to a person of his sensitivity and intuition much about the personality of his daughter with whom he could not manage to establish the close relationship he had with my two sisters.

My twin, Paola, who adored him, had shown from early infancy a great artistic talent which aroused in me unconditional admiration, unsullied by envy or regret, because I was completely lacking in her gift. This was only one of the differences between us evident from the first years of our lives. The others, no less significant and which revealed at first glance our nonidentical twinship, were manifest in our physical appearance, in our characters, and in our behavior. Her face differed from my own in shape and in its every feature. Beneath a high, slightly convex forehead, her laughing blue eyes denoted a disposition (in truth, more apparent than real) to a gaiety that enchanted our father. From an early age, which prevented one from guessing that still hidden design of her genes in the modeling of her facial features (a design puberty revealed to be entirely in keeping with one's expectations), her face bore an extraordinary resemblance to his own — a cause for joy and paternal pride. On the other hand, our mother was pleased to assert that I was the living image of her mother. She saw again in mine her mother's gray-green eyes with their melancholy gaze, the slight asymmetry of the face, the slender lines of the bone structure. My tendency to seek solitude and to flee from encounters with either sex reminded her of the sad, reserved character of her own mother whom she had adored and lost in adolescence. The deep affection linking Paola to our father, reciprocated with the most heartfelt tenderness, and that between myself and my mother date back to that early time. As for the relationship between Paola and myself, from our earliest childhood up to today — a period spanning over three quarters of a century — it has been characterized by an intensity of affection so great as to have created, especially while we were children, a sort of barrier against the intrusion of third parties.

Gino, our brother, seven years older than I, and Anna, five years older, came into the category of third parties. The barrier that excluded them from our secrets was to fall during adolescence when age differences were neutralized by the cultural inclinations and interests Paola shared with Gino and I with my elder sister. Gino had in common with Paola a strong artistic personality which made him choose architecture as a career. His natural talents manifested themselves in an exceptional aptitude for drawing — already evident, as in Paola, from childhood — and in a passion for modeling clay and plasticine (the smell of this malleable, gray-green, rubbery substance, which I believe can no longer be found in the shops, was noticeable on everything he touched and left permanent traces — among the most pleasant — on my olfactory neurons); these talents led him, after he had completed his high school studies with honors, to want to become a sculptor. Our father, however, whose dream it was that Gino would follow in his footsteps and take a degree in engineering, opposed a choice that offered no guarantees for the future. He yielded somewhat grudgingly to his son's clear preference for architecture, which offered a compromise between sculpture and engineering, the latter having no attraction for Gino whatsoever. The choice, as Gino himself later acknowledged, was a happy one. His natural artistic talents combined with passionate dedication made him one of the most prominent Italian architects of the mid-century and, at the same time, allowed him to express in his architectural constructions the innate sensibility of the sculptor. Our sister Anna (or Nina, as she was known to us and to friends) had literary interests similar to my own; yet neither she nor I were ever to fulfill our vague adolescent aspirations. In her case, marriage, pregnancies following one after another, and maternal duties took her away from the career she dreamed of: to become a writer like the Swedish Selma Lagerlöf, her favorite author and chosen model. Anna had passed on to me an unbounded admiration for Lagerlöf's books, and together we dreamed of the long nordic winters and shivered at the reading of Swedish sagas. Lagerlöf's 1891 novel *Gösta Berling* was our favorite subject of conversation, until we discovered in Emily Brontë's *Wuthering Heights* and Virginia Woolf's *To the Lighthouse* other models to emulate.

The alliance established between Paola and myself during our early childhood mitigated but did not free me from the anxieties I suffered as a child. These had their roots in extreme timidity, lack of self-confidence, and fear of adults in general and of my father in particular, as well as of monsters that might suddenly pop out of the dark and throw themselves upon me. To reach our bedroom and bathroom in the apartment where we then lived, one had to walk the whole length of a long hallway connecting the playroom of our preschool days to the bedrooms. The moment dusk began to fall, ignoring Gino's joking remarks, I would ask Paola, who didn't suffer from these torments, to accompany me whenever I had to face the ordeal. This fear of the dark, and of malevolent beings who might take advantage of it to attack me, was not the only manifestation of my insecurity and anxious nature. A form of terror of which I have a vivid memory was that caused by the motion of wind-up toys. One of these arrived as a present from my father's sister, who lived in London and enjoyed great prestige in the eyes of us children because she spoke English and married — as Mother put it — a high-class journalist. This particular toy was a small English gentleman wearing a black bowler hat, such as is still in fashion many decades later and was immortalized in photographs of Chamberlain, Eden, and Churchill. Our gentleman, no more than twenty-five centimeters tall, had a handsome mustache and a starched collar and held, in his gloved right hand, a walkingstick which he shook whenever he was set in motion by winding a little handle. The Britishness of his appearance was emphasized by a flannel jacket in black and white check (very tweedy, Agatha Christie would have said) and by the slow and dignified manner in which he advanced. When Gino wound him up and maliciously sent him toward me, panic would overwhelm me, and I would back away to reestablish distance between myself and "him" — to the great amusement of Gino and the family. "And yet," maintained my mother, who always protected me, "Rita is not easily frightened." And she would recall my easy acquaintance with animals much larger than myself and the pleasure I took in provoking a little goat in the country, exulting whenever it butted me and knocked me down. I think that the difference in my behavior derived from the fact that the little goat was a living creature. Fortunately for me, neither electronic mechanisms nor the possibility of activating machines or puppets by remote control had yet been thought of. I don't know how I would have reacted in the face of one of these if some force entirely mysterious to me had sent one in my direction.

Even if from early childhood I was bound by a far more vivid affection to my mother than to my father, it was he rather than she who had a decisive influence on the course of my life, both by transmitting to me a part of his genes and eliciting my admiration for his tenacity, energy, and ingenuity; and, at the same time, by provoking my silent disapproval of other aspects of his personality and behavior. . . . From him, too, I inherited seriousness and dedication to work, and a secular, Spinozan conception of life. The difficulty my father and I had in communicating — a cause of pain to him no less than to me — continued until death cut him off prematurely when Paola and I had just turned twenty-three. His sudden death left an ineradicable mark on Paola who had adored him, and filled me with a sense of regret and remorse for having so disappointed him in being what he would tenderly define, trying to overcome the barrier between us, as his "shrinking violet." Given our fundamental similarities, I think that today he would recognize me as his daughter and not only as his "shrinking violet," and that the harmony missing in the difficult years of my childhood and adolescence would immediately spring up between us, repaying us for the suffering we had involuntarily caused each other.

—◦◦◦—

Cell biologist *Rita Levi-Montalcini* (1909 –) was born in Turin, Italy. She earned her medical degree from the Institute of Cell Biology of the Consiglio Nazionale Richerche in Rome, Italy, in 1936. She began her academic career as a researcher at the University of Turin in neurobiology and psychiatry, and in 1947 she was invited to Washington University in St. Louis, Missouri, to work. She remained there until 1977. In 1986 she was awarded the Nobel Prize in medicine for the discovery of growth factors. This excerpt is from her autobiography, *In Praise of Imperfection*.

Dolores Huerta

Una mujer con compacion y gran fortaleza
A Woman of Fortitude and Compassion

It's funny about my mother. When I think about her, I don't necessarily remember what a great mom she was per se. Instead, I remember the things she did while I was growing up that have stayed with me to this day. I remember the things that in some way or another have inextricably shaped my life.

I was born in Dawson, New Mexico, in 1930, one of three children. My parents were divorced when I was five years old, and my mom, Alicia Chavez (no relation to César), moved me and my two brothers to Stockton, California, where she did everything from waitress to work in a cannery. Between taking care of the kids as a single mom before anyone coined the phrase, and holding down two, sometimes three, jobs, she always had time to do things for her kids and others . . . and that usually meant getting involved in her community, although what she did was not necessarily recognized as community service. Whether she was leading a Girl Scout troop, taking in a family who happened to have less than we did, or registering minorities to vote, she did so with a humbleness and naturalness that complemented her deep Catholic conviction that helping people is simply something that you do. In her humbleness she emerged as a real leader.

Eventually Mom opened a small restaurant and hotel in a mixed neighborhood primarily composed of Latinos, blacks, and Native Americans. I say that I "inherited" her passion for altruism and probably my fondness of farmworkers because she would often let farmworkers, or really anyone less fortunate than ourselves, stay in the hotel for free. In her service to others, and to the community in which we lived, I saw a woman dedicated to a goal: to feed the hungry, clothe the homeless, and serve in any way possible. My second husband always told me to keep an eye on my mom. If we didn't watch her carefully, he professed, she would give away the just-purchased auction lamb before he had time to even think about *berria* for dinner. And often we kids would come to learn all the wonderful things my mom did only after she died, because she would never talk about the fact that she had done something, only that we had to do something. "Don't be afraid to do new things, and always, always be yourself" was her motto, and it's something that still rings true to me to this day.

I remember one time when I was about five years old, it must have been in 1934 or 1935, my Aunt Mary had just lost her five children in a labor camp fire in Wyoming. When my mother heard about this, she went and got my aunt and brought her back to California and there she stayed until she could find the strength to start a new life. I remember sitting in the living room, hearing the pain in my aunt's voice and hearing only words of comfort and courage from my mother's mouth. Maybe it was because my mom was orphaned at age eight that she developed a strong work ethic and necessary independence, which saw her through her years of hardship growing up in a small New Mexico town. And maybe it was from that background that she talked about getting through even the most difficult times with a true sense of compassion and hope. It is that same sense of compassion and hope she shared with my aunt in the living room that day that allowed her to work with the Blue and Gold Community Group to feed destitute families, to pay for a stray kid's Girl Scouts dues, to raise funds to fight discrimination of Hispanics and other minority groups, and to initiate and organize the refurbishing of the community center.

When I look at my eleven kids (I had my first child at twenty and my last at forty-six) and how I have raised them among the farmworkers' cause during the 1960s and 1970s, I see a lot of parallels between my life as a working mother and my mother's life. Sexism was never a part of my world, because I was taught to be self-sufficient just like my brothers, much like I have taught my children. Rather than choose either my kids or my cause, I brought my kids to work with me, which I am certain comes from my mother's choice always to bring us kids along to whatever she was doing and encourage us to participate. I had the courage to walk away from two bad marriages, and I have taught my daughters that they do not need to stay in any relationship that is not respectful and completely fulfilling. The extent to which my sheer determination and desire to rise above my circumstances is generational, I firmly believe that I could not have survived the early union years without my mother's backbone and her true entrepreneurial spirit. And, I hope, these are the gifts I give to my sons and daughters as they find their own ways in life.

Often described as one of the best known women in the United States civil rights movement, *Dolores Huerta* (1930 –) is the cofounder and secretary-treasurer of the United Farm Workers of America (UFW), AFL-CIO. The mother of eleven children, fourteen grandchildren, and four great-grandchildren, Huerta has played many key roles in the UFW, including negotiating the first collective bargaining agreement for farmworkers, heading the UFW's national grape boycott, and directing the UFW's political and lobbying efforts. In championing farmworkers' rights, Huerta has often confronted "grower goons" and has been arrested more than twenty-two times for disobeying illegally imposed injunctions. In 1993 Huerta was inducted into the National Women's Hall of Fame. Currently she is the vice-president both of the Coalition for Labor Union Women and for the California AFL-CIO.

Judith Wicks

"A Table for 6 Billion, Please!"™

Bringing people together around food is a family tradition. As far back as I can remember, my parents Jack and Betty Wicks entertained with summer picnics on the patio, holiday gatherings, campfire sings, ladies luncheons, and their monthly Friday night Hungry Club, formed in 1947, the year I was born. In Winter Haven, Florida, my grandmother Grace turned her home into a guest house, renting out the bedrooms of her five daughters to put my mother and her sisters through college. Grandma's picture with Tricksy, a fox terrier, hangs on the dining room wall of the White Dog, along with her business card, which reads, "House of the Seven Gables — a good night's rest for every guest. Grace Scott, Proprietress." A cheery, spontaneous woman, she once slept in the bathtub, giving her bed to a weary soldier on his way home during World War II. I remember her most in the kitchen, cooking up big meals for our visiting family, sometimes of fresh fish she had caught in the lake and always with her favorite home-baked sticky buns, which she constantly nibbled. My other grandmother, Eleanor Wicks, was much more formal, though no less social. Nana set the perfect table at the many elegant dinner parties she hosted in her big house in Pittsburgh, and it was from her I learned to appreciate the details of good service.

We always dressed up when we went to Nana's house for dinner, with faces clean and hair combed, because we knew that Nana would notice everything. During the meal, she would make sure that we used the right utensil for each course and that we never put our elbows on the table. When I talk to servers about the expectations of our customers, I'm often reminded of the lessons Nana taught me as a child. It wasn't just about doing things right, though, that I remember most about the meals at Nana's house, it was more about the excitement and fun of family traditions. Holiday meals at Nana's house were times our family looked forward to with great expectation. The importance of traditions is another part of my childhood that I've continued at the café year after year, with the many annual events that customers come back to enjoy time after time.

When I was five, we moved to Ingomar, a small town north of Pittsburgh, where I grew up. The first thing I did was to run a string of extension cords down the driveway to hook up my record player. I turned it up full volume and sat on a little chair beside it to see who might come along. In a way, it was my first restaurant, and I'll never forget the delight I felt when my first customer, Johnny Baker, a boy my age with big feet and big ears, walked shyly up the driveway. By the time I was twelve I had numerous business startups. Success with the record player led to theater productions in the garage followed by a miniature golf course up in our woods, which I built with elaborate tunnels and ramps. With an early interest in design, I painted scenes on scraps of wood gathered from construction sites and sold them from my wagon down by the highway. With the larger scraps, I built clubhouses up in the woods — my favorite pastime and a foreshadowing of my future career. Each spring I'd ask for nails and tarpaper for my birthday and would tear down the old shack and build a bigger and better one every year until I went off to college. Just as I do now in the restaurant, I would take great care in creating comfortable and interesting places to sit — hanging pictures, designing curtains, and planting flowers around the entrance. Still building, I've kept up my childhood passion by adding or redoing a new room each year at the White Dog or in our shop next door, the Black Cat. Building clubhouses and miniature golf courses were not typical activities for girls growing up in the 1950s. My grandmother always tried to get me interested in a doll or new dress, but I had no interest in anything but building supplies. I'm grateful that my parents supported my nontraditional interests, and it was always a highlight when I led my parents up the path to the woods to show off my latest creation.

As the first child of three, I was born into the leadership position for organizing childhood games — from the Adventure Club to Halloween raiding parties. Although there were few female role models in my town for anything other than homemaking, my mother provided much of what I needed to become an entrepreneur with a commitment to community service. A great outdoorswoman, she was the leader of our town's

Girl Scouts troop and the volunteer director of our summer day camp. She led us on camping and white water canoe trips into the wilds, teaching us how to build a fire and pitch a tent, how to fend for ourselves and how to work in a group. I watched as she conducted the morning program at camp, and organized work assignments for each unit, always with fairness and enthusiasm. Mom planned our family camping trips, which Dad navigated by boat and canoe to a remote island in Canada. She packed supplies for two weeks and cooked meals over the campfire for eleven people. As it turns out, campfire cooking is the only method I have ever mastered. Rebelling against the 1950s practice of forcefeeding home economics to female students, while I longed to take woodshop, I refused to learn to cook and once leaped out the window of the classroom. My mother was concerned that I would not have the skills to feed a family, but no cause for worry — living above a restaurant has solved the problem!

A vision of blue-and-white-checked café curtains was the first thing I pictured when I thought of opening a restaurant. I found the fabric, my babysitter, Sita, who later became our first dishwasher, made the curtains, and I hung them in the front windows. Then I developed everything else around the style of the curtains! With a homey look of old lamps and antique oak furniture, and simple, flavorful food made from high quality, fresh ingredients, the White Dog began as an old fashioned kind of place where people gathered to discuss the issues of the day over a cup of coffee and a homemade muffin. Having spent a total of thirteen years in the French restaurant up the street where I had worked the gamut from waitress to coproprietor, I now only wanted American food, especially the favorites of childhood like hot fudge sundaes and root beer floats, Mom's marinated beef kabobs that Dad had grilled over charcoal, and Nana's strawberry pie. Call it luck or instinct, I caught the wave of popularity for American cuisine that was about to sweep the country, but to me I was simply doing what I wanted, bringing back the happy memories of meals our family enjoyed together.

Before long we had grown from serving simple food cooked on a charcoal grill behind the café to becoming a nationally recognized restaurant specializing in contemporary American cuisine. Although I'm proud of that accomplishment, I realized my dream was not simply a restaurant full of happy customers. I needed more than that to feel satisfied with my work, and I developed another dream, one in which everyone in the whole world would sit at one big table and enjoy the earth's abundance. I imagined walking into a restaurant and saying to the maitre d', "Table for 6 billion, please!" This is the name I gave our international sister restaurant project started in 1987 to promote world understanding through the universal love of eating.

I've always had a strong interest in those denied a place at the table. My father used to call it my passion for the underdog, which I think began with a traumatic experience in grade school. When I was ten, I first experienced the destructive feeling of being excluded. I loved to play softball and back in fifth grade was as good as the boys. I couldn't wait for the season to begin each spring, and one sunny morning our gym teacher announced, "Class, it looks like a great day out there — time to play softball." I jumped from my seat with excitement. "Guys down to the field," he said. "Girls go over there somewhere and practice cheerleading." I was dumbfounded and dejectfully stood behind the backstop watching the boys play. I didn't know enough to be mad about it. I accepted the fate of being a girl, of being a second-class citizen, and I developed contempt for myself and the other girls just for being girls. This taught me a lifetime lesson that discrimination causes self-destructiveness, and I began to understand that the whole community loses when some are left out of the game.

At first I saw business as a game I didn't want to play. I was offended by the profit-at-any-cost, winner-takes-all value system of corporate America. Drawn to small business entrepreneurship for the personal freedom it provided, I gradually developed my own idea of what business should be — contrary to business school traditions. Eventually, I came to the realization that a successful and sustainable economy was not one based on hoarding, but on sharing; not on excluding, but on finding a way for everyone to play the game according to everyone's individual strengths and interests.

Our international sister restaurant program uses food as a nonthreatening way to promote understanding between U.S. citizens and countries that have misunderstandings with our government. Traveling with our customers to such places as Nicaragua, Vietnam, and Cuba, I have seen the effect of U.S. foreign policy on the lives of others and realize that it is through dialog and understanding , rather than through isolationism or military confrontation, that we achieve world peace. Also, the trips have provided the opportunity to experience other economic systems as I continued to struggle with questions about capitalism that I developed as a college student in the 1960s. Convinced by my travels and my own experience in business that the free enterprise system works best in channeling creativity and energy into the workplace, I envisioned a combination of capitalism with concern for the common good found in socialist societies. I named this hybrid Capitalism for the Common Good. Now I finally understood what it was that I had been practicing, and at last stopped doubting my career in business, knowing that I had figured a way to connect my entrepreneurial energy with my commitment to social change. The possibilities were endless. I was filled with great hope and excitement as I began to create new programs at work for building a more inclusive community at home and around the world.

Realizing there were cultural misunderstandings right here in Philadelphia, I began a local sister restaurant program that promotes evenings in various ethnic neighborhoods to dine at minority-owned restaurants and attend cultural events such as an art opening at the Puerto Rican cultural center or a play at one of America's oldest African-American theatres. Concerned about citizen apathy, I began scheduling Table Talks at dinner and breakfast, featuring speakers on issues of public concern to encourage discussion and civic involvement in health care reform, public education, and environmental protection. On Saturday afternoons I added talks by and for teens to inspire student activism and discussion among diverse groups of youth. The Native American Thanksgiving Dinner, *Noche Latina*, and the Freedom Seder are among the many multicultural events held annually at the café, as well as birthday dinners each year in memory of Dr. Martin Luther King,

Jr. and Mahatma Gandhi and a celebration of organic gardening with the Farmers' Sunday Supper in the fall.

Looking back, I see that so much of what I've done at the café began with my childhood. My mother and grandmothers taught me the importance of having annual traditions to look forward to, of how to use food to gather people together, about the importance of attention to detail, and about fairness and cooperation in getting the job done. Most important, in watching my mother and grandmothers, I saw the joy they found in serving others. That's what our mission has become at the White Dog Café — to serve fully and in doing so to discover the meaning and joy of life. In serving fully, we not only think of ourselves as serving customers but also of serving our fellow employees, serving our natural world, and serving our community. After I began to find opportunities to run my business in ways that make a profit and serve others at the same time, I discovered this to be better known as "socially responsible business." I'm happy to find myself a part of the national movement that sees business as a vehicle for creating a just society, bringing new meaning to our work lives. And who knows? If the powerful institution of business is directed toward including everyone in the game, maybe someday there will be a world where everyone has a place at the table. What a great party that would be!

⌒◌◌⌒

What *Judith Wicks* (1947 –) began in 1983 as a muffin-and-coffee take-out shop in a Victorian brownstone on Sansom Street in Philadelphia is now the White Dog Café. According to Wicks, the name came from the story of a nineteenth-century occupant of the brownstone. Madame Helena Petrovska Blavatsky, cofounder of the Theosophical Society, apparently fell ill with an infected leg and was confined to bed. Legend says that a white dog slept on her leg, curing her of the malady. Hence, the White Dog Café, which Wicks owns and operates along with the Black Cat, a retail gift store. Wicks is best known for blending food, fun, and social activism. Including the nonprofit projects

Wicks runs herself, she contributes approximately 10 percent of profits after taxes to nonprofit organizations and charitable events.

Front and center, kneeling:
Judith Wicks

Faye Wattleton

Preacher's Daughter

In the summer of 1953, Mama was asked to preach at a revival for a white congregation in Nebraska. Daddy was not going to join us, so for the first time in my short life, I would be in the midst of only white people. The only other colored face that I would see for the two weeks of the revival would be my mother's.

Mama and I took the train to Albion, a small farming community in the middle of the corn and alfalfa fields of central Nebraska. We would be staying in the home of the host pastor, and Mama, anxious to make a good impression, reminded me during the train ride that we must not reinforce the negative racial stereotypes of blacks as unclean, unkept, or speaking in dialect; and I must be a polite and helpful guest.

"Help with the dishes and don't leave your washcloth on the sink," she instructed. "And I brought the hot comb to take care of that nappy hair of yours."

At ten, I was an old hand at adapting. Still, I had no idea what to expect in Albion, no comparable experience to draw on. I wasn't afraid, because I was with my mother, but I was anxious. First sight of our Alabama-born hosts, the McCulloughs, did much to calm my anxieties. Sister McCullough was a big, tall woman with laughing, vivid blue eyes. Her husband, rosy-cheeked and ever smiling, exuded enthusiasm. "Sister Wattleton, I can't tell you how happy we are to have you," he blurted out as he energetically pumped Mama's hand.

The McCullough sons, David, Ron, and Dale, were fresh-scrubbed, all-American teens. As they rounded out the reception line of smiles, I suspected that, like me, they had gotten some parental priming for our arrival. Here, far from the South, the hand of fellowship within the Church of God was being extended freely and kindly across racial lines. Nevertheless, I vaguely sensed that our hosts' effusiveness flowed in part from their own anxieties.

They took our bags and led us to the second-floor guest room. As I sat down cautiously on the double bed and looked out the window at the bright sunlight reflecting off the white steepled church outside, I wondered about what lay ahead.

My worries were soon forgotten in play with the McCullough boys and other neighborhood children and in riding borrowed bicycles on the wide, mostly empty, tree-shaded streets of the small town. Sometimes we played jacks or fiddlesticks on the concrete porch, or frequented the neighborhood confectionery. Mama, as was her custom, stayed in the guest room throughout the day, praying, reading the Bible, and preparing her sermons.

Every day at noon, lunchtime was announced by a siren blaring from the town's water tower and we children ran back to the parsonage for what were, to me, marvelous delicacies — banana and mayonnaise sandwiches on white bread, cottage cheese, potato chips, and raw vegetables. After the meals, faithful to my mother's instruction, I helped clean up. Then I returned to my outdoor adventures, which soon included sailing down the street at high speed without holding on to the handlebars.

While we were in Albion, I was introduced to the trials of conforming to a standard of beauty that did not value my African features. A day of vigorous play under the hot summer sun in that pre-chemical straightener era meant sweaty, kinky hair. Mama's thick, heavy, straight hair was unaffected by the heat, but she'd packed all the necessary equipment to tame my own soft but rambunctious mass of corkscrew curls. Late each afternoon, the preparation of my exterior for nightly services became a ritual. The companion odors of burning hair and roasting alfalfa, the latter wafting from the processing plant on the edge of town, filled the still afternoon air.

These secular ministrations began with bathing, dousing my emerging underarm pubescence with liquid Avon deodorant, rubbing Vaseline on my legs, "so that these white people won't see the ash on your legs," and pulling out a small can of liquid fuel to heat the straightening comb. I would sit on the floor between my mother's legs, facing out, my arms wrapped around her knees to anchor me while she tugged at my resistant hair.

"Hold still!" Mama would command as I tried to dodge the searing sweep of the comb.

"Hold your ear down," she'd order to avoid inflicting third-degree burns on me with the heated metal. Not only would a burn hurt me; more important, it might reveal our efforts to transform our looks into a semblance of white folks'.

Keeping my hair straightened was all but impossible since the spiral strands would reappear as soon as I began to perspire.

During the nightly services, members of the Church of God from Columbus, a small town nearby, used to come to hear "the colored lady preacher." They talked of needing a pastor for their church, and before we headed east, they asked my mother if she would consider the post.

Without hesitation, she accepted. Again, the invitation was for her a demonstration of "God's calling." It simply would not have done to question the details or the wisdom of it. My father would acquiesce. I was not asked. I was thrilled by the prospect of my parents' settling in one place for a little while and my being able to stay with them. Maybe I'd even be able to get a bicycle, I thought.

We drove into the town of ten thousand inhabitants in the middle of the night. Like Albion, its streets were wide, and the silhouettes of the broad-trunked trees and houses set behind large lawns gave a sense of elegance and tranquillity. But when we pulled up in front of the four-room house attached to the back of the stucco-and-brick church, my heart sank. It sank even deeper when we opened the door and beheld a living room and two bedrooms slightly larger than the double beds and dressers that filled them. In my room was a dressing table made from wooden crates and a sheet of wood that rested on top. It was draped in pink cotton. At the back of the apartment was a kitchen, a minuscule closet with a commode and a sink, and a shower in the basement. Or, if we preferred, we could use a galvanized metal washtub for baths. The members of the church had stocked the small refrigerator with cold milk. A package of Oreo cookies sat on the cabinet. There was no television, and the only other amenities were a piano, which became the site of my torture as I practiced endless scales on its keys, and a small Bakelite radio that my mother kept tuned to the homilies of commentator Paul Harvey at lunchtime and soap operas after I returned from school. But, such as it was, this was my first stable home since we'd pulled up stakes in St. Louis, and far better than any place I'd been since.

Everything seemed so charming, so orderly and predictable, in that quiet little town. But when my father went in search of construction and janitorial jobs, he was turned down repeatedly. Only then did a church member reveal to him one of the town's unwritten rules: No blacks were to be hired in Columbus.

Since my mother's resigning her position was out of the question, Daddy had no choice but to commute some eighty miles to Omaha to find work. For two years, he'd leave early Monday mornings and come home late Friday nights, and Mama and I would stay behind in a town where we knew black people were unwelcome.

I never heard Daddy complain. I have since wondered whether this situation provided him with an easy escape from Mama's ministry. Though devoted to Mama, he was still a proud man. I can imagine that the spring in his manner when it was time for him to depart came from the satisfaction of being able to hold onto his identity.

Members of my mother's congregation tried to downplay the significance of our color. One member, when asked her opinion about having a black pastor, disingenuously replied, "Oh, is she black? We really hadn't noticed." I still remember the first time Mama and I went to shop for groceries. We were walking down the tree-lined street when suddenly we found ourselves in the midst of a sea of white faces pointing, snickering, whispering, and staring at us. In every direction, people had stopped in their steps to gawk. Some were surely seeing black people for the first time. I was not a stranger to this mutual sense of otherness, but I was overwhelmed by the strength and lopsidedness of the feeling. I remembered my father telling us how members of his segregated army unit had their coats lifted so that their "tails" could be examined; this was not so different. We tried to go about our shopping as though this arm's-length assault weren't happening. Finishing our grocery shopping, we walked on to the dry goods store. The curious eyes tracked us. People stepped to the side and peered out the window to watch us as we passed.

My mother was incensed by the callous rudeness of the stares. As for me, while I had seen signs that had read "Colored" and "White" in the

South, this experience was altogether different. At ten years old, I felt humiliated and isolated. Nothing could have prepared me for this experience, and I cried all the way back to our small apartment. Once there, I ran into my room, closed the door, fell on the bed, buried my face in the pillow, and wept uncontrollably, distraught by the idea that we would be living in this town indefinitely. All I wanted to do was to go back to St. Louis, back to the security of the familiar — to be back in the house on Walton Street, playing with Miss Sue or reading the funny papers with Aunt Alice; back to smell the grass of Forest Park; to see the monkey show at the zoo; to drink a cool, bitter lemonade while sitting through a boring aria at Forest Park Opera, where Evie and Ola took me to escape the sweltering night heat and humidity of our brick house on Walton. But they were gone, too — Evie was married and supporting her husband while he attended Meharry Medical School in Nashville, Tennessee, and Ola was married and living in Indiana.

But it didn't matter what I felt. To rebel against my mother's calling would have been to rebel against God. I remembered the Sunday school song that Sister Epps had taught us, "Jesus loves me, this I know, for the Bible tells me so," and to its refrain, repeating over and over in my mind, I curled up and drifted into a sorrow-induced slumber.

I did enjoy going to school. The schools in Columbus were better than any I'd attended before — cleaner, with better books, and with teachers who gave me more attention than any I'd ever known. I even made a few friends — all girls. I was rarely invited to parties, however, or other social events by my classmates. In the seventh grade I tried out for a spot on the cheerleading team, figuring that it would unquestionably establish status with my peers. I was not chosen. Somehow, I knew all along that I wouldn't be. I'd practiced the chants over and over, but when it had come time to audition before the entire junior high, I was struck by stage fright. I managed to go through the motions, but not with the same exuberant abandon I'd mustered in the church basement. Maybe I wasn't good enough to be a cheerleader, but I'll always believe that it was more than that.

During our second year in Columbus, when I was in the seventh grade, I had a crush on a blond, blue-eyed boy named Steven. He'd been quite friendly to me, but then someone informed me that, while he liked me, he didn't want to go steady. I was hurt and frustrated by his rejection. Just like any other eleven-year-old, I was searching for acceptance and approval, and I was out of luck. In the adolescent social world of Columbus, Nebraska, I was neither openly rejected nor embraced; neither hated nor loved, recognized nor ignored.

I turned inward for comfort, and used fond memories of my reigning status at 1241 Walton to buoy my confidence. And I found a sense of importance and worldliness in talking with my classmates about a city they had only read about — big, faraway St. Louis. I substituted hard work and academic achievement for social companionship.

Mama and Daddy bought me a set of the *Encyclopedia Britannica*, and I'd leaf through the burgundy, leather-bound volumes every day. Once, by accident, I happened upon a sequence of diagrams showing the stages of a fetus developing within the uterus. About to enter pubescence, I was transfixed by the images. I'd hardly begun to examine the diagrams when my mother entered the room, and I slammed the book shut. For days after, I searched for those pictures, but I never found them again.

Racial seclusion affected my mother, too, but differently. Mama was accustomed to preaching before audiences that responded with encouraging "Amens" or an occasional "Sister Wattleton, preach the gospel!" In Columbus, she had to learn to stand before a roomful of silently attentive people — people who listened to her sermons with nary an amen, save as a ritual response. And in Columbus, realizing the distraction caused by the contrast between the dark color of the back of her hand and the paleness of her palm, she kept the back of her hand toward the audience, mitigating the issue of her color. Whatever sacrifices needed to be made to lead a Christ-like life, Mama was more than willing to make. . . .

I often imagine how different things would have been for me had my childhood not been divided between the road tours and the shuttling back and forth between Church of God families. But the truth is that, despite her frequent absences, my mother had a clear — and for the time, unconventional — vision of the woman she wanted me to become and the opportunities she wanted me to have. She was committed to making that vision a reality, and to doing so while still meeting the demands of her ministry. Her own example utterly bypassed the feminine stereotyping of that era, whether it confined women to the house in the Ozzie and Harriet model or stuffed them into the racial pigeonhole that assigned black women, especially, to labor as household servants. And in a conviction fostered by her father's belief in the value of education, Mama was determined that I receive the best possible education. . . .

In the emotional turbulence of my preadolescence, I cried a lot of tears in Nebraska. And yet the whole of life wasn't contained in that midwestern town. The world beyond its borders seemed to be changing. Americans were dying in the Korean conflict. Senator Joe McCarthy was conducting his communist witch-hunts, ruining careers and lives. A polio epidemic raged uncontrollably, crippling and killing thousands. But still, the 1950s were different from the anguished 1930s and wartime 1940s. There was growth, a sense of change, of hope. There was more talk about greater rights for women. And a few years later, in 1957, a movement that would shake America began with Rosa Parks, a bus seat, a young minister named Martin Luther King, Jr., and a boycott.

I recall one afternoon in Columbus, when I arrived home from school and found my mother listening to the radio. The Supreme Court had just announced its ruling in *Brown v. Board of Education*. Mama told me that segregation in public schools had been outlawed. Only eleven years old at the time, I had no knowledge of how or why the Court had decided to mandate school integration. It was my mother's exuberance and pride that impressed me. And I was old enough to understand that the Court had confirmed to society what my parents had often told me to make it through my time in Columbus: I might be the only black child in school, but I mustn't in any way feel unworthy of sitting in a classroom with white children. I had a right to be there.

Faye Wattleton (1943 –) has a distinguished career of service and advocacy for women's health issues, including her fourteen-year term as president of the

Planned Parenthood Federation of America. As the first woman, first African American, and youngest person to head Planned Parenthood, Wattleton worked on the forefront of some of the most important issues of this century — including those involving children and families, civil rights, women's reproductive rights, and health care. Wattleton continues to advocate on behalf of women today and recently established the Center for Gender Equality, a think tank focusing on women's issues. This excerpt is from her autobiography, *Life on the Line*.

Jody Williams
A Letter for My Parents

In this two-part letter, Jody Williams writes of her relationship with her older brother Stephen, who was born deaf and not correctly diagnosed as schizophrenic until his early forties. Williams speaks to her family's difficulties at the height of Stephen's disorder, shortly before he was correctly diagnosed and successfully treated with medication. In a moving narrative, Williams remembers her adolescence, a time rich in personal relationship with her brother, as a cornerstone to her life choices.

Sunday, 21 October 1990

Dear Mom and Dad,

Sometimes when we love someone and they are hurting and in pain, we are sure that if we could just find "one magic word" we could make it all better for them. I wish I could find that magic word to make it better for you and for Stephen. Unfortunately, after forty-three years, it is pretty clear that for him, there is no magic word.

We as a family have certainly been affected by having grown up with him. As hard as it may be to believe sometimes, I think that being with him has made us grow and learn as human beings as well as bring great sorrow, pain, and anger. Obviously, all of those feelings have been much more intense for you two as his parents.

I wish I could find the magic word that would make you really believe that you did everything that you could for him. As parents, as human beings, you have always done the best you could do for your children. You have always given up things for yourselves so that you could give to your children — and now sometimes for your children's children. For Stephen, you gave up everything — the warmth of your family and friends in Poultney, your house, your business. Unfortunately, he was not, nor will he ever be, a Hellen Keller. No one can definitively say what makes a Helen Keller or what makes a Stephen Williams. I hope you know I write this letter as much for myself as I do for you. . . .

_ﾟﾟ_

Monday, 3 December 1990

This part of the letter might not seem very connected to what I wrote six weeks ago — and obviously did not finish or send then. But I want to try to make sense with what I will write now.

This past weekend I had the privilege of spending a weekend of reflection on the tenth anniversary of the killings of the four North American churchwomen in El Salvador. Of the participants at the conference, probably 90 percent were nuns, with a few priests thrown in (for good measure?). They represent the new Church — the Church that has chosen to walk with the poor. The conference was attended by the nun who was the head of the Maryknoll order at that time, other nuns who knew and worked with them, some of their family members and Fr. Jon Sobrino — a Jesuit who would have been killed along with the six Jesuits and their housekeeper and her daughter in El Salvador last November had he not been on tour in Thailand. He is one of the world's foremost theologians in the area of Liberation Theology.

One of the themes of the weekend was martyrdom — no great surprise, I'm sure. Growing up as Catholic children, saints and martyrs were great mysteries to us all — as they were made to be by the institutional Church. The saints and martyrs were very esoteric to me. Often what was said about them made very little sense to me. "Giving their lives for God" was usually part of the description of their lives. But that never seemed concrete, never related to flesh and blood people nor grounded in concrete acts that made me understand what that really meant at all. In fact, they seemed a little crazy to me.

As you certainly know, for a decade now I have worked in Central America issues. In my own small way, I have sometimes walked with the poor. In that process, I have come to learn about the lives of Archbishop Romero, of the four Churchwomen, of the Jesuits — and of countless other nameless martyrs. I finally have come to understand what martyrdrom really means. It finally makes sense.

As Melinda Roper, head of the Maryknoll order at the time of the killings, said to us this weekend, "They did not go there to die. They went there to live." When I was growing up in the Church, I always somehow got the impression that martyrs wanted to die and that made no sense at all to me. These women, the Archbishop, the Jesuits did not want to die; they wanted to live. They wanted to live to help make life better for others. They understood that they might die in the process and certainly felt fear. But they knew what was right and what was wrong and they continued their work in spite of their fear. They gave their lives for the poor and in so doing, they gave their lives for God. That is what martyrdom is. (Please don't get the impression that I am reconverting. I understand all of this in a spiritual sense for sure, but not in a sense that can only be understood through the Catholic Church.)

Such martyrdom is also the example of strength and commitment that gives others the inner fortitude to continue their own work. As one of the speakers said this weekend, "When the killers kill, they expect to make everyone else too afraid to do anything. But that is not what happened in El Salvador. When they killed Rutilio Grande (a close friend of and priest under Romero), what did they produce? They produced Archbishop Romero (prior to Rutilio Grande's murder, Romero had been very conservative, but after Rutilio's death, Romero began to speak out against the oppression). When they killed Archbishop Romero, what did they produce? They produced a martyr who continues to inspire thousands through his death to walk with the poor."

As Father Jon Sobrino said to us this morning, "The Institutional Church tries to take our martyrs away from us, to turn them into mystery and remove them from the people. What saint spoke from a bush and said to build a church where the bush stood? What is that? Romero was a real saint. He walked with the poor. He gave of himself, as did the four women and the Jesuits, so that others could live better. And the Institutional Church wants to take him, to take them, a step away from the people too. We must not let that happen. We must not forget their real history and let them be turned into 'tradition'. We must never forget that what started this Church was a martyr — Christ himself. A real being who had a real history. He was a real man. A martyr — not a 'saint' speaking from a bush."

Why do I say all of this? What does this have to do with Stephen? I'm not sure, exactly. But if we try to find the good even in the most painful of things, maybe we can see some reason to find solace in Stephen's presence on this planet. The examples of the martyrs affect living people in their work. For me, I firmly believe that one of the absolutely pivotal and fundamental reasons for the choices that I have made in life are some of the early experiences that I remember with Stephen as a child in Poultney.

Mom, you know this already, but I will say it again here to try to pull all of this together to make some sense out of it. Watching how other kids treated Stephen made no sense to me. When they were cruel to him because of his "weakness" — a weakness imposed upon him by some outside force, a weakness he did not choose — it made me angry. It made me want to defend him. (As I later did with Michael against David [classmates] in the fourth grade. I remember trembling with rage and fear but not questioning for a moment that the right thing to do was defend Michael. That was because of Stephen.) I think that that transferred to being angry when any larger power is "mean" to any weaker power. That translated into wanting to find ways to "defend" them. That wanting to "defend" them has translated into the work that I have done over the past ten years.

And I am not trying to say that I am a saint or a martyr (or would want to be). I am not trying to say that I am in any way heroic or that because I do "good work" that makes it somehow okay that Stephen's life has been miserable. What I am trying to say is that the experience has led me to a lifestyle that has helped many, many people. And I know that that example has made other people think twice about their own choices.

I think of the twenty-seven children wounded in the war in El Salvador that I have brought to the U.S. for medical treatment. Some of them would be dead today without that help. I think particularly of the incredibly beautiful little five-year-old girl who had been made almost deaf when the bombing of her village resulted in her eardrums exploding. She became voluntarily mute because of the trauma. I sat on the plane with her and her mother on our way to her surgery in Cleveland. The child could hear a little but never spoke to anyone but her mother. But I spoke with her anyway — I could not get Stephen out of my mind. An hour or so into the flight, she began to speak back to me. A miracle? Not likely, but it certainly shocked the pants off her mother! She had surgery and today she hears. And then there was Dolores with the bomb shrapnel embedded in her skull. Little Carlos who had lost an arm during an air attack on his village, who got surgery and a new prosthetic arm. And the list of lives affected directly goes on and on.

Again, there is no way to try to "trade" the lives of these children for the sad, sad life of Stephen. But if it were not for Stephen, if he had not been my brother and affected me the way that he did, these children would be deaf or dead or god knows what. So, his pain and suffering has brought joy and life where it otherwise might not have been. So I guess I am trying to say to you, thank you for the gift of Stephen — all the joy and sorrow and everything that knowing him has been and will continue to be. But because of him, the lives of others who don't even know him have been changed — for the better — forever.

I love you deeply,

Jody

—⟋◌⟍—

Corecipient of the 1997 Nobel Peace Prize, human rights activist *Jody Williams* (1950 –) was the founding coordinator of the International Campaign to Ban Landmines (ICBL), which was formally launched by six nongovernmental organizations in October 1992. In only six years, Williams, who served as the chief strategist and spokesperson for the campaign, oversaw the growth of the ICBL to more than one thousand nongovernmental organizations in more than seventy-five countries. Working in a unprecedented cooperative effort with governments, United Nations bodies, and the International Committee of the Red Cross, the ICBL achieved its goal of an international treaty banning antipersonnel landmines during the diplomatic conference held in Oslo, Norway, in September 1997. Williams now serves as an "ambassador" for the ICBL, speaking on its behalf all over the world.

Linda Sanford

Lessons from the Farm

A couple of years ago I was lucky enough to be managing IBM's mainframe business. That means big computers for big companies. Often, at the end of the day, I would find myself walking to the back of the plant and watching the computers being loaded onto trucks, ready for delivery to customers. After a while I would wonder why I did this. I could see the shipping details in my office. I knew how many orders we had and how many computers we had in production. It occurred to me that this need to see for myself the actual product of my department was rooted in a life lesson I had learned as a child.

I was the eldest of five girls in a tight-knit family. We all lived on the family's small working farm on the north shore of Long Island. We grew mainly produce — potatoes, shallots, strawberries, and such — which was sold to local distributors or at a roadside produce stand I would run with my sisters.

Every day after school and during school holidays, we would all pitch in around the farm — planting or cultivating the crops, or working on the stand. This was just part of life on a small, family-run farm. We thrived in the knowledge that we were an integral part of the business and always wanted to participate. I firmly believe now that many of the personal characteristics that have served me well from a career perspective were honed in this environment. And these characteristics go beyond the typical "hard work ethic" that one would expect of this kind of upbringing.

One particular characteristic I developed at an early age was accountability — not necessarily accountability from a strict job responsibilities perspective, but more a sense of personal and collective achievement. Accountability is just a fact of life on a farm. There's a certain amount of work that needs to get done within a defined period of time. This could mean planting crops before the frost starts, picking them while they are perfectly ripe, or selling them to coincide with the tourist season on Long Island. Whatever the season, we could always look back at the end of the day and see what we had done. It was instantly measurable, and we all immediately knew the value of our contribution. We could look back at ten rows of potatoes picked, or an empty strawberry stand and a bucket full of dollar bills. Even today, this sense of immediate job feedback is something I strive to find. I think this is why I often go to the back of the factory at the end of the day and see how many of these massive computers were loaded onto trucks. I want to see for myself the results of my team's efforts.

Also, on a small farm you have no choice but to figure out how to work effectively as a team for the collective good. At the same time, you learn that people are most effective when challenged with something they enjoy and find fulfilling, whether it's harvesting rows of potatoes, marketing your wares on the produce stand, or acting as bank manager as sales are made. So working with a team was, even then, a delicate balance between common goals and personal motivations. I have yet to find a team in any professional environment, in either a participatory or a management role, in which this is not true.

Accountability and teamwork are two traits I have inherited from my parents that were instilled in me during childhood. With everything I have experienced in life since those days, these are characteristics that have served me well and enabled me to meet many personal and professional ambitions. I think we all have elements of our upbringing we bring to bear in our later lives. Sometimes it's not until we are watching them haul the computers out the back door that we realize how sound those lessons are.

—◦◦◦—

Linda Sanford (1953 –) is one of five sisters who all work in science and mathematics fields. Their father jokes about starting a family consulting team. But the Sanford sisters were brought up to believe they could excel in any field. "It never occurred to any of us there were things we couldn't do," Sanford says. Sanford is general manager of Global Industries, IBM's worldwide industry-specific sales units. Global Industries manages relationships with IBM's large customers; develops industry-specific applications to solve supply chain, payment, and customer care business problems; and helps customers implement their business strategies through the application of information technology. As such, Sanford's organization is responsible for generating about 70 percent of IBM's revenue. Sanford joined IBM in 1975 as an engineer in the typewriter division and has held several executive positions, including executive assistant to the chairman of the board and director of IBM Networking Systems. One of the four highest-ranking women and the highest-ranking technical woman at IBM, Sanford is a member of the Women in Technology International Hall of Fame and the National Association of Engineers.

Anne Hill Keiter

Summer Mama

I can remember coming home
on soft summer afternoons,
the loose screen door gently banging
behind me,
shutting out the world
of skinned knees and warm clover;
welcomed summer days
of endless hummings of
June bugs and bike wheels.
Coming in to the
sunny-as-outdoors indoors,
I'd listen just for a second
to the change of sounds:
replacing the June bug's song
was my mother's,
soft and light,
bouncing against the yellow
kitchen walls and clean muslin curtains.
Then the warmest smile
that ever came fresh
from a too-old oven,
and the warmest eyes
that ever learned favor
in a southern garden,
would sneak a glance
around the carefully painted door.
And taking in at once
my burnt nose and
summer tarred feet,
those arms that could open so wide

and gather in the whole room
if they wanted,
would fold around
just me.

⁓ஓ⁓

Anne Hitt Keiter has been published in numerous anthologies, including *Preposterous: Poems of Youth* (1991). A high school English teacher, Keiter has taken the last few years off from teaching to travel the world. She is currently at work on a collection of poems.

Seated in high chair
Anne Hitt Keiter

Girlfriends

So closely interwoven have been our lives, our purposes, and experiences that, separated, we have a feeling of incompleteness — united, such strength of self assertion that no ordinary obstacles, differences, or dangers ever appear to us insurmountable.

— Elizabeth Cady Stanton

Naomi Wolf

Girlfriends

Genevieve loved her girlfriends. A girl with straight dark hair cut in a pageboy, she was my best friend at age twelve. The sense of style she showed, the confidence she took in her compact body, helped to redeem me a little from the triple stigma of bookishness, awkwardness, and shapelessness. We all looked up to Genevieve. A small, scheming diplomat, she seemed polite and engaging to grown-ups; all the parents liked her. Little did they know she was rolling around with their daughters during slumber parties.

For most of us, these games really were, I suppose, "just a stage." But it would be many years before we fell in love with boys the way we were infatuated with one another.

For Genevieve, this passion was more absorbing than it was for any of the rest of us. Her interest in other girls started at ten, when she fell in love with her first older woman: a nineteen-year-old Japanese college student named Grace. Grace lived in the apartment across the hall. She let Genevieve come over to feed her cat while she was away. Genevieve was allowed to loll on the bed with Grace when she was bored and had no date for the night. The younger girl got to wait on Grace as she watched *The Mary Tyler Moore Show*. The child painted Grace's nails and brushed her hair. Genevieve did not know that Grace only wanted her there because the girl made her feel glamorous and less lonely. She thought Grace knew that she was not just a kid from next door but a suitor. Grace thought Genevieve wanted to learn to be like her. She did not understand that Genevieve wanted to possess her, vague as that notion was to the child; to lie next to her and look into her eyes.

Late one night in the winter of sixth grade, after Grace had moved away, Genevieve was at a sleepover with me and a group of other girls. A girl we hardly knew, Shari, asked, "Do you know how to do a French kiss?" We didn't. "Watch." All the girls were watching. Everyone held her breath. The girl took a pillow and inexpertly mauled it with her mouth.

Everyone agreed that a pillow was not the best educational tool: you really couldn't learn properly that way, and boys would laugh at you if you didn't learn how to do it right. So, "for pretend," my new acquaintance, the golden Shari, looked around, considering whom to demonstrate upon. She chose Genevieve. And Genevieve let herself be taken into Shari's arms. Shari's hair fell all over Genevieve's face as she demonstrated "how to kiss a boy." Genevieve thought: Why ever leave this behind? It was girls she loved. There was nothing shocking to us in this kiss or her excitement about it. It was girls we loved, too. . . .

Genevieve's father was one of the ones who had recently left home. But he still sent money. Of all our rooms, Genevieve's provided the best stage for rehearsals. It has a soft, long-haired shag throw rug, a guest bed with satin covers, and a full-length mirror. There were more different kinds of softness in Genevieve's room than we had in our whole house. Irritable Cath, golden Shari, and I would gather there with Genevieve.

Shari and Cath, who were a year older than I and far more sophisticated, joined Genevieve in setting the script and the scene. Shari was imperious, critical, statuesque, usually coy, and sometimes somewhat cruel. An ex-rich girl with white skin, freckles, and floating yellow-white hair, she was situated at the pinnacle of the gang of kids we knew who lived close by. She was the first girl I knew whose mother shopped as a pastime and taught her how to do the same. Cath was her sidekick, more stolid and devoted, a dark presence, the daughter of people who ran a contracting business. I was so far below their status, with girls as well as boys, that it felt like a miracle or an accident to me that they noticed me at all. But they took me in for a few months, and I held my breath, waiting to be ejected.

The afternoons began with ritual food: when Genevieve's mom had gone for the day, we mould make margarine-soaked grilled-cheese sandwiches in a devise with two molded plates we called the toaster bra. We often held it up to our chests and pranced around the kitchen.

Then we would push the twin beds together. We would lie stretched out or all curled together like cats. We free-associated about boys. That conversation would last a good hour.

"Craig likes you," I might say to Genevieve while braiding her wet-looking black hair.

"Oh, he does not," Genevieve would reply. "I heard from my brother's friend at Galileo" — another high school, a tougher one — "that he likes this freshman on the drill team at Lincoln."

"But he leaned over you like that when he asked that question about English class in the hall yesterday."

"What question? What?"

"Well, he acted like he was asking a question, but I know he was just trying to get a better look down your shirt."

At which Genevieve would leap onto my back and pummel me with a pillow. That was the signal for everyone to pillow-wrestle. We all tumbled together until we could not stand any more, then we separated and resumed talking.

As we gossiped, the throat of one girl would press against the back of another girl's hand or a hipbone would nudge the underside of a neck. We would all smell the Love's Baby Soft ("Because Innocence Is Sexy") mingling with Jovan Musk and Revlon's Charlie, and with the scent of freshly washed hair (Clairol's Herbal Essence) and cotton fabric. We were great believers in the powers of scent. We had to be: perfume was, we believed, just as the magazines promised us, a way for us, all still virgins, to connect seductively without touching.

All this talk about boys was still a pretext. The truth was that we were not ready to splinter off into love relationships with the opposite sex. We talked about crushes on boys because we knew it was forbidden to breathe a word about the way we felt about one another. Everyone was in love with clever, observant Genevieve, and Genevieve flirted with me and with Shari, Genevieve's rival for the role of the alpha female. Shari and Genevieve were wary of each other, as two stars must be. But when we were all together, it was a group crush. We were giddy with the charm of ourselves. . . .

In a way, there will be nothing as exciting as this love between girls ever again. This love has codes and repression, innocence and distant obsession, all intensified by the secrecy of the feelings involved and the knowledge of the world's disapproval "if they only knew." These are all parameters of love that, by the time we were coming of age, had died out everywhere but in our all-girl subculture. . . .

But our loving other girls was still the stuff of great dramas or nineteenth-century novels, rather than of women's magazines, for a simple reason: it was doomed. We understood already that the price of being intimate with women beyond that first stage of early adolescence was just too high and that if there were another path we could take, we should do so, with all the strength we could muster, and not look back. Even as we flirted and left little love notes filled with sparkle in one another's lockers ("My lady of celadon eyes," read a favorite note, addressed to me by an older girl with long blond hair and a car, as she must have known, I had to look up the word "celadon"), we knew that time was running out on us. But our regret at the separation was wrenching as we began to move away from our infatuations with girls, whom we saw as captivating, civilized beings, into the world of sex with boys, those ill-spoken, skateboard-wielding Visigoths. It was like moving a love life from a Henry James novel into a Spiderman comic.

—◌◌—

Writer, lecturer, and Rhodes scholar, *Naomi Wolf* (1963 –) is the author of numerous essays and books on feminist social commentary. Her first two books, *The Beauty Myth* (1991) and *Fire with Fire* (1993), placed Wolf in the limelight of literary criticism and made her one of the most visible feminist writers in the country. The *New York Times* called *The Beauty Myth* one of the seventy most significant books of the century. In her best-selling *Promiscuities: The Secret Struggle for Womanhood* (1997), Wolf takes a candid historical and cultural look at the confusion surrounding girls' sexual coming of age and reveals the secrets associated with awakening sexuality: forbidden crushes, loss of virginity, rites of initiation. Her essays appear widely in *The New Republic*, the *New York Times*, the *Wall Street Journal*, the *Washington Post*, *Ms.*, and other publications. Wolf lectures widely on women's issues and recently taught a course on the language of politics at George Washington University, where she is a visiting scholar. This excerpt is from *Promiscuities*.

Teresa Cader

The Strand Theatre

Lovesick girls, old men in foul underwear
inhabit this movie theatre
in Trenton, New Jersey, in the fifties,
before the riots, before debutantes
are murdered in their town houses.
The most beautiful man we have ever seen
is making love to a woman we envy.
She lifts her thigh, we are breathless.
When they are not making love,
she cries, he drives his Ferrari
to an empty beach where he paces
the cliffs, imagining how he will leave
his wife. She waits in a back room,
as if she would wait there her whole life,
until one night coming to see her,
he crashes the Ferrari into a parked truck,
dies in her arms. We sob, lurching
in our seats. Old men yell at us
from the balcony, only I can't stop,
neither can you. You make syncopated snorts,
I hiccup as if on a megaphone.
Then you whisper *we sound like toads*,
and we are laughing, bleating like little goats
through the funeral all the way to the cemetery,
and God knows what will happen to the woman
whose man just died, because we are ushered
from the theatre, returned to the street,
where on the littered sidewalk
we stand astonished and thirteen.

꧁

Teresa Cader (1947 –) is the author of *Guests* (1991), which won both the Norma Farber First Book Award from the Poetry Society of America and the Ohio State University Press/*The Journal* Award in Poetry. Her second collection of poems, *The Paper Wasp* (1998), contains the poem "Internal Exile," which won the 1997 George Bogin Memorial Award from the Poetry Society of America. Cader's poems have appeared in numerous publications, including *Poetry, The Atlantic Monthly, Poetry Review,* and the *Radcliffe Quarterly.* A graduate of Harvard University's John F. Kennedy School of Government, Cader is currently teaching in the literature department at the Massachusetts Institute of Technology.

Lt. Gen. Claudia J. Kennedy

Inner Inspiration

The United States Army has a long tradition of singing while it works. The songs sung by legion soldiers while they trained are referred to as cadences. Cadences can be short or long and fast or slow depending upon the type of work they accompany. They are melodic as well as harmonic and are often placed against the backdrop of a familiar American folk song. They are usually about funny stories or uplifting experiences in life, thereby raising the morale and spirit of everyone who hears them. Typically, a senior, noncommissioned officer responsible for troop leadership will lead a formation of running soldiers while singing or chanting cadences. The leader will cast one line of the cadence to the troops, who will then echo back the appropriate response.

As I reflect upon my career in the army, I remember the sense of unity and teamwork cadences provided. As a young adult, I especially enjoyed running with soldiers, singing cadences. The cadence fortifies me when I run and strengthens my resolve to achieve my goals. For me, physical fitness is a physical, mental, and spiritual joy. And running to a rhythm intensifies the experience and provides meditation and discipline at the same time.

Many young women enter the army seeking a sense of structure and camaraderie, especially among their peers. Young soldiers say that the cadences help them identify with their peers, and begin planting the seeds for a lifelong career of mutual respect and friendship between them. When you can work with other girls toward a common goal, and share a common experience, even share a bit of the effort of disciplining yourself for rigorous physical and mental activity, then your relationship among yourselves is strengthened. As girlfriends together in the barracks, maturing into woman who will uphold the philosophy and regulations of the military, the cadence is one tool among many for building confidence and respect.

In some ways, I think it's even more important for young women, rather than young men, to deliberately embrace activities that promote cohesion and bonding. In the scope of U.S. history, women's bonding has been viewed with ambivalence, and anything leaders of young women can do to reinforce a young woman's standing among her peers and her girlfriends will help build her morale and shape her identity. For girls beginning to pave their way in life, inner strengtheners such as these cadences can fortify the soul and remind young women that they have a wealth of experiences and character traits to contribute to traditionally male-oriented environments.

The following double-time cadence was written with a sense of camaraderie and almost exuberance in mind. It's one the young women really enjoy, and we hope that, like American folk songs, they will modify and pass on to the next generation. . . .

Came into the Women's Army Corps
Came into the Women's Army Corps
I wanted a life that gave me more!
I wanted a life that gave me more!

Went to school to learn my trade
Went to school to learn my trade
Knowing that's how leaders are made
Knowing that's how leaders are made.

Sound off! One-two
Sound off! Three-four
Break it down, one-two-three-four.

I worked real hard and did PT
I worked real hard and did PT
'Cause I know what's good for me
'Cause I know what's good for me.

The army's merged and so are we
The army's merged and so are we
Now we fight as one military
Now we fight as one military.

Training together side by side
Training together side by side
We're America's Number One pride
We're America's Number One pride.

Sound off! One-two
Sound off! Three-four
Break it down, one-two-three-four.

Served overseas and in our own country
Served overseas and in our own country
Now I'm wearing three stars bright as can be
Now I'm wearing three stars bright as can be.

In my shoes you can follow
In my shoes you can follow
To give our land a bright tomorrow
To give our land a bright tomorrow.

Sound off! One-two
Sound off! Three-four
Break it down, one-two-three-four
One-two-three-four.

—◦◦◦—

A three-star general and the U.S. Army's deputy chief of staff for intelligence, *Lt. Gen. Claudia J. Kennedy* (1947 –) is the army's highest-ranking female and its senior intelligence official. Kennedy began her military career in 1969 as a lieutenant in the Women's Army Corps at a period in military history when men and women served in separate branches and women were prohibited from attending military academies such as West Point. She was a cryptologic officer working with the National Security Agency when the WAC was integrated into the U.S. Army in 1978. In her twenty-eight-year career, she has served two tours in Germany and one in Korea, rising quickly through the ranks. Through her highly decorated career, Kennedy became one of the first women in the army to command men, and currently has gained national prominence for speaking up about women's rights in the armed forces. She has received awards and decorations to include the Legion of Merit, the Defense Meritorious Service Medal, the Army Meritorious Service Medal, and the Army Commendation Medal.

Dorianne Laux

Rites of Passage

When we were sixteen, summer nights in the suburbs sizzled
like barbecue coals,
the hiss of lawn sprinklers,
telephone wires humming above our heads.
Sherry and me walked every block within five miles that year,
sneaking into backyards, peeking through windows,
we dared and double-dared each other from behind the red
      wood slats.
Frog-legged, we slid down street lamps,
our laughter leaving trails of barking dogs behind us.
One night we came home the back way,
perfectly sexy walks and feeling "cool,"
and found my little sister on the side porch,
hiding between the plastic trash bins in her nightgown,
smoking Salems,
making Monroe faces in a hand-held mirror.

Dorianne Laux (1952 –) is the author of two poetry collections, *Awake* (1990) and *What We Carry* (1994), the latter a finalist for the National Book Critics Circle Award. She is also co-author, with Kim Addonizio, of *The Poet's Companion: A Guide to the Pleasures of Writing Poetry* (1997). Among her awards are a Pushcart Prize for poetry and a fellowship from the National Endowment for the Arts. Her recent poems can be read in the *Harvard Review*, the *Alaska Quarterly Review*, the *Southern Review*, the *Kenyon Review*, the *American Poetry Review*, and *DoubleTake*. Currently, Laux is at work on a libretto with composer

Wally Brill, as well as on a new book of poems. She is director of the University of Oregon's creative writing program.

Margaret Atwood

Cat's Eye

The light fades earlier; on the way home from school we walk through the smoke from burning leaves. It rains, and we have to play inside. We sit on the floor of Grace's room, being quiet because of Mrs. Smeath's bad heart, and cut out rolling pins and frying pans and paste them around our paper ladies.

But Cordelia makes short work of this game. She knows, instantly it seems, why Grace's house has so many *Eaton's Catalogues* in it. It's because the Smeaths get their clothes that way, the whole family — order them out of the *Eaton's Catalogue*. There in the Girls' Clothing section are the plaid dresses, the skirts with straps, the winter coats worn by Grace and her sisters, three colors of them, in lumpy, serviceable wool, with hoods: Kelly Green, Royal Blue, Maroon. Cordelia manages to convey that she herself would never wear a coat ordered from the *Eaton's Catalogue*. She doesn't say this out loud though. Like the rest of us, she wants to stay on the good side of Grace.

She bypasses the cookware, flips through the pages. She turns to the brassieres, to the elaborately laced and gusseted corsets — foundation garments, they're called — and draws mustaches on the models, whose flesh looks as if it's been painted over with a thin coat of beige plaster. She pencils hair in, under their arms, and on their chests between the breasts. She reads out loud the descriptions, snorting with stifled laughter: "'Delightfully trimmed in dainty lace, with extra support for the mature figure.' That means big bazooms. Look at this — *cup* sizes! Like teacups!"

Breasts fascinate Cordelia, and fill her with scorn. Both of her older sisters have them now. Perdie and Minnie sit in their room with its twin beds and sprigged-muslin flounces, filing their nails, laughing softly; or they heat brown wax in little pots in the kitchen and take it upstairs to spread on their legs. They look into their mirrors, making sad faces — "I look like Haggis McBaggis! It's the curse!" Their wastebaskets smell of decaying flowers.

They tell Cordelia there are some things she's too young to under-stand, and then they tell these things to her anyway. Cordelia, her voice lowered, her eyes big, passes on the truth: the curse is when blood comes out between your legs. We don't believe her. She produces evidence: a sanitary pad, filched from Perdie's wastebasket. On it is a brown crust, like dried gravy. "That's not blood," Grace says with disgust, and she's right, it's nothing like when you cut your finger. Cordelia is indignant. But she can prove nothing.

I haven't thought much about grown-up women's bodies before. But now these bodies are revealed in their true, upsetting light: alien and bizarre, hairy, squashy, monstrous. We hang around outside the room where Perdie and Minnie are peeling the wax off their legs while they utter yelps of pain, trying to see through the keyhole, giggling: they embarrass us, although we don't know why. They know they're being laughed at and come to the door to shoo us away. "Cordelia, why don't you and your little friends bug off!" They smile a little ominously, as if they know already what is in store for us. "Just wait and see," they say.

This frightens us. Whatever has happened to them, bulging them, softening them, causing them to walk rather than run, as if there's some invisible leash around their necks, holding them in check — whatever it is, it may happen to us too. We look surreptitiously at the breasts of women on the street, of our teachers, though not of our mothers, that would be too close for comfort. We examine our legs and underarms for sprouting hairs, our chests for swellings. But nothing is happening: so far we are safe.

Cordelia turns to the back pages of the catalogue, where the pictures are in gray and black and there are crutches and trusses and prosthetic devices. "Breast pumps," she says. "See this? It's for pumping your titties up bigger, like a bicycle pump." And we don't know what to believe.

We can't ask our mothers. It's hard to imagine them without clothes, to think of them as having bodies at all, under their dresses. There's a great deal they don't say. Between us and them is a gulf, an abyss, that goes down and down. It's filled with wordlessness. They wrap up the garbage in several layers of newspaper and tie it with string, and even so it drips onto the freshly waxed floor. Their clotheslines are strung with underpants, nighties, socks, a display of soiled intimacy, which they have washed and rinsed, plunging their hands into the gray curdled water. They know about toilet brushes, about toilet seats, about germs. The world is dirty, no matter how much they clean, and we know they will not welcome our grubby little questions. So instead a long whisper runs among us, from child to child, gathering horror.

Cordelia says that men have carrots, between their legs. They aren't really carrots but something worse. They're covered with hair. Seeds come out the end and get into women's stomachs and grow into babies, whether you want it or not. Some men have their carrots pierced and rings set into them as if they are ears.

Cordelia's unclear about how the seeds get out or what they're like. She says they're invisible, but I think this can't be so. If there are seeds at all they must be more like bird seeds, or carrot seeds, long and fine. Also she can't say how the carrot gets in, to plant the seeds. Belly buttons are the obvious choice, but there would have to be a cut, a tear. The whole story is questionable, and the idea that we ourselves could have been produced by such an act is an outrage. I think of beds, where all of this is supposed to take place: the twin beds at Carol's house, always so tidy, the elegant canopy bed at Cordelia's, the dark mahogany-colored bed in Grace's house, heavily respectable with its crocheted spread and layers of woolen blankets. Such beds are a denial in themselves, a repudiation. I think of Carol's wry-mouthed mother, of Mrs. Smeath with her hairpinned crown of graying braids. They would purse their lips, draw themselves up in a dignified manner. They would not permit it.

Grace says, "God makes babies," in that final way of hers, which means there is nothing more to be discussed. She smiles her buttoned-up disdainful smile, and we are reassured. Better God than us.

But there are doubts. I know, for instance, a lot of things. I know that *carrot* is not the right word. I've seen dragonflies and beetles, flying around, stuck together, one on the back of the other; I know it's called *mating*. I know about ovipositors, for laying eggs, on leaves, on caterpillars, on the surface of the water; they're right out on the page, clearly labeled, on the diagrams of insects my father corrects at home. I know about queen ants, and about the female praying mantises eating the males. None of this is much help. I think of Mr. and Mrs. Smeath, stark-naked, with Mr. Smeath stuck to the back of Mrs. Smeath. Such an image, even without the addition of flight, will not do.

I could ask my brother. But, although we've examined scabs and toe jam under the microscope, although we aren't worried by pickled ox eyes and gutted fish and whatever can be found under dead logs, putting this question to him would be indelicate, perhaps hurtful. I think of JUPITER scrolled on the sand in his angular script, by his extra, dexterous finger. In Cordelia's version it will end up covered with hair. Maybe he doesn't know.

Cordelia says boys put their tongues in your mouth when they kiss you. Not any boys we know, older ones. She says this the same way my brother says "slug juice" or "snot" when Carol's around, and Carol does the same thing, the same wrinkle of the nose, the same wriggle. Grace says that Cordelia is being disgusting.

I think about the spit you sometimes see, downtown, on the side-walk; or cow's tongues in butcher's shops. Why would they want to do such a thing, put their tongues in other people's mouths? Just to be repulsive, of course. Just to see what you would do.

⸺⸱⸺

A varied and prolific writer, *Margaret Atwood* (1939 –) has many acclaimed books to her credit, including the novel *Cat's Eye* (1988), the children's book *For the Birds* (1990), and two volumes of short fiction, *Wilderness Tips* (1991) and *Good Bones* (1992). In 1993 Atwood published *The Robber Bride*, one of her most extraordinary and intricate novels to date, which was cowinner of Ontario's Trillium Book Award and won the City of Toronto Award. However, the phenomenal success of *The Handmaid's Tale* (1985) has won Atwood greater renown as a novelist than perhaps any of her other work. In all her writing her careful craftsmanship and precision of language, which give a sense of inevitability and a resonance to her words, are clear. Atwood's latest novel is *Alias Grace* (1996). This excerpt is from *Cat's Eye*.

Katherine Soniat

Matinees

By twos we flocked
to the Mecca movie matinee,
growing breathless over the word "censored."
Fuchsia-lipped and solemn,
we aged our way into *The Moon Is Blue*
and felt our hearts' collective thump

as the redhead mouthed the culprit
word "seduce." In the dark
we straightened with a nudge,
forgetting that summer of huddles
in the lightning-hollowed oak.
There, staring up that charred alley

to the sky, we vowed,
"I would never do *that*. Even with my brother."
And we scurried from the tree and on
to our hideout
in leafy summer bush to glimpse
the neighborhood weight lifter

in his loose-legged shorts.
At four-thirty his dumbbells clanged
through the open garage window,
the work whistle shrilled for evening
from the old molasses factory,
its dark vats coating the air we breathed.

According to *Katherine Soniat* (1942 –   ), the starting point for this poem was the memory of exactly how tantalizing the word *censored* was, stamped across the movie title *The Moon Is Blue*. Soniat says, "We smeared lipstick and age on our young faces and raced to the show!" Her third and most recent collection of poems, *A Shared Life* (1993), from which this poem is taken, won the Iowa Prize and a Virginia Prize for Poetry. Other awards include a 1998 Virginia Fellowship in Poetry grant, the 1984 Camden Poetry Prize, and the Faulkner Award. Soniat's other books include *Notes of Departure* (1984), *Winter Toys* (a chapbook, 1989), and *Cracking Eggs* (1990). She is currently an associate professor of English at Virginia Polytechnic Institute and State University in Blacksburg, Virginia.

Mentors & Heroes

My father took me to a shoe store when I was twelve.
I was used to people mistaking me for a boy.
I was the last girl in my class to get her period, and as for a figure, forget it.
"Scout," an old lady once called me.
"Scout, could you help me across the street?"
This time I saw myself in a full-length mirror and started crying.
Big calves. Big ears. Big feet.
"I'm always going to look like a boy," I cried.
My father had to hustle me out of the store.
"Don't worry, " he told me. "You're a late bloomer. I can tell you're going
to be pretty when you grow up."

My father also told me about tennis.
Told me to play aggressively.
Like a boy.
I already did.
Rush the net.
Put it past them.
Take a chance. Invent shots.
He told me I would win Wimbledon some day.
I believed that part.

— Martina Navratilova, from her autobiography

Alice Walker

To Hell with Dying

"To hell with dying," my father would say. "These children want Mr. Sweet!"

Mr. Sweet was a diabetic and an alcoholic and a guitar player and lived down the road from us on a neglected cotton farm. My older brothers and sisters got the most benefit from Mr. Sweet for when they were growing up he had quite a few years ahead of him and so was capable of being called back from the brink of death any number of times — whenever the voice of my father reached him as he lay expiring. "To hell with dying, man," my fathering would say, pushing the wife away from the bedside (in tears although she knew the death was not necessarily the last one unless Mr. Sweet really wanted it to be). "These children want Mr. Sweet!" And they did want him, for at a signal from Father they would come crowding around the bed and throw themselves on the covers, and whoever was the smallest at the time would kiss him all over his wrinkled brown face and begin to tickle him so that he would laugh all down in his stomach, and his moustache, which was long and sort of straggly, would shake like Spanish moss and was also that color.

Mr. Sweet had been ambitious as a boy, wanted to be a doctor or lawyer or sailor, only to find that black men fare better if they are not. The South was a place where a black man could be killed for trying to improve his lot; the laws of segregation kept most black people from ever having decent schools, housing, or jobs. Since he could become none of these things he turned to fishing as his only earnest career and playing the guitar as his only claim to doing anything extraordinarily well. His son, the only one that he and his wife, Miss Mary, had, was shiftless as the day is long and spent money as if he were trying to see the bottom of the mint, which Mr. Sweet would tell him was the clean brown palm of his hand. Miss Mary loved her "baby," however, and worked hard to get him the "li'l necessaries" of life, which turned out mostly to be women.

Mr. Sweet was a tall, thinnish man with thick kinky hair going dead white. He was dark brown, his eyes were very squinty and sort of bluish, and he chewed Brown Mule tobacco. He was constantly on the verge of being blind drunk, for he brewed his own liquor and was not in the least a stingy sort of man, and was always very melancholy and sad, though frequently when he was "feelin' good" he'd dance around the yard with us, usually keeling over just as my mother came to see what the commotion was.

Toward all of us children he was very kind, and had the grace to be shy with us, which is unusual in grown-ups. He had great respect for my mother for she never held his drunkenness against him and would let us play with him even when he was about to fall in the fireplace from drink. Although Mr. Sweet would sometimes lose complete or nearly complete control of his head and neck so that he would loll in his chair, his mind remained strangely acute and his speech not too affected. His ability to be drunk and sober at the same time made him an ideal playmate, for he was as weak as we were and we could usually best him in wrestling, all the while keeping a fairly coherent conversation going.

We never felt anything of Mr. Sweet's age when we played with him. We loved his wrinkles and would draw some on our brows to be like him, and his white hair was my special treasure and he knew it and would never come to visit us just after he had had his hair cut off at the barbershop. Once he came to our house for something, probably to see my father about fertilizer for his crops because, although he never paid the slightest attention to his crops, he liked to know what things would be best to use on them if he ever did. Anyhow, he had not come with his hair since he had just had it shaved off at the barbershop. He wore a huge straw hat to keep off the sun and also to keep his head away from me. But as soon as I saw him I ran up and demanded that he take me up and kiss me with his funny beard which smelled so strongly of tobacco. Looking forward to burying my small fingers into his woolly hair I threw away his hat only to find he had done something with his hair, that it was no longer there! I let out a squall which made my mother think that Mr. Sweet has finally dropped me in the well or something and from that day I've been wary of men in hats. However, not long after, Mr. Sweet showed up with his hair grown out and just as white and kinky and impenetrable as it ever was.

Mr. Sweet used to call me his princess, and I believed it. He made me feel pretty at five and six, and simply outrageously devastating at the blazing age of eight and a half. When he came over to our house with his guitar the whole family would stop whatever they were doing to sit around him and listen to him play. He like to play "Sweet Georgia Brown," that was what he called me sometimes, and also he liked to play "Caldonia" and all sorts of sweet, sad, wonderful songs which he sometimes made up. It was from one of these songs that I learned that he had to marry Miss Mary when he had in fact loved somebody else (now living in Chica-go or De-stroy, Michigan). He was not sure that Joe Lee, her "baby," was also his baby. Sometimes he would cry and that was an indication that he was about to die again. And so we would all get prepared, for we were sure to be called upon.

I was seven the first time I remember actually participating in one of Mr. Sweet's "revivals" — my parents told me I had participated before, I had been the one chosen to kiss him and tickle him long before I knew the rite of Mr. Sweet's rehabilitation. He had come to our house, it was a few years after his wife's death, and was very sad, and also, typically, very drunk. He sat on the floor next to me and my older brother, the rest of the children were grown up and lived elsewhere, and began to play his guitar and cry. I held his woolly head in my arms and wished I could have been old enough to have been the woman he loved so much and that I had not been lost years and years ago.

When he was leaving, my mother said to us that we'd better sleep light that night for we'd probably have to go over to Mr. Sweet's before daylight. And we did. For soon after we had gone to bed one of the neighbors knocked on our door and called my father and said that Mr. Sweet was sinking fast and if he wanted to get in a word before the crossover he'd better shake a leg and get over to Mr. Sweet's house. All the neighbors knew to come to our house if something was wrong with Mr. Sweet, but they did not know how we always managed to make him well, or at least stop him from dying, when he was often so near death. As soon as we heard the cry we got up, my brother and I and my mother and father, and put on our clothes. We hurried out of the house and down the road for we were always afraid that we might someday be too late and Mr. Sweet would get tired of dallying.

When we got to the house, a very poor shack really, we found the front room full of neighbors and relatives and someone met us at the door and said that it was all very sad that old Mr. Sweet Little (for Little was his family name, although we mostly ignored it) was about to kick the bucket. My parents were advised not to take my brother and me into the "death room," seeing we were so young and all, but we were so much more accustomed to the death room than he that we ignored him and dashed in without giving his warning a second thought. I was almost in tears, for these deaths upset me fearfully, and the thought of how much depended on me and my brother (who was such a ham most of the time) made me very nervous.

The doctor was bending over the bed and turned back to tell us for at least the tenth time in the history of my family that, alas, old Mr. Sweet Little was dying and that the children had best not see the face of implacable death (I don't know what "implacable" was, but whatever it was, Mr. Sweet was not!). My father pushed him rather abruptly out of the way saying, as he always did and very loudly for he was saying it to Mr. Sweet, "To hell with dying, man, these children want Mr. Sweet" — which was my cue to throw myself upon the bed and kiss Mr. Sweet all around the whiskers and under the eyes and around the collar of his nightshirt where he smelled so strongly of all sorts of things, mostly liniment.

I was very good at bringing him around, for as soon as I saw that he was struggling to open his eyes I knew that he was going to be all right, and so could finish my revival sure of success. As soon as his eyes were open he would begin to smile and that way I knew that I had surely won. Once, though, I got a tremendous scare, for he could not open his eyes and later I learned that he had had a stroke and that one side of his face was stiff and hard to get into motion. When he began to smile I could tickle him in earnest because I was sure that nothing would get in the way of his laughter, although once he began to cough so hard that he almost threw me off his stomach, but that was when I was very small, little more than a baby, and my bushy hair had gotten in his nose.

When we were sure he would listen to us we would ask him why he was in bed and when he was coming to see us again and could we play with his guitar, which more than likely would be leaning against the bed. His eyes would get all misty and he would sometimes cry out loud, but we never let it embarrass us, for he knew that we loved him and that we sometimes cried too for no reason. My parents would leave the room to just the three of us; Mr. Sweet, by that time, would be propped up in bed with a number of pillows behind his head and with me sitting and lying on his shoulder and along his chest. Even when he had little trouble breathing he would not ask me to get down. Looking into my eyes he would shake his white head and run a scratchy old finger all around my hairline, which was rather low down, nearly to my eyebrows, and made some people say I looked like a baby monkey.

My brother was very generous in all this, he let me do all the revivaling — he had done it for years before I was born and so was glad to be able to pass it on to someone new. What he would do while I talked to Mr. Sweet was pretend to play the guitar, in fact pretend that he was a young version of Mr. Sweet, and it always made Mr. Sweet glad to think that someone wanted to be like him — of course, we did not know this then, we played the thing by ear, and whatever he seemed to like, we did. We were desperately afraid that he was just going to take off one day and leave us.

It did not occur to us that we were doing anything special; we had not learned that death was final when it did come. We thought nothing of triumphing over it so many times, and in fact became a trifle contemptuous of people who let themselves be carried away. It did not occur to us that if our father had been dying we could not have stopped it, that Mr. Sweet was the only person over whom we had power.

When Mr. Sweet was in his eighties I was studying in the university many miles from home. I saw him whenever I went home, but he was never on the verge of dying that I could tell and I began to feel that my anxiety for his health and psychological well-being was unnecessary. By this time he not only had a moustache but a long flowing snow-white beard, which I loved and combed and braided for hours. He was very peaceful, fragile, gentle, and the only jarring note about him was his old steel guitar, which he still played in the old sad, sweet, down-home blues way.

On Mr. Sweet's ninetieth birthday I was finishing my doctorate in Massachusetts and had been making arrangements to go home for several weeks' rest. That morning I got a telegram telling me that Mr. Sweet was dying again and could I please drop everything and come home. Of course I could. My dissertation could wait and my teachers would understand when I explained to them when I got back. I ran to the phone, called the airport, and within four hours I was speeding along the dusty road to Mr. Sweet's.

The house was more dilapidated than when I was last there, barely a shack, but it was overgrown with yellow roses which my family had planted many years ago. The air was heavy and sweet and very peaceful. I felt strange walking through the gate and up the old rickety steps. But the strangeness left me as I caught sight of the long white beard I loved so well flowing down the thin body over the familiar quilt coverlet. Mr. Sweet!

His eyes were closed tight and his hands, crossed over his stomach, were thin and delicate, no longer scratchy. I remembered how always before I had run and jumped up on him just anywhere; now I knew he would not be able to support my weight. I looked around at my parents, and was surprised to see that my father and mother also looked old and frail. My father, his own hair very gray, leaned over the quietly sleeping old man, who, incidentally, smelled still of wine and tobacco, and said, as he'd done so many times, "To hell with dying, man! My daughter is home to see Mr. Sweet!" My brother had not been able to come as he was in the war in Asia. I bent down and gently stroked the closed eyes and gradually they began to open. The closed, wine-stained lips twitched a little, then parted in a warm, slightly embarrassed smile. Mr. Sweet could see me and he recognized me and his eyes looked very spry and twinkly for a moment. I put my head down on the pillow next to his and we just looked at each other for a long time. Then he began to trace my peculiar hairline with a thin, smooth finger. I closed my eyes when his finger halted above my ear (he used to rejoice at the dirt in my ears when I was little), his hand stayed cupped around my cheek. When I opened my eyes, sure that I had reached him in time, his were closed.

Even at twenty-four how could I believe that I had failed? that Mr. Sweet was really gone? He had never gone before. But when I looked up at my parents I saw that they were holding back tears. They had loved him dearly. He was like a piece of rare and delicate china which was always being saved from breaking and which finally fell. I looked long at the old face, the wrinkled forehead, the red lips, the hands that still reached out to me. Soon I felt my father pushing something into my cool hands. It was Mr. Sweet's guitar. He had asked them months before to give it to me; he had known that even if I came next time he would not be able to respond in the old way. He did not want me to feel that my trip had been for nothing.

The old guitar! I plucked the strings, hummed "Sweet Georgia Brown." The magic of Mr. Sweet lingered still in the cool steel box. Through the window I could catch the fragrant delicate scent of tender yellow roses. The man on the high old-fashioned bed with the quilt coverlet and the flowing white beard had been my first love.

Best known for her Pulitzer Prize–winning novel *The Color Purple* (1982), *Alice Walker* (1944 –) depicts black women struggling for sexual as well and racial equality and emerging as strong, creative individuals. Both her parents were tenant farmers, and as a child she witnessed violent racism as well as severe economic oppression of the sharecropping system. When Walker was eight, her right eye was injured by one of her brothers, resulting in permanent damage and facial disfigurement that isolated her as a child. Walker is the author of *Third Life of Grange Copeland* (1970), *Meridian* (1976), *The Temple of My Familiar* (1989), *Possessing the Secret of Joy* (1992), *The Same River Twice: Honoring the Difficult* (1996), and *Anything We Love Can Be Saved: A Writer's Activism* (1997). She has published several volumes of poetry, including *Revolutionary Petunias and Other Poems* (1971) and *Her Blue Body Everything We Know* (1991), as well as numerous short stories and books of essays on women's issues. This short story is from *In Love & Trouble: Stories of Black Women* (1973).

Lydia Minatoya

Transformation

When we lived in Albany, I was always the teachers' pet. "So tiny, so precocious, so prettily dressed!" They thought I was a living doll and this was fine with me.

My father knew that the effusive praise would die. He had been through it with my sister. After five years of being a perfect darling, Misa had reached the age when students are tracked by ability. Then the anger started. Misa had tested into the advanced track. It was impossible, the community declared. Misa was forbidden entry into advanced classes as long as there were white children being placed below her. In her defense, before an angry rabble my father made a presentation to the Board of Education.

But I was too young to know of this. I knew only that my teachers praised and petted me. They took me to other classes as an example. "Watch now, as Lydia demonstrates attentive behavior," they would croon as I was led to an empty desk at the head of the class. I had a routine. I would sit carefully, spreading my petticoated skirt neatly beneath me. I would pull my chair close to the desk, crossing my swinging legs at my snowy white anklets. I would fold my hands carefully on the desk before me and stare pensively at the blackboard.

This routine won me few friends. The sixth-grade boys threw rocks at me. They danced around me in a tight circle, pulling at the corners of their eyes. "Ching Chong Chinaman," they chanted. But teachers loved me. When I was in first grade, a third-grade teacher went weeping to the principal. She begged to have me skipped. She was leaving to get married and wanted her turn with the dolly.

When we moved, the greatest shock was the knowledge that I had lost my charm. From the first, my teacher failed to notice me. But to me, it did not matter. I was in love. I watched her moods, her needs, her small vanities. I was determined to ingratiate.

Miss Hempstead was a shimmering vision with a small upturned nose and eyes that were kewpie-doll blue. Slender as a sylph, she tripped around the classroom, all saucy in her high-heeled shoes. Whenever I looked at Miss Hempstead, I pitied the Albany teachers whom, formerly, I had adored. Poor old Miss Rosenberg. With a shiver of distaste, I recalled her loose fleshy arms, her mottled hands, the scent of lavender as she crushed me to her heavy breasts.

Miss Hempstead has a pet of her own. Her name was Linda Sherlock. I watched Linda closely and plotted Miss Hempstead's courtship. The key was the piano. Miss Hempstead played the piano. She fancied herself a musical star. She sang songs from Broadway revues and shaped her students' reactions. "Getting to know you," she would sing. We would smile at her in a staged manner and position ourselves obediently at her feet.

Miss Hempstead was famous for her ability to soothe. Each day at rest time she played the piano and sang soporific songs. Linda Sherlock was the only child who succumbed. Routinely, Linda's head would bend and nod until she crumpled gracefully onto her folded arms. A tousled strand of blond hair would fall across her forehead. Miss Hempstead would end her song, would gently lower the keyboard cover. She would turn toward the restive eyes of the class. "Isn't she sweetness itself!" Miss Hempstead would declare. It made me want to vomit.

I was growing weary. My studiousness, my attentiveness, my fastidious grooming and pert poise: all were failing me. I changed my tactics. I became a problem. Miss Hempstead sent me home with nasty notes in sealed envelopes: Lydia is a slow child, a noisy child, her presence is disruptive. My mother looked at me with surprise, *"Nani desu ka?* Are you having problems with your teacher?" But I was tenacious. I pushed harder and harder, firmly caught in the obsessive need of the scorned.

One day I snapped. As Miss Hempstead began to sing her wretched lullabies, my head dropped to the desk with a powerful CRACK! It lolled there, briefly, then rolled toward the edge with a momentum that sent my entire body catapulting to the floor. Miss Hempstead's spine stretched slightly, like a cat that senses danger. Otherwise, she paid no heed. The linoleum floor was smooth and cool. It emitted a faint pleasant odor: a mixture of chalk dust and wax.

I began to snore heavily. The class sat electrified. There would be no drowsing today. The music went on and on. Finally, one boy could not stand it. "Miss Hempstead," he probed plaintively, "Lydia has fallen asleep on the floor!" Miss Hempstead did not turn. Her playing grew slightly strident but she did not falter.

I lay on the floor through rest time. I lay on the floor through math drill. I lay on the floor while my classmates scraped around me, pushing their sturdy little wooden desks into the configuration for reading circle. It was not until penmanship practice that I finally stretched and stirred. I rose like Sleeping Beauty and slipped back to my seat. I smiled enigmatically. A spell had been broken. I never again had a crush on a teacher.

Lydia Minatoya's (1950 –) coming-of-age travel memoir, *Talking to Monks in the High Snow* (1992), from which this excerpt is taken, weaves memories of childhood, graduate-school study, and travels in Asia. For this work Minatoya won numerous awards, including the American Pen Center's Jerard Award for emerging woman authors. After earning a doctorate in counseling and psychology, Minatoya began an assistant professorship in the field of counseling psychology and taught and traveled throughout Asia. Her novel, *The Strangeness of Beauty* (due out in 1999) is set in Japan and America, in the period between the world wars, and has been described as a fascinating, funny, and moving exploration of love and courage. Currently, she is a faculty member in the counseling department of North Seattle Community College and is at work on her second novel.

Wilma Mankiller

Child of the Sixties

The San Francisco I experienced as a young girl in the late 1950s and early 1960s was not the sophisticated city of palatial Nob Hill mansions, picturesque cable cars, fancy restaurants, and elegant hotels. My family did not lunch amid the tourists at Fisherman's Wharf or dine at Trader Vic's. We did not meet friends to watch from the Crown Room high atop the Fairmont Hotel as the mists rolled in on the bay. Folks who did those things were on a much higher rung of the economic and social ladder than we were. Our family was more familiar — and comfortable — with the crowd that shopped for bargains at Goodwill or St. Vincent de Paul. We ate simple meals at home, wore hand-me-down clothes, and got by from paycheck to paycheck. Our family's meager budget could not handle any nonessentials or luxuries.

After we lived in San Francisco for a little more than a year, my father, with help from my older brother Don's salary contributions, was able to scrape together enough money for a down payment on a small house. So we left the crowded flat in the Potrero Hill District and moved into a new home in Daly City, just south of San Francisco on the southern peninsula in San Mateo County. Daly City had come into being as a result of the earthquake and fire of 1906, when many San Franciscans fled to John Daly's dairy ranch. It grew into a residential area that mushroomed during the boom years after World War II, when it became one of California's fifty most populous communities.

Our new residence looked as if it had come straight out of a cookie-cutter mold. There were three small bedrooms, a full basement, and not many frills. My sisters and I shared bunk beds. I would describe it as modest, just like the hundreds of other ticky-tacky houses in the endless rows that climbed up and down the landlocked hills flanked by the Pacific Ocean and San Francisco Bay.

For our family as a whole, the move to Daly City was a good one. It represented a marked improvement over our first dwelling. We were moving up in the world. At about the same time, my father started to become active at the San Francisco Indian Center, where we met and spent time with other native people living in the area. That had a positive impact on the family. But for me, nothing had changed. I still loathed being in California, and I particularly despised school.

I was uncomfortable. I felt stigmatized. I continually found myself alienated from the other students, who mostly treated me as though I had come from outer space. I was insecure, and the least little remark or glance would leave me mortified. That was especially true whenever people had to teach me something basic or elementary, such as how to use a telephone. I was convinced that they must think it odd to be teaching an eleven- or twelve-year-old how to pick up a phone, listen for a tone, and then dial a number.

In Daly City, I was getting ready to enter the seventh grade. The thought of that depressed me a great deal. That meant having to meet more new kids. Not only did I speak differently than they did, but I had an unfamiliar name that the others ridiculed. We were teased unmercifully about our Oklahoma accents. My sister Linda and I still read out loud to each other every night to lose our accents. Like most young people everywhere, we wanted to belong.

Also, there were changes going on inside me that I could not account for, and that troubled me very much. I was experiencing all the problems girls face when approaching the beginning of womanhood. I was afraid and did not know what to do. Besides having to deal with the internal changes, I was also growing like a weed and had almost reached my full adult height. People thought I was much older than twelve. I hated what was happening. I hated my body. I hated school. I hated the teachers. I hated the other students. Most of all, I hated the city.

I did not hate my parents or the rest of the family. I always loved them very much. But it was a time of great confusion for me. I was silently crying out for attention, but nobody heard me. My dad was constantly busy trying to make a living and, at the same time, deal with his own frustrations and confusion about city life in California. My mother was doing her best to help all of us with our problems while she kept us fed and clothed. Then on top of everything, my oldest brother, Don, announced that he was going to get married. He had met a nice young Choctaw woman named LaVena at the Indian Center. They had fallen in love. Everyone was very happy about the news, but there were long discussions about Don leaving home with his bride and how that loss of income would affect the rest of the family.

With so much going on, I felt like nobody had any time for me. I felt there was not one single person I could confide in or turn to who truly understood me. My self-esteem was at rock bottom. That is when I decided to escape from all of it. I would run away from home. At the time, that seemed my best and only option.

I ran off to Grandma Sitton, who lived at Riverbank. She was an independent woman. I had gotten to know her better since our move to the West Coast, and I liked her very much. I thought perhaps my grandmother would understand and comfort me and help with my problems. Also, I liked Riverbank because Oklahoma families who had come out during the Dust Bowl period were living in the area. I felt more comfortable around them.

My younger sister Linda and I had stashed away a little bit of money saved from baby-sitting jobs we had gotten through meeting other families at the Indian Center. We did not have much, but it was enough to buy a bus ticket. Of course, as soon as I got to her house, my grandma called my folks and said, "Pearl's here, you better come get her." My parents were upset — very upset — and my dad drove out and took me back. But that did not end it. That first time was just the start of a pattern of behavior that lasted until I became a teenager.

I waited a little while, and then I ran away a second time and went straight to my grandmother's house. My parents and I went through the same routine. But I did not stop. I did it again. Once more, my dad drove to Riverbank and took me back to Daly City. One time my sister Linda ran away, too. She took off for somewhere on her own. I am not sure where she went. My folks found her and brought her home. But I kept running away. Every single time, I went to Grandma Sitton's. Over a year or so, I guess I ran away from home at least five times, maybe more.

My parents could not control me. Eventually, they decided that I had become incorrigible. They saw that I truly did not want to live in the city. I wanted no part of it. So they gave in and let me stay with my grandmother. By then she had outlived another husband. She sold her home and gave the money to her son and his wife — my Uncle Floyd Sitton and Aunt Frauline. They had moved to California after Uncle Floyd's return from World War II and his discharge from the service. He used the money my grandmother gave them to buy a dairy ranch north of Riverbank, near the town of Escalon. In exchange for helping them buy their "dream place," Grandma Sitton moved in with my uncle and aunt and their four children, Tommy, Mary Louise, and twins about my age, Eddie and Teddie.

I was preparing to begin the eighth grade when I joined my grandmother and the other Sitton relatives at their ranch. The agreement was for me to stay with them for one year. Ultimately, it turned out to be a very positive experience, but at first there were difficulties. There was a fair amount of conflict between my cousins and me, but they finally got used to my living there. Our problems sprang not from my Native American blood, but from a rivalry between the four of them and me. In a nutshell, we were all competitive kids. We were pure country, too, and that meant we would not run from a fight. When I arrived, it took only the slightest agitation to provoke me. I was highly sensitive and self-conscious.

One time in particular, I recall, several of us were walking back from the fields following Uncle Floyd. My cousin Teddie kept taunting and teasing me until I could not take it any more. When he pulled my hair again, I whirled around and punched him in the jaw so hard that he dropped to the ground. I got in trouble over that incident, and there was some talk about shipping me back home to the city. That finally passed, I settled down, and the teasing stopped. The conflict faded. My life seemed to improve.

I began to gain some confidence. As I felt better about myself, I felt better about others. My grandmother deserves much of the credit. Even though she was strict, she was never judgmental. At a very critical point in my life, she helped me learn to accept myself and to confront my problems.

School even seemed more palatable. When I moved to the farm, I did not have one single friend my age at school. I relied on my tough demeanor to protect myself, and I found that this really turned off people. My cousins had told all the other kids at the small community school we attended that my parents had sent me to live with them because they could not handle me. That was not a good way for me to begin. During lunch and recess, I was usually by myself. Although I got off to a bumpy start, I had made some friends and had developed a routine by the close of the school year. I got along better with my cousins and enjoyed the work on the farm.

All in all, the year I spent on the dairy farm was just what I needed. I slept in the same bed with my grandmother, and we all got up every day at 5:00 A.M. to milk the cows and take care of chores. My main job was to help keep the barn clean. Besides the dairy cows, my uncle and aunt had some pigs and a horse. There was a big vegetable garden. I even helped my Aunt Frauline deliver a calf during a difficult birth. The hard work and fresh air at the farm were so good. We also found time to explore the fields and swim in the creeks.

During our year together, my grandmother helped shape much of my adolescent thinking. I spent much of my time with her, and never considered a single moment wasted. Although she was small, only about four feet ten inches tall, she was solidly built. She was also opinionated, outspoken, tough, and very independent. She was deeply religious and sang from her hymnbook every day. Her favorite song was "Rock of Ages." My grandmother also loved to garden, raise chickens, and pick peaches. Grandmother Sitton and my father — two of the people I most admired as a young woman — valued hard work. I believe it was their examples more than anything else that contributed to my own work ethic.

I continued to visit the farm every summer during my high school years. Some of my brothers and sisters usually came too, and we would help tend the crops or pick fruit to earn money for new school clothes. We worked alongside some white people in the fields, and my mistrust of whites certainly did not apply to them. The people whom some Californians derisively called Oakies or Arkies were great friends — hardworking people, close to the land, and quick to share what little they had with others who had even less. The farm work was demanding, but those were summers of freedom. We swam in the canals, went to drive-in movies, and sipped cherry Cokes or limeades at the local Dairy Queen. Sometimes we headed to the nearby town of Modesto to cruise the streets. Later, Modesto was the setting for *American Graffiti*, the film about teenage life in small-town America directed by George Lucas, a native son.

I looked forward to those visits with my grandmother. After I was married, I still went to see her. I would sit on her lap, and we teased each other and laughed. Full of spirit and energy, my grandmother married her third and last husband when she was in her eighties. During their courtship, she had me dye her hair black because she believed it would make her look her best. I obliged. Later, I helped her get all prettied up before they went to Reno, Nevada, for a quick wedding. Pearl Halady Sitton never stopped enjoying life. She canned vegetables and fruit, kept chickens, worked in the garden, and sang those hymns until shortly before she died. I am inspired whenever I think of her and all those good times we had.

—⚬⚬—

In a historic tribal election in 1987, the members of the Cherokee Nation of Oklahoma elected their first woman principal chief, *Wilma Mankiller* (1945 –). In 1991 she was reelected with nearly 83 percent of the vote. The effect of Chief Mankiller's political success has been an unprecedented worldwide interest in Native Americans that has enabled her to share her philosophy and the story of her tribe with the rest of the world. She devotes much time, energy, and expertise to intergovernmental relations to bring about an enlightened state and congressional response to American Indian concerns. Mankiller attributes her understanding of her people's history partially to her family's forced removal to California, as part of the government's Indian relocation policy, when she was a young girl. This excerpt is from her autobiography, *Mankiller: A Chief and Her People*.

Dr. Antonia Coello Novello

They Will Dream of Greatness

During the years I was surgeon general of the United States, I learned many things. I learned that although the world may love you, it owes you nothing. To expect the world to treat you fairly because you're a woman or, for that matter, a surgeon general, is like expecting a bull not to charge you because you are a vegetarian.

I also learned that having a vision is tremendously important because, after all, if you don't know where you're going, you're already there.

I learned that when you get to the top of the ladder, you don't forget your roots, your culture, or your language. But what I learned more than anything is that if we are to succeed in the years ahead, as women, once and for all we must unite in putting an end to damaging stereotypes, and in reminding America that to be a Hispanic woman means love of family, love of honor, love of country, love of heritage, and, of course, love of children.

It is said that five messages must be given to girls as they grow up through their adolescent years: They are loved and special; they can do anything they want; they can dream of greatness; they are able to take risks; they are able to use creative aggression and still remain feminine. However, only that they are loved and special is the message that girls get in today's society. And often they don't hear it enough.

I often reflect on my childhood and think about these messages — messages that I was fortunate to receive from Ana Delia, my mother; Doña Paula, my grandmother; and Mami Lolin, my favorite aunt. They were among the most influential women role models in my life. And as family members, what they spoke over me helped shape my character. And I firmly believe what these strong women instilled in me: that the measure of a leader is not always found in what he or she has done, but in the measure of his or her character. Basically, as it has been said, the kind of character that becomes apparent when the spotlight has been turned off, the applause has died down, and no one is around to give him or her credit. I was taught to believe that leadership is not merely a goal and character is not merely a word, but in reality a true way of life, for it touches on how we women conduct our lives, how we see ourselves in relation to those around us, and, most important, how we offer our help and services to those in need, when the going gets tough and there is no one to give us credit.

As a young girl I saw firsthand that as women, with our tradition of caring for our families and our communities while doing our work, we face many challenges. The ones I remember most involved how to retain our pride — without lingering at the altar of personal ambition — and learn to *transform* without *transgressing, share* without *imposing,* and *integrate* without *interrupting.* What a challenge, to make our way in this life and contribute the best we know how, hoping that what we do today for this generation of young women will pave the way for the next, just as those women who came before did for us.

And now I place, more than I ever did growing up, great value on women's caring, women's intuitiveness, women's empathy, women's attention to details, women's tendency to solve problems peacefully and through teamwork, women's ability to listen, and women's strength in the face of adversity. Experience tells me that most women — women of all cultures and social classes — have these characteristics in abundance, and that such characteristics are traditionally not given room for expression or reward.

From the earliest age, I was taught to be proud of who I was. I saw my family and my friends with a deep sense of heritage and honorable demeanor. Many of my extended family believe that honor is more important than life itself. For the Hipanics I know, maintaining a sense of honor is the lifeblood of the people — there can be no true respect without it. As Hispanics, as Americans, we understand very well that, in the words of Benito Juarez, "The road to respect for others is the very road to peace." As a girl I was taught not to confuse honor with weakness. It was my very strength as a child; it is my very strength as an adult. I trust that my three nieces and four godchildren will see their honor as a sense of their strength.

Values are easier caught than taught. Family partnerships, grounded in mutual respect and Christian values, would, by their example, help children to grow up being loved. I will teach any child what it means to be proud of her heritage, what to expect of herself, and what the world expects of her. Girls need a vision of life worth living, of dreams worth aspiring to, and of possible goals to be reached. Many need to be told that they are important, strong, and powerful people. Society tells them quite the opposite. Unless we convince our children that there is hope for them in the future, they will drop out — not only from school, but from society as well.

And as women who strive to be accepted and blended into this society, we cannot allow our children to lose their sense of heritage. Everything we do to improve our lives and that of future generations must be done with great care for our traditional values. For how can we expect to raise our children to value our traditions, customs, and ethics, to respect their cultural and character traits that shape their individuality, when we ourselves lose our identity and self-respect? I need to remind myself that I am deserving of all the positive messages I was given, and the values that are part of my heritage, and that I cannot only add to them but must pass them along to the next generation. I trust they will dream of greatness, but never lose sight of who they are or where they are headed.

―◦◦◦―

Antonio Coello Novello (1944 –) was sworn in as the fourteenth surgeon general of the United States Public Health Service in 1990. The historic event marked two firsts: Dr. Novello became the first woman and the first Hispanic to hold the position. During her tenure from 1993 to 1996, Dr. Novello advised the public on health matters ranging from AIDS to the importance of immunization. Novello then served as

United Nations Children's Fund (UNICEF) special representative for health and nutrition, where she provided leadership toward the global efforts to eliminate iodine and vitamin A deficiency disorders, immunize the world's children, and prevent smoking and substance abuse among teens. Currently, Dr. Novello is a visiting professor of health policy and management at the Johns Hopkins University School of Hygiene and Public Health and special director for community health policy.

Antonia Coello Novello
and her scout troop

Jackie Joyner-Kersee
My Guiding Light

People have always assumed I succeeded at sports because I was a natural talent. Not quite. I had talent and determination, but I needed someone to help me develop it. Nino Fennoy was that person. He encouraged me to imagine myself doing great things and worked with me to turn my fantasies into reality.

I met Mr. Fennoy on a spring day in 1973. Mr. Ward piled the girls he'd been coaching into his car and drove us to the field at Hughes Quinn Junior High, some eight blocks from my house. Every evening Mr. Fennoy worked with a group of boys and girls from Lilly Freeman Elementary at the Hughes Quinn playground. The two men had decided to divide the coaching duties of the Franklin-Freeman squad, with Mr. Ward taking the boys and Mr. Fennoy the girls.

To determine our skill level, they asked us all to run 120 yards, then circle around and run back, and repeat the drill several times. I did it easily. I still wasn't the fastest, but after almost a year of training with Mr. Ward, I had lots of stamina. I stood about 5' 5" tall and weighed a lean 120 pounds — all arms and legs.

"What else are we going to do?" I asked the two coaches when we were done. Mr. Fennoy looked at me and smiled.

The longer I worked with him, the stronger and faster I became. But I still wasn't in the front of the pack at the end of the races — my 440 time was well over a minute. In my first race with Mr. Fennoy as my coach, I didn't finish last, but I was well back. I hoped he wouldn't be disappointed and drop me from the team.

"I tried," I said, shrugging my shoulders apologetically afterward.

He responded with a reassuring smile: "That's all I ask."

Over time, lots of girls started the Railers track program. But as training drills intensified, sessions lasted longer and the temperature rose, many of them dropped out. A group that included Gwen Brown, Deborah Thurston, Carmen Cannon, Tina Gully, Danette, Cindy and

Mona Onyemelukwe, Devlin Stamps, Pat Riggins, and me stuck it out that summer and all the seasons thereafter. We formed the core of the girls' athletic program on the south side of East St. Louis. That program included volleyball, basketball, and track squads. Most of us played two sports. I was one of the few who played all three. In summers, we competed as East St. Louis Railers. During the school year, we competed for our respective junior high teams, and later, as Lincoln Tigerettes in senior high.

Mr. Fennoy, the son of an East St. Louis political leader, was a high school classmate of Daddy's. After an undistinguished athletic career at Lincoln, he realized his future was in coaching, rather than competing. He studied physical education in college and earned a master's degree from Southern Illinois University. He got the idea of using sports to help youngsters in East St. Louis after administering the President's Physical Fitness Test to a group of Lilly Freeman students early in the school year. When they scored in the top percentile, without any preparation or coaching, he knew he'd found the seeds of a potentially fruitful program. The influx of federal funds to East St. Louis for educational and recreational programs in the 1970s, coupled with passage of Title IX, provided the fertilizer.

Mr. Fennoy was only about 5' 7", but his ideas were lofty. The skin beneath his afro, mustache, and beard was the color of parchment and he dressed like many of the other thirtysomething men in town. But he spoke like a wise, old man — a combination sociologist, philosopher, and motivational speaker. With his index finger jabbing the air and his hazel eyes staring intently at us, he peppered his speeches at team meetings with phrases like "making maximum use of minimal resources" and "the parameters of acceptable behavior."

He had a broad vision of what he wanted to accomplish through the track program. He encouraged us to work hard in practice, as well as in class. With a solid foundation in athletics and academics, he told us, the possibilities were unlimited — college scholarships, graduate school, good-paying jobs, and productive lives.

In one of his first speeches to us after practice when we were still in elementary school, he explained that success in sports could open doors for us and set us on the path to broader success. "Doing well in sports is fine. But in order to compete and get any portion of what this country has to offer, you have to have an education. You can't get a job if you can't fill out an application."

Like my parents, he stressed that there was a world beyond East St. Louis and that life in that world wouldn't be a struggle if we were properly prepared. "You have alternatives," he said. "You don't have to just be housewives. You don't have to settle for staying here."

Other than my parents, Mr. Fennoy was the major influence on my attitudes and outlook. He inspired me to make the most of my talent, to withstand peer pressure, and to avoid the traps into which others fell.

He was a constant force in our lives, serving as our AAU coach from elementary school through junior high. By the time we entered Lincoln High, he was the head track coach there as well. He got to know us almost as a parent would — sometimes even better. Beginning in junior high, he asked us to record everything we were thinking and doing and eating in a daily journal. I recorded my times on sprint and endurance drills, as well as my long-jump distances. I reviewed the day's activities at school. I wrote that I hated typing class and that I was flunking home economics because I couldn't cook. I described how excited I was to be involved in the History Club's program to bring Donald McHenry, the United Nations ambassador and Lincoln High alumnus, back to campus for a lecture to the student body. I also related my experiences with my boyfriend.

Every week until my senior year, Mr. Fennoy reviewed what I wrote and discussed it with me. Nothing got by him. After hearing about my ex-boyfriend's new girlfriend being pregnant, I was melancholy and uninspired. Mr. Fennoy talked to me about it away from the others.

"What's wrong?" he asked.

When I told him, he said, "I figured that was it. You shouldn't be upset. Breaking up with him was the best thing that could have happened to you," he said. "Now, let's get back to work."

As protective as my parents were, they allowed me to go to out-of-town meets with Mr. Fennoy because they knew I was in good hands. He was like a father away from home. Mr. Fennoy always seemed to know what we needed, without our having to ask. He gave me my first pair of track shoes and never asked for any money.

When it was time to travel to meets out of state or across country, we sometimes raised the money for travel expenses by holding bake sales and raffles. But Mr. Fennoy often turned down huge donations from people in town, even though expenses could run as much as $5,000 when several of us and a coach had to travel out of town. We heard about some of the offers and asked why he'd refused them. "You never want anyone to think you owe them something," he said. Also, he reminded us, eligibility rules prohibited gifts to high school and college athletes.

Mr. Fennoy, assistant coach Arlander Hampton and Mr. Ward drove us to meets in their cars when the Railers were first organized. After the program became successful and our victories were publicized, the school board agreed to fund the summer track program. From that point on, we rode to meets in chartered buses and rented vans.

On one of the trips I took with the Railers, I didn't have any money for lunch. My father wasn't working and my mother said she just didn't have anything to give me. If I went, she said I'd have to wait until I got back home that night to eat. When the van carrying us pulled into the McDonald's parking lot at lunchtime, my mouth watered and my stomach gurgled. I'd exerted myself all morning and I was starving. But when it was time to get off the bus, I was too embarrassed to say I didn't have any money, so I told everyone I wasn't hungry.

While my teammates rushed inside with bills clutched in their hands, I waited on the bus. No sense torturing myself by going inside and smelling the french fries. Mr. Fennoy walked back to the bus and asked why I wasn't inside. I told him I wasn't hungry. Without inquiring further, he said, "Come on inside with me and order what you want."

"Thanks!" I said, flashing a big, grateful grin. We walked in side by side.

After that, whenever Momma was running short and a trip was approaching, I saved my lunch money during the week or bought candy bars at the store for a nickel and sold them at school for a dime. At mealtime after the meets, I rolled down my socks, pulled out and the ball of money hidden there and walked in with everyone else, carrying a fistful of money.

With Mr. Fennoy, I got a taste of life away from East St. Louis. It was, at times, a bittersweet experience. But he tried to insulate us from the most painful aspects. In most cases, the only way white schools would agree to compete against us was if we traveled to their schools. East St. Louis had such a bad reputation, people were afraid to come into town. One white coach told Mr. Fennoy he was afraid his bus would be vandalized. It made me sad to hear what people thought of the place I lived.

Some of our trips took us to remote towns in Illinois and Missouri. Without explaining why, when the driver stopped for gas in those places, Mr. Fennoy said we should stay on the bus. Whenever a ticklish situation arose at a meet that indicated prejudice or a racial bias, Mr. Fennoy handled it diplomatically and taught us to do the same.

During the preliminary round of an AAU meet in Poplar Bluff, Missouri, in 1976, when I was fourteen, I landed a jump in my last turn during the qualifying round, which should have been long enough to put me in the final round. But the official failed to record it. As a result, I was out of the competition. At the time I thought it was a deliberate oversight. The disappointment was all the more bruising because I had to finish in one of the top three spots to advance to the AAU Regional competition, and to have a chance at ultimately competing in the AAU National meet. When the official told me I'd failed to qualify, tears welled up in my eyes and my body stiffened. I was ready to yell at someone. Mr. Fennoy saw my face and called me over.

"It's not fair . . ." I started to rant.

"Don't say another word," he ordered, pointing his finger at me. "Let me handle it. And you better not cry, either."

He didn't make a scene. He huddled with the officials, discussing the issue calmly. Then he walked back over to me and told me the decision was final. I wanted to scream about the injustice of it all. I felt as if someone had stolen something from me. While he was gone, I had heard some of the chaperones say that Mr. Fennoy had run into trouble with one of the judges at the meet in the past. The conversation made it sound like it was a racial issue. When I asked him about it, he said whether the oversight was racially motivated or not wasn't the point.

"Rather than looking for someone to blame or to be mad with, let's learn from this," he said. The idea of blame and anger appealed to me more, but I listened.

"From now on, after every jump, always make sure that the judges have recorded your mark. And let's work harder on your jumping so that next time, one jump won't mean the difference between qualifying and not qualifying."

The lessons stuck with me. Watching Mr. Fennoy, I learned to handle controversy and adversity calmly. And at each long-jump competition I enter, I walk by the judges after every jump and, while pretending to look at the standings, make sure they've recorded the result.

_⟨∂∘∂⟩_

"I like the heptathlon," three-time Olympic Gold medalist *Jackie Joyner-Kersee* (1962 –) once said of her seven-event sport, "because it shows you what you're made of." Although it is one of the most varied disciplines in women's athletics, the heptathlon was virtually ignored by the American public until the performances of Joyner-Kersee, who in 1986 dominated the sport. Her exploits that year, including the setting of two world records in twenty-six days, won her the 1986 Sullivan Award as the best athlete in the United States and began to draw media and public attention to her sport's two-day trial: a 200-meter dash; a 100-meter hurdles race; competitions in the high jump, shotput, long jump, and javelin throw; and an 800-meter run. In addition to establishing her heptathlon world record of 7,161 points, Joyner-Kersee holds the United States record in the long jump at twenty-three feet nine inches. She now has six Olympic medals, more than any other U.S. woman. Most recently, the college basketball star has taken to the court, lending her name and efforts to the recently formed Women's National Basketball Association. This excerpt is from her autobiography, A Kind of Grace.

Christy Haubegger
An Idea of My Own

People ask me about the genesis of my career, which essentially began when I launched *Latina,* and I tell them that the idea for creating a magazine by and for Latinas really germinated when I was a ten-year-old kid. I used to pick up teen magazines and notice a lack of images and information that related to my experience as a Mexican-American growing up in a middle-class Houston neighborhood. As an adopted Mexican-American daughter of white parents who always stressed the importance of my heritage and encouraged a bicultural, bilingual lifestyle, I was always in tune with my identity. But because I was living in the United States speaking English at school and at home, and my roots were Mexican-American, I was really living between two cultures and two languages. These circumstances were often true for my school-age friends and still remain true for the majority of Hispanic women today.

I remember going to the grocery store with my mom and waiting for her at the big magazine racks near the check-out counter. I always wondered why the models were always blonde haired and blue eyed. I remember that I clearly didn't see myself, or my issues, portrayed on those pages. For me it was a matter of inclusion. I was wondering, Why don't they include us? Why don't they ever show anyone with brown eyes and brown skin?

What I didn't realize at the time, of course, was that fashion and lifestyle magazines, and the media at large really, were simply a reflection of society's views during the 1970s, which was that Hispanic women had no distinct identity. They were thought of as stupid, or lazy, or any of those other horrible terms used to label people. And as far as the popular culture was concerned, Hispanic women definitely had no place or real representation in the professional world.

I distinctly remember wanting to defy those stereotypes and fight what I felt was an injustice about how Hispanics were being viewed. I knew — even then — that somehow I was going to do something different to address girls my age and older who were told by society that they couldn't be leaders, or doctors, or lawyers. What I have always wanted to do was create a forum in which the Hispanic success story can be told, a place where women can identify with their potential to become doctors, or lawyers, or astronauts. Had some of my teachers and the people I really looked up to told me how powerful I was, how much potential I had, my self-esteem and whole identity would have been strengthened tenfold.

And that's what I tell teens today. I tell them that just because you're African American, or Hispanic, or Asian, or poor, or rich, or young and female, people may conclude that you are not capable. But always remember that you are so amazing and strong *just as you are*. There's power in the fact that you are young and female. And if you don't like something about what is being said about you, or about the world in general, you can change it. That's one idea my parents gave me. They knew I was going to confront stereotypes and that people's expectations of me would be artificially lowered because of the color of my skin. But they convinced me that I was capable of doing anything — no matter what anyone said.

That is why I really think mentors are important. I had several in my childhood — my mom, my brother, and a lawyer whose firm I did legal research for during my last year of high school. Each person gave me something different: my mother modeled true strength and was a living example of a working mom who managed to balance home and work life; my brother (my primary playmate for many years) taught me, albeit unknowingly, that I could do anything a boy could do (as evidenced by my scraped knees); and my employer trusted me and believed I was smart and ultimately convinced me that it was within my reach to pursue a law career if I chose to. These people each taught me certain values, and I was able to pick and choose from each of them. The perfect person who models all character traits will seldom come your way (who is perfect, after all?), but if you can develop your own "composite" mentor, so to speak, you are free to admire the strengths of each unique individual and absorb them.

And in some way, I hope my magazine functions like a mentor to the women I aim to reach. They are Latina like me, with one foot in each culture. Some live with their mothers who don't speak English; others have kids who don't speak Spanish. And they are trying to navigate between two worlds, and once in a while they would like to have a mentor, a listening ear, a roadmap, that says we are here to support you. And someday, when some little girl tries to visualize an astronaut, I trust she will close her eyes and see [Hispanic astronaut] Ellen Ochoa.

⌐☙☙⌐

Having launched *Latina* in 1996, the first bilingual magazine catering exclusively to Hispanic women in the United States, Latina entrepreneur *Christy Haubegger* (1968 –) is breaking barriers and providing a voice for Hispanics in the U.S. mainstream media. As president of Latina Publications, L.L.C., Haubegger oversees the production and publication of the magazine, which enjoys the backing and resources of joint venture partner Essence Communications, Inc., publishers of *Essence*, the leading magazine for American women of color. Haubegger was chosen as one of the Top Ten Role Models of 1997 by the Ms. Foundation for Women and one of the Most Inspirational Women of 1996 by *NBC Nightly News with Tom Brokaw*. Hailed by *Crain's New York Business* as one of the youngest businesswomen in the United States, Haubegger's desire is to make *Latina* the number one Hispanic publication for women.

Vivian Gornick

Fierce Attachments

In recounting her 1940s Bronx childhood, Vivian Gornick relates her strange relationship with her Ukrainian neighbor Nettie, whose calculating sexuality fascinates the pre-adolescent Gornick. As an adult reflecting on her coming of age, Gornick claims Nettie as a key force in her awakening identity.

A year after my mother told Mrs. Drucker she was a whore the Druckers moved out of the building and Nettie Levine moved into their vacant apartment. I have no memory of the Druckers moving out or of Nettie moving in, no truck or moving van coming to take away or deposit the furniture, dishes, or clothes of the one or of the other. People and all their belongings seemed to evaporate out of an apartment, and others simply took their place. How early I absorbed the circumstantial nature of most attachments. After all, what difference did it really make if we called the next-door neighbor Roseman or Drucker or Zimmerman? It mattered only that there was a next-door neighbor. Nettie, however, would make a difference.

I was running down the stairs after school, rushing to get out on the street, when we collided in the darkened hallway. The brown paper bags in her arms went flying in all directions. We each said "Oh!" and stepped back, I against the staircase railing, she against the paint-blistered wall. I bent, blushing, to help her retrieve the bags scattered across the landing and saw that she had bright red hair piled high on her head in a pompadour and streaming down her back and over her shoulders. Her features were narrow and pointed (the eyes almond-shaped, the mouth and nose thin and sharp), and her shoulders were wide but she was slim. She reminded me of the pictures of Greta Garbo. My heart began to pound. I had never before seen a beautiful woman.

"Don't worry about the packages," she said to me. "Go out and play. The sun is shining. You mustn't waste it here in the dark. Go, go." Her English was accented, like the English of the other women in the building, but her voice was soft, almost musical, and her words took me by surprise. My mother had never urged me not to lose pleasure, even if it was only the pleasure of the sunny street. I ran down the staircase, excited. I knew she was the new neighbor. ("A *Ukrainishe* redhead married to a Jew," my mother had remarked dryly only two or three days before.)

Two evenings later, as we were finishing supper, the doorbell rang and I answered it. There she stood. "I . . . I . . ." She laughed, a broken, embarrassed laugh. "Your mother invited me." She looked different standing in the doorway, coarse and awkward, a peasant with a pretty face, not at all the gorgeous creature of the hallway. Immediately, I felt poised and generous. "Come in." I stepped courteously aside in the tiny foyer and let her pass into the kitchen.

"Sit down, sit down," my mother said in her rough-friendly voice, as distinguished from her rough I-really-mean-this voice. "Have a cup of coffee, a piece of pie." She pushed my brother. "Move over. Let Mrs. Levine sit down on the bench." A high-backed wooden bench ran the length of one side of the table; my brother and I each claimed a sprawling space on the bench as fast as we could.

"Perhaps you'd like a glass of schnapps?" My handsome, gentle father smiled, proud that his wife was being so civil to a Gentile.

"Oh no," demurred Nettie, it would make me dizzy. And please" — she turned ardently toward my mother — "call me Nettie, not Mrs. Levine."

My mother flushed, pleased and confused. As always, when uncertain she beat a quick retreat into insinuation. "I haven't seen Mr. Levine, have I," she said. In her own ears this was a neutral question, in anyone else's it was a flat statement bordering on accusation.

"No, you haven't." Nettie smiled. "He isn't here. Right now he's somewhere on the Pacific Ocean."

"*Oy vay*, he's in the army," my mother announced, the color beginning to leave her cheeks. It was the middle of the war. My brother was sixteen, my father in his late forties. My mother had been left in peace. Her guilt was extravagant.

"No," said Nettie, looking confused herself. "He's in the Merchant

Marine." I don't think she fully understood the distinction. Certainly my mother didn't. She turned an inquiring face toward my father. He shrugged and looked blank.

"That's a seaman, Ma," my brother said quickly. "He works as a sailor, but he's not in the navy. He works on ships for private companies."

"But I thought Mr. Levine was Jewish," my mother protested innocently.

My brother's face brightened nearly to purple, but Nettie only smiled proudly. "He is," she said.

My mother dared not say what she wanted to say: Impossible! What Jew would work voluntarily on a ship?

Everything about Nettie proved to be impossible. She was a Gentile married to a Jew like no Jew we had ever known. Alone most of the time and apparently free to live wherever she chose, she had chosen to live among working-class Jews who offered her neither goods nor charity. A woman whose sexy good looks brought her darting glances of envy and curiosity, she seemed to value inordinately the life of every respectable dowd. She praised my mother lavishly for her housewifely skills — her ability to make small wages go far, always have the house smelling nice and the children content to be at home — as though these skills were a treasure, some precious dowry that had been denied her, and symbolized a life from which she had been shut out. My mother — secretly as amazed as everyone else by Nettie's allure — would look thoughtfully at her when she tried (often vaguely, incoherently) to speak of the differences between them, and would say to her, "But you're a wife now. You'll learn these things. It's nothing. There's nothing to learn." Nettie's face would then flush painfully, and she'd shake her head. My mother didn't understand, and she couldn't explain.

Rick Levine returned to New York two months after Nettie had moved into the building. She was wildly proud of her tall, dark, bearded seaman — showing him off in the street to the teenagers she had made friends with, dragging him in to meet us, making him go to the grocery store with her — and she became visibly transformed. A kind of illumination settled on her skin. Her green almond eyes were speckled with light. A new grace touched her movements: the way she walked, moved

her hands, smoothed back her hair. There was suddenly about her an aris-
tocracy of physical being. Her beauty deepened. She was untouchable.

I saw the change in her, and was magnetized. I would wake up in the
morning and wonder if I was going to run into her in the hall that day.
If I didn't, I'd find an excuse to ring her bell. It wasn't that I wanted to
see her with Rick: his was a sullen beauty, glum and lumpish, and there
was nothing happening between them that interested me. It was *her* I
wanted to see, only her. And I wanted to touch her. My hand was always
threatening to shoot away from my body out toward her face, her arm,
her side. I yearned toward her. She radiated a kind of promise I couldn't
stay away from, I wanted . . . I wanted . . . I didn't know *what* I wanted.

But the elation was short-lived: hers and mine. One morning, a week
after Rick's return, my mother ran into Nettie as they were both leaving
the house. Nettie turned away from her.

"What's wrong?" my mother demanded. "Turn around. Let me see
your face." Nettie turned toward her slowly. A tremendous blue-black
splotch surrounded her half-closed right eye.

"Oh my God," my mother breathed reverently.

"He didn't mean it," Nettie pleaded. "It was a mistake. He wanted to
go down to the bar and see his friends. I wouldn't let him go. It took a
long time before he hit me."

After that she looked again as she had before he came home. Two
weeks later Rick Levine was gone again, this time on a four-month
cruise. He swore to his clinging wife that this would be his last trip.
When he came home in April, he said, he would find a good job in the
city and they would at long last settle down. She believed that he meant
it this time, and finally she let him pull her arms from around his neck.
Six weeks after he had sailed she discovered she was pregnant. Late in
the third month of his absence she received a telegram informing her
that Rick had been shot to death during a quarrel in a bar in port somewhere on the Baltic Sea. His body was being shipped back to New York,
and the insurance was in question.

Nettie became intertwined in the dailiness of our life so quickly it
was hard later for me to remember what our days had been like before

she lived next door. She'd slip in for coffee late in the morning, then again in the afternoon, and seemed to have supper with us three nights a week. Soon I felt free to walk into her house at any hour, and my brother was being consulted daily about the puzzling matter of Rick's insurance.

"It's a pity on her," my mother kept saying. "A widow. Pregnant, poor, abandoned."

Actually, her unexpected widowhood made Nettie safely pathetic and safely other. It was as though she had been trying, long before her husband died, to let my mother know that she was disenfranchised in a way Mama could never be, perched only temporarily on a landscape Mama was entrenched in, and when Rick obligingly got himself killed this deeper truth became apparent. My mother could now sustain Nettie's beauty without becoming unbalanced, and Nettie could help herself to Mama's respectability without being humbled. The compact was made without a word between them. We got beautiful Nettie in the kitchen every day, and Nettie got my mother's protection in the building. When Mrs. Zimmerman rang our bell to inquire snidely after the *shiksa* my mother cut her off sharply, telling her she was busy and had no time to talk nonsense. After that no one in the building gossiped about Nettie in front of any of us.

My mother's loyalty once engaged was unswerving. Loyalty, however, did not prevent her from judging Nettie; it only made her voice her reservations in a manner rather more indirect than the one to which she was accustomed. She would sit in the kitchen with her sister, my aunt Sarah, who lived four blocks away, discussing the men who had begun to appear, one after another, at Nettie's door in the weeks following Rick's death. These men were his shipmates, particularly the ones who had been on board with him on his last voyage, coming to offer condolences to the widow of one of their own, and to talk over with her the matter of the seaman's life insurance, which evidently was being withheld from Nettie because of the way in which Rick had died. There was, my mother said archly, something *strange* about the way these men visited. Oh? My aunt raised an interested eyebrow. What exactly was strange? Well, my mother offered, some of them came only once, which was normal, but some of them came twice, three times, one day after another, and those who came two, three times had a look about them, she must surely be wrong about this, but they looked almost as though they thought they were getting away with something. And Nettie herself acted strangely with these men. Perhaps that was most troubling: the odd mannerisms Nettie seemed to adopt in the presence of the men. My mother and my aunt exchanged "glances."

"What do you mean?" I asked loudly. "What's wrong with the way she acts? There's nothing wrong with the way she acts. Why are you talking like this?" They would become silent then, both of them, neither answering me nor talking again that day about Nettie, at least not while I was in the room.

One Saturday morning I walked into Nettie's house without knocking (the door was always closed but never locked). Her little kitchen table was propped against the wall beside the front door — her foyer was smaller than ours, you fell into the kitchen — and people seated at the table were quickly "caught" by anyone who entered without warning. That morning I saw a tall thin man with straw-colored hair sitting at the kitchen table. Opposite him sat Nettie, her head bent toward the cotton-print tablecloth I loved (we had shiny, boring oilcloth on our table). Her arm was stretched out, her hand lying quietly on the table. The man's hand, large and with great bony knuckles on it, covered hers. He was gazing at her bent head. I came flying through the door, a bundle of nine-year-old intrusive motion. She jumped in her seat, and her head came up swiftly. In her eyes was an expression I would see many times in the years ahead but was seeing that day for the first time, and although I had not the language to name it I had the sentience to feel jarred by it. She was calculating the impression this scene was making on me. . . .

Nettie was a talented lacemaker. She had in fact been working in a lace factory when she met Rick Levine. She could make dresses and coats, cloths and spreads, but she never undertook such major enterprises. She only made doilies, pillow covers, antimacassars, small bits and pieces to brighten the tiny apartment. She never had a specific idea of a fixed design in mind when she sat down to make lace, she just worked at lace. She would sink into a chair at the kitchen table whenever Richie [her newborn son] finally keeled over late in the afternoon or at night (he was never put to bed, he simply went unconscious), wind a length of the smooth, silky cotton thread around her wrist and forefinger, pick up the fine steel crochet hook, and begin. She worked to comfort herself, to entertain and mollify her ruffled spirits (there was no moment when Nettie wasn't recovering from motherhood). She did not take her talent seriously. If you watched her working you could see that it interested her — the designs seemed to emerge from her hook, they took her by surprise, she wanted to know how a piece of work would come out — but the interest was not sustained: one moment intent and concentrated, the next shrugged off, discarded, easily forgotten. Lacemaking was only a mildly valued companion, company when she was nervous or relaxed or hopeful or tense, winding up or winding down.

If I counted the hours I sat at the kitchen table while Nettie made lace, they would add up to a good two or three years. I was usually there in the late afternoon, and often in the evening after supper. She worked at the lace and I watched the movement of her hook, and we fell into a way of being together. She would fantasize out loud as she worked, and I would listen, actively, to her fantasizing.

"Wouldn't it be wonderful if . . ." was her ritual beginning. From this sentence she would spin out a tale of rescue involving love or money as easily as she unwound the silky thread from around her fingers. Like the plots of the paperback romances she read (her lips moving as her eye traveled slowly across the page), her fantasies were simple, repetitious, and boring. The ones that turned on money usually went: "Wouldn't it be wonderful if an old lady was crossing the street and a truck nearly ran her down and I saved her and she said, 'Oh my dear, how can I thank you, here, take this' and she gave me the necklace she was wearing and I sold it for a thousand dollars." Or: "Wouldn't it be wonderful if I was sitting on a bench in the park and tucked between the slats was a brown paper bag nobody would touch, it was so crumpled and dirty, and I opened it and inside was a thousand dollars." (In the late 1940s, in certain circles, a thousand was as good as a million.)

The stories that turned on love were infinitely more appealing to her, and these she entered into with great elaboration: "Wouldn't it be wonderful if I'm coming off the trolley car and I slip and sprain my ankle and they take me to the hospital and the doctor who comes to help me is tall and so handsome, and kind and gentle, and he looks into my face and I look into his, and we can't tear our eyes away from each other, it's as though we're glued together, we've been looking for each other all our lives and now we're afraid to look away even for a minute, and he says to me, 'I've been waiting such a long time for you, will you marry me?' and I say, 'But you're a doctor, an educated man, and I'm a poor woman, ignorant and uneducated, I'll embarrass you,' and he says, 'I must have you, life is not worth living if I can't have you,' and that's it, we're together from then on."

Sometimes, after an hour or so of this, she would say to me, "Now you say what you would like to have happen." And I would say, "Wouldn't it be wonderful if there was a flood or an epidemic or a revolution, and even though I'm this little kid they find me and they say to me, 'You speak so wonderfully you must lead the people out of this disaster.'" I never daydreamed about love or money, I always daydreamed I was making eloquent speeches that stirred ten thousand people to feel their lives, and to act.

Nettie would stare at me when I said what I would like to have happen. The sparkle in her eyes would flicker and her quick-moving fingers would drop into her lap. I think she was always hoping that this time it would be different, this time I'd come back with a story more like her own, one that made her feel good, not puzzled and awkward. But she must have known it was a long shot. Otherwise she would have asked me more often than she did to tell her what magic I longed for.

When I was fourteen years old, Nettie's lace figured strongly in a crucial development in my inner life. It was the year after my father's death, the year in which I began to sit on the fire escape late at night making up stories in my head. The atmosphere in our house had become morgue-like. My mother's grief was primitive and all-encompassing: it sucked the oxygen out of the air. A heavy drugged sensation filled my head and my body whenever I came back into the apartment. We, none of us — not my brother, not I, certainly not my mother — found comfort in one another. We were only exiled together, trapped in a common affliction. Loneliness of the spirit seized conscious hold of me for the first time, and I turned my face to the street, to the dreamy melancholy inner suggestiveness that had become the only relief from what I quickly perceived as a condition of loss, and of defeat.

I began sitting on the fire escape in the spring, and I sat there every night throughout that immeasurably long first summer, with my mother lying on the couch behind me moaning, crying, sometimes screaming late into the night, and my brother wandering aimlessly about, reading or pacing, the only conversation among us that of barely polite familiars: "Get me a glass of water," or "Shut the window, there's a draft," or "You going down? Bring back milk." I found I could make myself feel better simply by swinging my legs across the windowsill and turning my face fully outward, away from the room behind me.

The shabby tenement streets below our windows were transformed by darkness and silence. There was in the nighttime air a clarity, a softness and a fullness, indescribably sweet, that intensified the magical isolation I sought and that easily became a conduit for waking dreams. A hungry fantasizing went instantly to work as soon as I was seated with my back to the apartment, my eyes trained on the street. This fantasizing was only one step removed from Nettie's "Wouldn't it be wonderful," but it was an important step. Mine began "Just suppose," and was followed not by tales of immediate rescue but by imaginings of "large meaning." That is: things always ended badly but there was grandeur in the disaster. The point of my romances was precisely that life is tragic. To be "in tragedy" was to be saved from what I took to be the pedestrian pains of my own life. These seemed meaningless. To be saved from meaninglessness, I knew, was everything. Largeness of meaning was redemption. It was an adolescent writer's beginning: I had started to mythicize.

Late in the summer a woman I had never seen before appeared in the neighborhood, and began to walk up our block, late at night, across the street from the fire-escape window where I sat. I never saw her during the day, but she appeared promptly every night at eleven. She was thin and white-skinned. A mass of tangled black hair framed her face. Her shoulders were narrow and bony. She wore makeup and high heels. Her nylon stockings were loose and wrinkled around her ankles, and there was in her walk some muscular disconnect, as though she had been knocked apart like a puppet and put back together again badly. Sometimes she wore a thin shawl of tropical print. She was an altogether peculiar creature to have appeared on those streets, brimful as they were with working-class respectability, but I accepted her appearance as unthinkingly as I did the other human oddities on the block. Or at least I thought I did.

One night early in the fall as I was watching her walk jerkily up the block, I turned back into the living room where my brother was reading and my mother lying on the couch. I called my brother to the window and pointed to the woman in the street.

"Have you seen her?" I asked.

"Sure," he said.

"Who is she?"

"She's a prostitute."

"A what?"

"That's a person without a home," my mother said.

"Oh," I said.

In that moment I became aware that the woman on the street had moved me. I was stirred by her presence, her aspect. I felt her as a broken creature, broken and diseased, and I had begun to imagine myself healing her. This image now pushed through the scrim of half-conscious thought, and quickly developed itself. As I healed her she became changed, her shoulders widened, her skin cleared, her skin neatened; above all, her eyes became grave and purposeful. But still, the nights were growing colder and she shivered in her thin dress and torn shawl. I imagined myself draping her in some lovely material that was both warming and magically possessed of the power to increase the healing process. I couldn't see the material clearly for the longest time. Was it thin or thick, solid or print, light or dark? Then one night I looked closely at it and saw that it was lace. A series of flash images confused me. I saw Nettie's face cradled on a piece of her own lace. I saw myself and the prostitute and Nettie, all of us with our faces laid sadly against small pieces of lace. Not a mantle of lace for any one of us, only these bits and pieces, and all of us sorrowing against the bits and pieces.

—◌◌—

Vivian Gornick (1935 –) has divided her life between teaching English and sustaining a career as a journalist, including holding a post as staff writer for the *Village Voice* for nine years. Her essays on literature and feminism have appeared in the *Village Voice*, the *New York Times*, *The Nation*, and other national publications. Gornick is the author of *In Search of Ali Mahmoud: An American Woman in Egypt* (1973), *The Romance of American Communism* (1977), *Essays in Feminism* (1979), *Women in Science: Portraits from a World in Transition* (1990), and *Approaching Eye Level* (1996). This excerpt is from her memoir, *Fierce Attachments* (1987).

Irreplaceable Moments

Life loves the liver of it.
— Maya Angelou

Devorah Major

A Line of Storytellers

I could fall asleep anywhere when I was a child. If I was tired I could curl up in the corner of a stranger's sofa, doze off leaning against an over-stuffed armchair, catnap in the back seat of a car, or snooze, chin couched in hand, at my school desk. Sleeping, then or now, was rarely a problem for me. That is, I could fall asleep anywhere if I was tired. If I wasn't sleepy, my eyes stayed open, and my mind concocted all kinds of tales. I saw mythological beings in the cracks on my walls, and landscapes in the shadows on the ceiling. Most of the time I could amuse myself with the scenery of darkness until, minutes or hours later, I dozed off to sleep. But for some reason, on this particular night, I would not fall asleep.

My father ran our house. What he said, went. My mother was ever present and certainly had some skill as a negotiator, but my father's tem-perament, or more accurately temper, my father's height and the light-ening way his growl could catch you at your throat and squeeze tight your windpipe before that sass you were planning to say got all the way out of your brain and onto your tongue, as well as my father's undeniable intelligence, which over the years has mellowed into a wide swath of salt and pepper wisdom, made him the absolute ruler of our domain. When my brother and I suggested that the democratic principles which he espoused should be a part of our household, my father explained the idea of a dictatorship. Then he put the notion of benevolent in front of the idea of dictatorship. Then he put his name in back of that to complete the thought. The world needed democracy, but our home was a dicta-torship and he was the dictator. There were no votes. There was only the possibility of getting a hearing. I believe this is where the idea of benev-olent came in.

Which is to say that bedtime was bedtime. You didn't pout. You did-n't whine. If you had anything negative to say about it, you could scream your head off, as long as it was inside your imagination. If you wanted to stay up more than five minutes longer, you could forget about it. Bedtime was bedtime.

This night it was past bedtime. It was way past bedtime. I went to bed as told, without voiced complaint. I had been in bed for hours. I had gone over my day and planned the upcoming weekend with several variations in the way it could go. I had spent time reconsidering the possibilities of finding a real pathway to Oz, the imaginary land I went to live in whenever San Francisco realities left me feeling lonely and abandoned. I had gone over some of the characters I would meet were I to find the particular sewer cover, windstorm, or hot air balloon that would carry me to that wonderland. I decided that even though Tic Toc had a nice sense of humor, he still didn't seem to be all that warm a friend. I definitely felt like Ozma had a lot more going for her then the very rotund and obviously recycled tin man. I had tried, unsuccessfully, to transform a particular paint crack in the wall from a foreboding witch into any number of more peaceable ideas, an upside-down flower, a tree by a river, a horse. The crack obstinately insisted on remaining a scary witch. I turned my back on her and looked at the slats under my brother's bunk. I counted them frontwards and then backwards and than frontwards again. I counted up the number of friends I had, less than five, and then the number of almost friends. I counted the people I wanted to be friends with until I realized that I was still wide awake. My older brother was fast asleep, but my parents were not. They were playing jazz albums in the living room. Someone was visiting and all the adults were laughing and having a good time, a much better time than me, laying in bed, eyes opened, toes wiggling, and heart racing. I had a dilemma. I was bored, a painful hazard of childhood. I was bored and ready for action. It was time to get up! But then, bedtime was bedtime. Bedtime was absolute. Bedtime was inviolate.

What could I do? I got up. I mean I had done everything I could do to make myself fall asleep, and everything had failed. I got up and went into the living room. I was depending on my little girl cuteness, and the presence of company, to save me from too harsh a rebuke. I was a sickly child and my getting up because of problems breathing or a low-grade fever was not unusual. As soon as I reached the living room door my mother began to make a fuss over me. Was I sick? Did I feel alright? What was the matter? The matter was that I could not sleep. Being awake seemed more fun. Being up very late, which was then and remains today one of my favorite pastimes, seemed full of enticing possibilities. "I can't sleep," I muttered hoping that my soft voice and doe eyes would charm my father once again. "I'm not tired. I tried to fall asleep." I kept the stream of words trickling out of my mouth as I crawled into my father's lap. It worked. He did not rage. Instead he held me gently expecting, I am sure, that a few minutes resting against his rumbling chest would cause me to doze off and get my "sweet little girl" reward of being carried back to my bed.

But I stayed awake, wide awake. Time passed and I was still wide awake. This would not do. Bedtime was bedtime. It was way past my bed-time. My father carried my very awake, and quietly protesting self back to bed. Then he sat on the edge of the bed and began to tell me a story. It was a story about a little girl who wouldn't go to sleep. I began to join in the storytelling. It wasn't just one night that she wouldn't go to sleep. No it was a lot more, it was days and days. She wouldn't go to sleep for weeks. My father added details. I added color. He created plot turns and turned her mischief into drama. Finally, I believe, the little girl fell into a dead sleep right in the middle of the sidewalk on her way to or from school. I don't remember how she escaped her predicament, but I remember being relieved that my father and I had gotten her home safe-ly. She found her bed, and from that day on she went to sleep when she was supposed to go to sleep. In fact, she looked forward to bedtime and sometimes went without being told. When we finished telling each other the story my father leaned down and gave me a kiss and told me it was time for me to go to sleep. Our smiles were moonlight on the shad-ows in the room. The witch on the wall turned into a starburst as I snug-gled under the covers and he stood up.

"But what about our story?" I remember asking.

"I'll type it up," he answered hovering in the doorway, well aware that I was trying to stall his exit.

"Really?"

"Goodnight," he laughed and closed the door behind him. I must have fallen asleep a few minutes after that.

Now the promise to type our story was a serious promise. After all, my father was a real writer, a real writer. He had a room with a desk, a big black Royal typewriter, and shelves and shelves of books. Sometimes people paid him for his words, which proved to outsiders that he was a real writer. He shared his workroom with my mother who had an easel, never quite dry oil paints, and finished and unfinished canvases all over the walls. My mother was a real painter. I was an ordinary child. I drew for fun. I wrote in school and it was fun. I wasn't a painter and I certainly wasn't a writer. A few days later, as promised, my father showed me our story. He had typed it up and added even more details. It was wonderful, and it was written by him and me.

After that we didn't write together. He went about in his very adult world, which included working, battling with the world and his family, and writing until close to dawn more days than not. I was in my child's world, which was often lonely and full of the quiet pains that many children, especially colored children, carry and do not share with their parents. I mean why, what can adults do about it anyway? I grew into dance and drama. I was going to be one of the great Negro actresses of the stage. I was going to be one of San Francisco's first Negro prima ballerinas.

My father continued to write, publishing a story here and an article there. My head became incredibly hard at the same time as my body became quite shapely. In that period I also mastered the act of not hearing what I did not want to hear. I became a teenager, and an inevitable gulf came between my father and me. He bridged the gulf with letters. When I protested his decisions over *my* life, my father wrote to me. He wrote his reasoning, he wrote his concern, and he wrote his love. I can't truly say I appreciated all of his logic at that time. But I appreciated the work, the effort of page after page after page of thoughts pointed at me, crafted for me.

In time I began to write too. I left home and wrote long letters back. I had lovers and wrote letters full of gush and passion and poems full of sugar and thorns. I got into arguments, and when I couldn't get through to someone else I wrote. I remembered the power of words. I remembered the magic of language. I remembered my father's letters. And when I had a little girl, I remembered the story that he and I wrote together.

I never planned to be a writer. I planned to be a dancer and actress. My mother was the painter. My brother the photographer, and briefly, filmmaker. My father was the writer. Years later writing swallowed me up like the ocean taking a cast-off soda bottle, breaking it into pieces, and smoothing out the edges until it became jewels to return to the sand. Years later I learned to swim in words, learned to breath under the water of their weight. Years later I became a writer too. And now, I am my father's daughter, a storyteller come down from a line of storytellers.

Devorah Major (1952 –) is a performer and writer. She has taught poetry to children, adolescents, and adults in schools, community centers, museums, and penal institutions for more than fifteen years. Her first novel, *An Open Weave* (1995), was awarded the First Novelist Award by the Black Caucus of the American Library Association. In 1996 Major released her first solo book of poetry, *street smarts*, for which she was awarded the PEN Oakland 1996 Josephine Miles Award for Excellence in Literature. Mayor's essays, poems, and short stories have been featured in numerous periodicals and anthologies. She is at work on a new novel and poetry manuscript, and still finds late nights a good time for writing stories.

Lauren Bacall

The spring before high school ended, Betty Kalb and I had read that Bette Davis was coming to New York. She always stayed at the Gotham Hotel. Traveling with her was her friend Robin Byron, who also happened to be a friend of my Uncle Jack's. I called him and asked him — begged him — to call Robin and try to arrange for me to meet my idol. While waiting for the answer, Betty Kalb and I stalked the Gotham Hotel. One afternoon when we were skulking in the lobby, Bette Davis came in — walked directly into the elevator. We rushed in after her and tremblingly rode to the tenth floor with her. She was wearing a small black hat, her hair was pulled back with a black ribbon — she was smaller than I'd thought she'd be, but that face was there, just as I'd seen it magnified so many times so far away on the screen. We stared at her openly. When the elevator stopped at ten, she got out. We asked the elevator operator to stop at eleven, rushed for the staircase, ran down one flight only to see her back as she walked through the door of her suite. We laughed weakly and waited awhile to compose ourselves before facing the questioning eyes of the elevator operator. But Bette Davis was wonderful — everything we had imagined. We *had* to meet her, we'd die if we didn't.

Finally my darling Uncle Jack called. He's spoken with Robin, and though Miss Davis had a very busy schedule, Betty and I could come to her hotel on Saturday afternoon at four o'clock. Betty and I were hysterical. We spent hours on the phone — what would we wear — how would we do our hair — what would we say? We did our imitations of her walk, speech — to get *that* out of our systems at least. It was so exciting — the high point of my life, a dream come true!

I was warned by Uncle Jack to make it brief — not to linger and for God's sake to behave. "Don't make a fool of yourself — this is a big favor Robin is doing, arranging this. Don't let me down, and tell Betty Kalb to keep calm." Keep calm? Ha! Well, we'd just have to *act*. Oh, I wished I looked more grown-up. Betty's figure was well developed — she was actually built not unlike Bette Davis — while I was this tall, gawky fifteen-year-old.

Saturday came — Mother and Grandma couldn't wait for it all to be over, they'd heard nothing but Bette Davis for days on end. Betty arrived to pick me up. I was trying to look my most sophisticated, but as nothing in my wardrobe suggested sophistication, I was wearing my best suit. My friend looked much better than I did, I thought — less like a stagestruck kid.

We went to the hotel and I asked the receptionist to call Miss Davis' room to announce that Miss Bacall was in the lobby with friend, we had an appointment. How would I keep from shaking — how would Betty keep from fainting? We were told to go right up. This time we looked the elevator operator squarely in the eye and said, "Ten, please." By then we were so caught up in thinking how to present ourselves — how to keep from falling apart until after the visit — that we couldn't speak. The elevator arrived at ten too quickly. Out we stepped and proceeded shakily down the long corridor to Suite 1009-10. We grasped each other's hands — took deep breaths — checked our hair — and finally I pressed the doorbell. I was trembling from head to foot. Inside and out. The door opened — it was Robin. She smiled at me — I introduced Betty to her — and she ushered us into a living room. There was a sofa with two chairs facing it. I sat on the edge of one of the chairs, Betty on the other. At last the door to the bedroom opened and out walked Bette Davis with that Bette Davis walk — Queen of Films — the best actress in the world. Oh, God!

We stood up immediately — she shook our hands and moved to the sofa. I sat down again in the same chair — I was terrified to take a step — but Betty plunked herself down next to the Queen. Bette Davis was open, direct, easy, and sympathetic. She asked us about ourselves, said she had been told by Robin that I wanted to be an actress. In a voice barely audible, I said that I did and that I had been going to drama classes on Saturdays until I finished school. Betty was much more talkative than I — seemed to have more to say. I suppose I was literally tongue-tied. I was so nervous, my hands were shaking. She offered us tea, but I didn't dare pick up a cup and saucer for fear it would fall on the floor and spill all over me. She motioned me to come sit on the other side of her on the sofa. I don't know how I got there, but I did. Of course we told her we had seen all of her films many times over. The silences seemed endless, why was my mind so blank? I couldn't think of any words.

Bette Davis was very patient. She said, "Well, if you want to act, you should probably try to work in summer stock. That's the best way to learn your craft." "Oh, yes, that's what I want to do — I want to start on the stage and then go into films just as you did." "Well, be sure it's really what you want to do with your life. It's hard work and it's lonely." I remembered she had said in an interview when talking about her life, "I have two Oscars on my mantelpiece, but they don't keep you warm on cold winter evenings." More silence. Robin looked at me — I knew it was time to go. I said, "Thank you so much, Miss Davis, for your time — for seeing us — I am so grateful." Betty said much the same. Bette Davis shook our hands, wished us luck. Robin opened the door and out we went.

Betty had started down the corridor and near the end of it she fell into a heap of emotion. I panicked — Bette Davis mustn't hear us, mustn't know this was going on. I helped Betty up — we staggered to the elevator — rushed to the nearest drugstore so we could sit down. What a relief! Ordeal over. We both started talking at once. "I will never wash my hand again!" "Nor will I!" "Wasn't she wonderful — did you notice her walk as she came into the room?" "What do you think she thought of us?" "Why didn't I ask her what her favorite film was?" "Why didn't I ask her what it was really like to work in films — to be a star?" "Why was I so nervous? She must have thought I was a fool." "I want to be just like her." "We must write her and thank her." "We mustn't let her forget us." "Maybe next time she comes to New York she'll invite us to see her again."

It was truly generous of Bette Davis to have seen us. It meant so much. To be stage-struck and star-struck is an unbeatable, overpowering combination. Such emotion! Only kids who have wanted to be something really badly and have had a specific someone or something to identify with know that feeling. It's more than ambition. It comes at a time when you're still in school and your life work is still very far away, but you feel you're getting closer to the gold ring and maybe someday you'll not only catch the ring but keep it. Everything seems possible, but your life is all frustration because you can't do anything about it yet.

I reported to Jack that I would be forever indebted to him for making this happen. No crown of diamonds placed on the head of a fairy princess by a handsome prince could mean as much. I told Mother and Granny all about it, almost. I left out Betty's collapse — that didn't come out till years later. Then I wrote Bette Davis the fan letter to end all fan letters — I composed it at least twenty times, choosing only the best words from each version — thanking her and saying some things I'd been too nervous or shy to say when I saw her. Betty wrote her too. We sent the letters to Maine, as we knew from the fan magazines that she had a house there where she spent a good deal of time. About a week later the morning mail brought a blue envelope with unfamiliar writing. In it, a letter from Bette Davis thanking me for my flattering words — saying she had enjoyed our visit — wishing me luck — and at the end: "I hope we meet again sometime." I couldn't believe it — all in long-hand! I treasured that letter — read and reread it hundreds of times. Betty Kalb got one too. Writing us was another generous thing for that busy actress to do.

───⚬⚬───

Lauren Bacall (1924 –) was born Betty Joan Perske in the Bronx, New York. In her Hollywood debut, she appeared with Humphrey Bogart in *To Have and Have Not* (1944), for which she was highly praised. In 1945 she married Bogart, with whom she later appeared in three more films, *The Big Sleep* (1946), *Dark Passage* (1947), and *Key Largo* (1948). In 1970 she won the Tony Award for her performance in Broadway's *Applause*, a musical remake of the film *All About Eve*. She triumphed again on Broadway in 1981 in *Woman of the Year*. In 1996 she played Barbra Streisand's mother in *The Mirror Has Two Faces* (a performance for which she garnered a Golden Globe and an Oscar nomination). Perhaps the least likely person to sign up for a Royal Caribbean cruise, Bacall still does the commercials. This excerpt is from her autobiography, *Lauren Bacall: By Myself*.

Angela Davis

My childhood friends and I were bound to develop ambivalent attitudes toward the white world. On the one hand there was our instinctive aversion toward those who prevented us from realizing our grandest as well as our most trivial wishes. On the other, there was the equally instinctive jealousy which came from knowing that they had access to all the pleasurable things we wanted. Growing up, I could not help feeling a certain envy. And yet I have a very vivid recollection of deciding, very early, that I would never — and I was categorical about this — never harbor or express the desire to be white. This promise that I made to myself did nothing, however, to drive away the wishdreams that filled my head whenever my desires collided with a taboo. So, in order that my daydreams not contradict my principles, I constructed a fantasy in which I would slip on a white face and go unceremoniously into the theater or amusement park or wherever I wanted to go. After thoroughly enjoying the activity, I would make a dramatic, grandstand appearance before the white racists and with a sweeping gesture, rip off the white face, laughing wildly and call them all fools.

Years later, when I was in my teens, I recalled this childish daydream and decided, in a way, to act it out. My sister Fania and I were walking downtown in Birmingham when I spontaneously proposed a plan to her: We would pretend to be foreigners and, speaking French to each other, we would walk into the shoe store on 19th Street and ask, with a thick accent, to see a pair of shoes. At the sight of two young Black women speaking a foreign language, the clerks in the store raced to help us. Their delight with the exotic was enough to completely, if temporarily, dispel their normal disdain for Black people.

Therefore, Fania and I were not led to the back of the store where the one Black clerk would normally have waited on us out of the field of vision of the "respectable" white customers. We were invited to take seats in the very front of this Jim Crow shop. I pretended to know no English at all and Fania's broken English was extremely difficult to make out. The clerks strained to understand which shoes we wanted to try on.

Enthralled at the idea of talking to foreigners — even if they did happen to be Black — but frustrated by the communication failure, the clerks sent for the manager. The manager's posture was identical. With a giant smile he came in from his behind-the-scenes office saying, "Now what can I do for you pretty young ladies?" But before he let my sister describe the shoes we were looking for, he asked us about our background — where we were from, what we were doing in the States and what on earth had brought us to a place like Birmingham, Alabama? "It's very seldom that we get to meet people like you, you know." With my sister's less than elementary knowledge of English, it required a great effort for her to relate our improvised story. After repeated attempts, however, the manager finally understood that we came from Martinique and were in Birmingham as part of a tour of the United States.

Each time this man finally understood something, his eyes lit up, his mouth opened in a broad "Oh!" He was utterly fascinated when she turned to me and translated his words. The white people in the store were at first confused when they saw two Black people sitting in the "whites only" section, but when they heard our accents and conversations in French, they too seemed to be pleased and excited by seeing Black people from so far away they could not possibly be a threat.

Eventually I signaled to Fania that it was time to wind up the game. We looked at him: his foolish face and obsequious grin one eye-blink away from the scorn he would have registered as automatically as a trained hamster had he known we were local residents. We burst out laughing. He started to laugh with us, hesitantly, the way people laugh when they suspect themselves to be the butt of the joke.

"Is something funny?" he whispered.

Suddenly I knew English, and told him that he was what was so funny. "All Black people have to do is pretend they come from another country, and you treat us like dignitaries." My sister and I got up, still laughing, and left the store.

I had followed almost to the t the scenario of my childhood daydream.

Angela Davis (1944 –) became politically active growing up in Birmingham, Alabama, and later in New York City. She came to national attention when she was removed from her teaching position in the philosophy department at the University of California at Los Angeles because she was a member of the Communist party. In 1970 she was placed on the FBI's Ten Most Wanted list and was the subject of an intense police search that drove her underground and culminated in one of the most controversial trials in recent United States history. During her sixteen-month incarceration, an international "Free Angela Davis" campaign was organized, leading to her acquittal in 1972. Harnessing the campaign's momentum, Davis and her colleagues founded the National Alliance Against Racist and Political Repression, which remains active today. She is the author of five books, including the recently published *Blues Legacies and Black Feminism* (1998), and holds the University of California presidential chair in African-American and feminist studies at Santa Cruz, where she is a professor in the history of consciousness program. This excerpt is from her autobiography, *Angela Davis: An Autobiography*.

Dr. Nafis Sadik

Breaking Boundaries

I think it's fair to say that I was always one to speak my mind. My family, both immediate and extended, my girlfriends, my whole world as I knew it growing up was the former British India of the 1930s. Although girls generally were not educated at that time, in that place, and rarely spoke up, I was encouraged by my parents to speak the truth. I can remember sitting in my social studies classroom of the Catholic missionary school I attended, debating the moral issues of marriage. My teachers said that marriages are made in heaven, but I knew very well in my Muslim country that marriages are arranged and are a very definite social contract. I knew, although my mother was educated and my father believed very highly in educating his daughters, that not all parents of my school friends shared that mindset. And I also knew, intuitively at first, that these ideas had to be examined. That I challenged the teachers repeatedly on points of this nature doesn't surprise me, really, for my parents had always told me and my four brothers and sister to speak our minds — and be ready to defend our positions on issues.

Freedom to speak my mind was only one of the many liberties I enjoyed growing up, and for this I thank my father, who was really my mentor in my early childhood and adolescence. He taught me the value in respecting others and listening to other people's views, in treating people with respect and dignity. My father stretched my perception of the world and my imagination through books — indeed, the library of our home was the only room off limits to the many guests who visited our home every year. Although I frequently gave up my bed for a visiting aunt or cousin, I never had to give up our library, for that was the "children's room," and any book on the shelf was fair game. My father taught me the importance of relishing the moment and of reaping the rewards of life's tasks. Parts of this came alive through the pages of these books.

From the ability to speak my mind, pursue the goals of my choice, and hear the voices of those who imparted truth for me (from girlfriends to scholars, from novelists to world leaders) came my desire (from a twelve-year-old's point of view) to truly change the world. At that time I did not know the plight of developing countries, especially with regard to women's rights, reproductive freedom, the lack of health and medical care, and the rampant spread of disease. I did not know that the unmet needs of basic health and gynecological care within a large and relatively young age group had produced, for many of these populations, an increase in the number of people living in poverty. But I did know that I wanted to reach out, particularly to people in need.

I remember this decision as a true turning point in my young life, a moment of clarity. My volunteer work and a desire to contribute to the independence movement are a distinct image of my adolescence that clearly folded into this decision. I would rise at 5:00 A.M. to teach in orphanages before I had to be in school. Later I would impart emergency first aid to those women in need through the Pakistan Muslim League. When I was fifteen years old, I remember my aunt and uncle discussing a boy they felt I should "meet" (in preparation for marriage). To say that I objected would be phrasing my behavior politely. I shouted. I stomped. They could not believe that a girl my age put her foot down and refused to be married off as a teenager and that she was set on actually going to college, to study medicine no less. Was it a need to rebel against the best-laid plans of my dearest relatives? Perhaps. But more certainly it was a need to embark upon the world that was set before me — and that my parents wholeheartedly wished I'd pursue. Actually, it was much later in life that I realized my expressions of freedom would never have been realized had my parents not fully encouraged my independence as a young woman, *in her own right*.

The most important lesson of my lifework today is borne out of this fundamental value: Population growth and other demographic trends in developing countries can be affected only by investing in people and by promoting equality between women and men. The empowerment of individuals to make their own decisions is the very essence of all my work efforts.

I must say that through all my rather mature perceptions of the world, for all my reading and education, what became clear as I practiced medicine was that I was truly out of touch with the women of Pakistan. Women in this country, indeed throughout the world, even in countries where there are large families, want to have fewer children. I support family values and families, but I also support the right of a woman to choose when to have her children. Women want high-quality reproductive health care that includes not only family planning information and services, but also prenatal and postnatal care, prevention of sexually transmitted diseases and AIDS, and referrals for complications. My job is to address these needs. When the essential needs of the individual are addressed, those of larger groups — the family, the community, the nation, and indeed the planet — are more likely to be kept in the right perspective. One challenge of my work has been to find the balance between individual rights and responsibilities on the one hand, and the rights and obligations of the wider society on the other. Perhaps if I had not been treated as an individual, my desires today would be very different. Inherently, I know I must give back to women some of the individuality and freedom of choice that was so freely given to me.

_____

Nafis Sadik (1929 –) is the executive director of the United Nations Populations Fund, the world's largest source of multilateral assistance to population programs, and holds the rank of under-secretary general. With her appointment in 1987, she became the first woman to head one of the United Nations' major voluntarily funded programs. As chief executive, Dr. Sadik directs a worldwide staff of about eight hundred and manages $4 billion in donor pledges. Under her direction the fund provides assistance, education, and support to women in need in more than 140 countries and territories throughout the world. She has consistently called attention to the importance of addressing the needs of women and of involving women directly in making and carrying out development policy. Forty-four percent of the fund's professional staff are women, and it has promoted more women to leadership than has any other part of the United Nations system.

Marta Salinas

The Scholarship Jacket

The small Texas school that I attended carried out a tradition every year during the eighth grade graduation; a beautiful gold and green jacket, the school colors, was awarded to the class valedictorian, the student who had maintained the highest grades for eight years. The scholarship jacket had a big gold S on the left front side and the winner's name was written in gold letters on the pocket.

My oldest sister Rosie had won the jacket a few years back and I fully expected to win also. I was fourteen and in the eighth grade. I had been a straight A student since the first grade, and the last year I had looked forward to owning that jacket. My father was a farm laborer who couldn't earn enough money to feed eight children, so when I was six I was given to my grandparents to raise. We couldn't participate in sports at schools because there were registration fees, uniform costs, and trips out of town; so even though we were quite agile and athletic, there would never be a sports school jacket for us. This one, the scholarship jacket, was our only chance.

In May, close to graduation, spring fever struck, and no one paid any attention in class; instead we stared out the windows and at each other, wanting to speed up the last few weeks of school. I despaired every time I looked in the mirror. Pencil thin, not a curve anywhere, I was called "Beanpole" and "String Bean" and I knew that's what I looked like. A flat chest, no hips, and a brain, that's what I had. That really isn't much for a fourteen-year-old to work with, I thought, as I absentmindedly wandered from my history class to the gym. Another hour of sweating in basketball and displaying my toothpick legs was coming up. Then I remembered my P.E. shorts were still in a bag under my desk where I'd forgotten them. I had to walk all the way back and get them. Coach Thompson was a real bear if anyone wasn't dressed for P.E. She said I was a good forward and once she even tried to talk Grandma into letting me join the team. Grandma, of course, said no.

I was almost back at my classroom's door when I heard angry voices and arguing. I stopped. I didn't mean to eavesdrop; I just hesitated, not knowing what to do. I needed those shorts and I was going to be late, but I didn't want to interrupt an argument between my teachers. I recognized the voices: Mr. Schmidt, my history teacher, and Mr. Boone, my math teacher. They seemed to be arguing about me. I couldn't believe it. I still remember the shock that rooted me flat against the wall as if I were trying to blend in with the graffiti written there.

"I refuse to do it! I don't care who her father is, her grades don't even begin to compare to Martha's. I won't lie or falsify records. Martha has a straight A plus average and you know it." That was Mr. Schmidt and he sounded very angry. Mr. Boone's voice sounded calm and quiet.

"Look, Joann's father is not only on the Board, he owns the only store in town; we could say it was a close tie and —"

The pounding in my ears drowned out the rest of the words, only a word here and there filtered through. ". . . Martha is Mexican. . . . resign . . . . won't do it. . . ." Mr. Schmidt came rushing out, and luckily for me went down the opposite way toward the auditorium, so he didn't see me. Shaking, I waited a few minutes and then went in and grabbed my bag and fled from the room. Mr. Boone looked up when I came in but didn't say anything. To this day I don't remember if I got in trouble in P.E. for being late or how I made it through the rest of the afternoon. I went home very sad and cried into my pillow that night so Grandmother wouldn't hear me. It seemed a cruel coincidence that I had overheard that conversation.

The next day when the principal called me into his office, I knew what it would be about. He looked uncomfortable and unhappy. I decided I wasn't going to make it any easier for him so I looked him straight in the eye. He looked away and fidgeted with the papers on his desk.

"Martha," he said, "there's been a change in policy this year regarding the scholarship jacket. As you know, it has always been free." He cleared his throat and continued. "This year the Board decided to charge fifteen dollars — which still won't cover the complete cost of the jacket."

I stared at him in shock and a small sound of dismay escaped my throat. I hadn't expected this. He still avoided looking in my eyes.

"So, if you are unable to pay the fifteen dollars for the jacket, it will be given to the next one in line."

Standing with all the dignity I could muster, I said, "I'll speak to my grandfather about it, sir, and let you know tomorrow." I cried on the walk home from the bus stop. The dirt road was a quarter of a mile from the highway, so by the time I got home, my eyes were red and puffy.

"Where's Grandpa?" I asked Grandma, looking down on the floor so she wouldn't ask me why I'd been crying. She was sewing on a quilt and didn't look up.

"I think he's out back working in the bean field."

I went outside and looked out at the fields. There he was. I could see him walking between the rows, his body bent over the little plants, hoe in hand. I walked slowly out to him, trying to think how I could best ask him for the money. There was a cool breeze blowing and a sweet smell of mesquite in the air, but I didn't appreciate it. I kicked at a dirt clod. I wanted that jacket so much. It was more than just being a valedictorian and giving a little thank you speech for the jacket on graduation night. It represented eight years of hard work and expectation. I knew I had to be honest with Grandpa; it was my only chance. He saw me and looked up.

He waited for me to speak. I cleared my throat nervously and clasped my hands behind my back so he wouldn't see them shaking. "Grandpa, I have a big favor to ask you," I said in Spanish, the only language he knew. He still waited silently. I tried again. "Grandpa, this year the principal said the scholarship jacket is not going to be free. It's going to cost fifteen dollars and I have to take the money in tomorrow, otherwise it'll be given to someone else." The last words came out in an eager rush. Grandpa straightened up tiredly and leaned his chin on the hoe handle. He looked out over the field that was filled with the tiny green bean plants. I waited, desperately hoping he'd say I could have the money.

He turned to me and asked quietly, "What does a scholarship jacket mean?"

I answered quickly; maybe there was a chance. "It means you've earned it by having the highest grades for eight years and that's why they're giving it to you." Too late I realized the significance of my words.

Grandpa knew that I understood it was not a matter of money. It wasn't that. He went back to hoeing the weeds that sprang up between the delicate little bean plants. It was a time-consuming job; sometimes the small shoots were right next to each other. Finally he spoke again.

"Then if you pay for it, it's not a scholarship jacket, is it? Tell your principal I will not pay the fifteen dollars."

I walked back to the house and locked myself in the bathroom for a long time. I was angry with Grandfather even though I knew he was right, and I was angry with the Board, whoever they were. Why did they have to change the rules just when it was my turn to win the jacket?

It was a very sad and withdrawn girl who dragged into the principal's office the next day. This time he did look me in the eyes.

"What did your grandfather say?"

I sat very straight in my chair.

"He said to tell you he won't pay the fifteen dollars."

The principal muttered something I couldn't understand under his breath, and walked over to the window. He stood looking out at something outside. He looked bigger than usual when he stood up; he was a tall gaunt man with gray hair, and I watched the back of his head while I waited for him to speak.

"Why?" he finally asked. "Your grandfather has the money. Doesn't he own a small bean farm?"

I looked at him, forcing my eyes to stay dry. "He said if I had to pay for it, then it wouldn't be a scholarship jacket," I said and stood up to leave. "I guess you'll just have to give it to Joann." I hadn't meant to say that; it had just slipped out. I was almost to the door when he stopped me.

"Martha — wait."

I turned and looked at him, waiting. What did he want now? I could feel my heart pounding. Something bitter and vile tasting was coming up in my mouth; I was afraid I was going to be sick. I didn't need any sympathy speeches. He sighed loudly and went back to his big desk. He looked at me, biting his lip, as if thinking.

"Okay, damn it. We'll make an exception in your case. I'll tell the Board, you'll get your jacket."

I could hardly believe it. I spoke in a trembling rush. "Oh, thank you, sir!" Suddenly I felt great. I didn't know about adrenaline in those days, but I knew something was pumping through me, making me feel as tall as the sky. I wanted to yell, jump, run the mile, do something. I ran out so I could cry in the hall where there was no one to see me. At the end of the day, Mr. Schmidt winked at me and said, "I hear you're getting a scholarship jacket this year."

His face looked as happy and innocent as a baby's, but I knew better. Without answering I gave him a quick hug and ran to the bus. I cried on the walk home again, but this time because I was so happy. I couldn't wait to tell Grandpa and ran straight to the field. I joined him in the row where he was working and without saying anything I crouched down and started pulling up the weeds with my hands. Grandpa worked alongside me for a few minutes, but he didn't ask what had happened. After I had a little pile of weeds between the rows, I stood up and faced him.

"The principal said he's making an exception for me, Grandpa, and I'm getting the jacket after all. That's after I told him what you said."

Grandpa didn't say anything, he just gave me a pat on the shoulder and a smile. He pulled out the crumpled red handkerchief that he always carried in his back pocket and wiped the sweat off his forehead.

"Better go see if your grandmother needs any help with supper."

I gave him a big grin. He didn't fool me. I skipped and ran back to the house whistling some silly tune.

―⁊⁊⁊―

Stories by *Marta Salinas* have appeared in the *Los Angeles Herald Examiner* and *California Living*. Her work has been excerpted extensively, and this short story appears in several Mexican-American anthologies.

Ruth Colvin

Spinning the Globe

I spun the globe, with my eyes tightly closed. I pointed to a spot, and when the globe stopped spinning, I read the name I had pointed to: Hyderabad, India. I was fourteen years old, and I had never heard of this exotic-sounding place. I was from Chicago, Illinois.

When I was twelve years old my father died, leaving my mother alone with five children. Because I was the eldest, I had to grow up quickly and adjust to the new responsibilities resting on me. It wasn't until years later that I realized I was from a single-parent family. Although there was an abundance of love, there were financial problems — my teenage years were spent in the midst of the Great Depression. Through the hardships and stresses of growing up, who was the one person who made a difference in my life? My mother.

When I think back about things that now seem difficult, I realize that at the time they didn't seem like hardships to us. Because Mother couldn't drive, our car was put up on blocks in the garage. Because my youngest sister had polio and was in a cast for years, we all took the responsibility of helping her. Because we didn't have enough beds, we got used to sleeping two in each twin bed. Because we didn't always have coal in our coal bin, sometimes the winter nights were cold and long and we piled coats on top of us to keep warm. Because we had to take our turns scrubbing the kitchen and bathroom floors on our knees, we put newspapers down to keep them clean longer.

What was important to us? Crowding around the small kitchen table each night, sharing stories and each giving advice — wanted or unwanted. Chicken and mashed potatoes every Sunday after church. (I still don't know how Mother managed that on her very limited budget.) Sitting on the floor before the radio, listening to "One Man's Family," a family who seemed to have everything go right.

There never were lectures or spankings from Mom — but we knew right from wrong, and one look told us when we were in the "wrong."

How, then, did Mom get her standards and beliefs across to us? I honestly don't know, except by her actions.

Growing up seemed normal enough to me, but it wasn't until my own children were growing up, going away to school, getting married, that I realized the big gift Mom had given us. She gave each of us the freedom to become independent, allowing and encouraging each of us to follow our own dreams — and all five of us brothers and sisters *are* different.

My mother wrote "her stories" about our Swedish heritage (her mother — my grandmother — sailed without family on a ship to America when she was thirteen), and put it in booklet form for her family. That led my children to want "my stories," so over the past few years I've kept adding new ones. One of my favorites is about a special game I used to play with my brothers and sisters called "Spinning the Globe."

Because my mother never really learned how to drive, after we went to church Sundays were stay-at-home days. And what do you do with four children younger than yourself for an entire afternoon? We'd color. We'd read. (I loved to read and wanted my brothers and sisters to get the same thrill and excitement out of reading as I did.) We'd play. The girls would play paper dolls while the boys spent hours with their little cars, running them around the edge of the rug.

Often I was hard pressed to think of new and interesting things to do. But there's one game I well remember. I got out the world globe, and each youngster took turns spinning it. With eyes closed, they had to point to a spot. With the earnestness of a teenager, I forecast that each of them would someday visit that spot — that foreign city — so they'd better get out the encyclopedia and find out all they could about it. I doubt that my brothers and sisters remember their "spots," but I remember mine well. It was Hyderabad, India.

Never did I dream I'd really visit Hyberabad, but I did, in the mid-1980s when I gave a Literacy Volunteers of America workshop there. I have made other trips to India, encountering fascinating people and situations just miles from that exotic and crowded city.

I believe things happen for a purpose, that one contact or event leads to another in ways we cannot predict. My mother taught me to be prepared to go forward when doors are opened. To do this, she said, you must be ready and have some skills and talents to share. She said that everyone who touches your life has a possibility for opening doors, so treat everyone well because he or she may have the key to open another door. And this is how I eventually found myself in India.

On a plane between Kenya and Liberia, I met an Indian, Swami Hari Har, the holy man, head of all the Geeta Ashrams in the world; a gentle, mystical man who insisted I was his "daughter." Little did I realize that I would be the guest of the Swami at the International Geeta Ashram Conference in Jodhpur, India, after I had given literacy training in several Indian cities, including Hyderabad.

Because planes fly only twice a week to Jodhpur, and because my husband and I weren't sure of the kinds of accommodations we'd have (we'd been in many parts of India where facilities were quite primitive), we took only one small suitcase, together with soap, towels, and toilet paper, trying to prepare for whatever situation we had to face. We knew there was no alternative — we had to stay four nights.

Jodhpur is a fair-sized city in the western part of India, right on the Thar desert. We were pleasantly surprised to find the Swami and the conference held in a mammoth, brightly colored tent more than a block long, with thousands of people sitting on the ground, patiently waiting, or milling around. We were brought to the Swami, who seemed genuinely delighted to see us again. He gave us his blessing, then suggested we might like to clean up and see our accommodations — the services would start in an hour or so. Hesitantly, we agreed. We just weren't sure what those accommodations would be, but we were sure we could adjust.

Imagine our surprise when we were taken to a magnificent Indian palace to be the guest of Maharaj Swaroop and Maharani Usha Singh. In 1947, when India received independence from Great Britain, all the power was taken from the maharajs — the regional Indian leaders — but not all the wealth. However, since 1947 taxes have been very heavy and the royal families have found it very difficult, often nearly impossible, to keep up the huge palaces. Rani Usha explained that they, too, have converted part of their palace, Ajit Bhawan, to a hotel to accommodate travelers and to help pay part of the exorbitant expenses of the palace. We sipped tea in the elegant courtyard attended by Indian women in colorful saris and men in bright turbans.

We were brought back to the conference tent, resplendent in the dazzling colors of the geometric designs. The tent size alone overwhelmed us as we looked again at more than seven thousand Indians, men in their white pants and tunics on the right, women in brightly colored saris on the left, sitting quietly, patiently on the ground.

I was invited to sit on the stage with the Swami, now eighty-three years old, in his ocher robe, with his kind laughing eyes, the long red mark down the center of his forehead, sitting lotus position. Other dignitaries on the stage included the mother of the present maharajah, a charming, quiet, but elegant widow, and the Buddhist guru to the King of Thailand. The backdrop to the stage was designed to show the universality of the thinking and faith of those in the Geeta Ashram — one God over all. The center was a reverse swastika, a Hindu symbol for thousands of years, showing ongoing life. The Indians were surprised that the swastika disturbed us, not associating it as we westerners do with the Nazis. Colorfully displayed were the symbols of other religions — Hindu, Buddhist, Moslem, Taoism, Judaism, Christianity.

Prayers, songs, chants, words of inspiration — in Hindi — occasionally were translated for us. But as I watched the faces of the thousands of people sitting on the ground in rapt attention for each three-hour session, I felt their dedication and serenity. Their history — thousands of years as compared with the United States' mere hundreds — and their lives were something I was determined to learn more of. As an American, I felt I had so much to learn.

At that moment I recollected that time during my adolescence when I believed in opportunities like these because my mother taught me they were possible. She also instilled in me the belief that with opportunities come *responsibilities*. And so the opportunities I have had to travel to India and other faraway places have been filled with stories of growth, stories of people, and stories of change. And I realized, during travels like these and other not-so-glamorous situations, that we at Literacy Volunteers of America are not only teaching people to read and write, but to become independent. We are not just breaking down cultural, economic, and racial barriers in the process of spreading literacy, but in our own small way we are bringing tolerance and peace into the world. Had my finger pointed to Cleveland instead of Hyderabad, I wonder what doors would have opened. According to the lessons of my youth and all that I have learned in my travels, I am certain the experience would have been just as meaningful.

—⤸⤹—

In 1962 when *Ruth Colvin* (1916 –) learned that there were more than 11,000 adults who lacked basic reading skills in her own city of Syracuse, New York, she started Literacy Volunteers of America (LVA), a national, educational nonprofit organization that teaches basic literacy and English to people of all ages. Today, LVA has more than 375 programs in 42 states, working in conjunction with correctional facilities, adult basic educational programs, schools, universities, libraries, industries, and other community service programs. Approximately 120,000 volunteer tutors and students are currently involved in the LVA program. Over the past twenty-five years, Colvin has traveled the world with her husband, giving three months each year to a developing country where she adapts literacy methods to local country needs and teaches English to speakers of other languages. Her most recent trainings have been in Papua, New Guinea, and the Solomon Islands, as well as in Africa, China, India, and South America. The recipient of seven Honorary Doctors of Humane Letters, Colvin was awarded the United States of America's President's Volunteer Action Award in 1987 and was inducted into the National Women's Hall of Fame in 1993. She continues to write, train, and teach.

Gloria Wade-Gayles

For My Children's Remembering

It always happened during the summer. The children knew that. They also knew never to ask me when a southern heat owned the night and made even empty beds sweat. That would have been the logical time to "give in," but it was never about logic. It was about remembering my own childhood and making it magical for my own children. Only cool summer nights, I was convinced, were made for magic.

The steps were always the same. I would sit on the floor next to the bathtub while they played with their favorite animals or their imaginary friend who dressed in white suds and spoke in a little bitty voice. When they were so clean their brown bodies glistened like polished oak, they raced to their beds where Winnie the Pooh or Babar the Elephant lay waiting to cover the nakedness that felt good to them, and to me.

Dressed cuddly, they returned to the bathroom to stroke their teeth and sing the song I had composed just for them: "Mister Yellow, Mister Yellow. Won't you come out. Oh, Mister Yellow, you gotta come out."

And then the inspection. Tiny fingers stretched tiny lips to reveal tiny teeth we named "you-can't-find-any-cavities-here teeth."

"Story time!" The children would grab their books, usually too many, and race to the family room to the long leather sofa that had been reupholstered several times. We rarely used the small bedroom they shared because reading stories involved all four of us, and it required mov-ing-around-in space. We would read the stories and then turn them into dramas the children would act out to the background sounds their father and I provided. Reading bedtime stories and touching were inseparable.

On a cool night which promised magic, it would happen. I would give in, having decided to do so before the children asked. I would read the last story, announce that it was time for bed, and then the game would begin. On a cool night which promised magic.

"Mommie, tell us about the girl named Harriet," one of the children would request. "Harriet," they knew was the imaginary girl whose experiences in Memphis, Tennessee, were exactly the same as their mother's. Harriet is their mother.

I would, of course, say no. That was one of the rules of the game. We had to pretend that I didn't really want them to stay up later, but that they had succeeded in changing my mind.

"Not tonight," I would say in mock firmness. "It's already past your bedtime."

The rules called for them to beg for stories about Harriet by covering me with kisses and hugs.

"Please. Please. Please, Mommie," they would whine in unison. "Just a little bit. Please. Please. Pretty please."

I would give in.

"Okay, just a little bit. Just two minutes and that's all."

The children would quickly arrange themselves on the floor. The sofa would become the stage from which I would tell the stories about my childhood that the children had already heard many times.

"Once upon a time," I would begin.

"There lived a girl named Harriet," the children would say.

"How old is Harriet this time?" I would ask.

They were never in agreement, and they never chose the age I wanteded, which didn't matter because my remembering went in and out of years. The story was pretty much the same whether "Harriet" was seven or seventeen.

"Let's say she is twelve this time," I would tell them. The questions guiding me through my remembering would begin.

"Is she pretty?"

"Well, yes and no," I would answer. "Let me describe her for you, and you can decide whether or not she's pretty." Images of me as a young girl were always vivid.

"She is tall for her age, and she is small. The children tease her because she is small. They call her Skinny Harriet and sometimes Boney Maroney or Toothpick Tillie."

Making happy or sad faces throughout the story was the children's contribution, and they loved it. They made a sad face.

"Does she cry?" one of them asked.

"At first, yes, but that was before her grandmother, her mother, and her aunt teach her how to like herself just the way she is."

"Because she is special," one of the children would remember from my earlier remembering. "And there is only one Harriet like her in the whole wide world."

"Right," I would say and continue. "Besides, the other children are jealous of her."

Faces with question marks.

"Why are they jealous?"

"Because Harriet is happy. You see, when you are happy, you are pretty on the inside, and when you are pretty on the inside, you are also pretty on the outside."

I could hear the three women in my family talking to me, their voices a cacophony of love. In a world where being neither black nor female was an asset, I had incredible self-esteem. I owe it all to my socialization in a family of women who groomed my spirit and my mind. When I listen very closely to my remembering, I hear more references to my being "a girl" than my being a "Negro." No one talked then about women's empowerment, but that was precisely what I learned. Empowerment. According to their teaching, that meant loving myself and grooming both my spirit and my mind.

The children rarely began their questions with where "Harriet" lived. Children see people before they see places. Only after I described Harriet would they ask, "What kind of house does Harriet live in?" They knew the answer.

"She does not live in a house. She lives in a housing project."

"What's a housing project, Mommie?"

This was always a difficult question to answer. Children apply word descriptions to places they have seen either in life or in books. Jonathan and Monica had never seen a housing project, not like the one in which "Harriet" was reared. I could take them to one of the projects in Atlanta and say, "This is a housing project," but they wouldn't see the project I remember.

How could I explain that housing projects were stretches of red-brick units facing clean boulevards and beckoning to passersby with petunias, buttercups, and violets.

The flowers said, "This is our home. We love it." The flowers said, "We are a proud people." The flowers said also, "Do not trespass." These flowers were no ragged patches of wild blossoms scattered here and there throughout the community. They were gardens, designed and nurtured beauty representing the people's dignity and their hope.

The "project," my home, was a class-mixed community, a concept the children would not understand. Professionals, semi-professionals, skilled laborers, and unskilled laborers lived in my community. And regardless of class, the people worked hard, saved well, and, in time, moved into private homes, proud of their achievement, but remaining connected to friends in the old neighborhood. Whenever a family moved, their neighbors were jubilant, not jealous. The promise of upward mobility belonged to all of us.

I do not explain all of this to the children. Instead, I tell them about the many look-alike units and the large park in which community children played. I also tell them about my love for the Mississippi River. They remember my past remembering.

"It is long and wide," one of them says.

"And it is real, real deep," the other adds.

They demand that I tell them again about Harriet's skill in making flat rocks skip one, two, three across the muddy bosom of the river. I show them how she angled her hand, and for their delight I throw an imaginary rock across an imaginary river. The children count, "One, two, three, four . . ." I do not tell them that the real Harriet was rarely without pain when she skipped rocks. I do not tell them that I could skip rocks only from an area overgrown with weeds. Downstream. Away from the riverboats. Isolated. And without a park. The park near the river was a wonderland of flowers and white benches painted each spring. Where it ended and the river began, no one could measure. It received kisses from the Mississippi. It was a beautiful park open only to whites. I remember as a young girl wanting desperately to sit on one of the benches and pretend that I was giving orders to boat captains on the Mississippi through a walkie-talkie. I remember my mother's fear that, in my defiance, I would one day walk into Confederate Park and claim the whitest bench as my very own.

I loved the Mississippi River. It was grand, spectacular, powerful, and in charge of itself. It seemed to be lying on its back communing with the sky. Nothing stood between the river and the sky. I envied the freedom with which they spoke to each other.

How could I explain my love-hate relationship with the Mississippi? That I could love it passionately at one moment and, in the next, hate it intensely? That I loved its majesty and hated its cooperation with people of violence? For hundreds, perhaps thousands, of my people, it is a watery grave.

But it was the love of my youth, the source of my most exciting fantasies and dreams. Until I began my remembering with my children, many decades after my youth, only the Mississippi and I knew about our love affair.

The children become restless. I have not moved quickly enough to the remembering they like best. And so I call for the question that will move me where they want me to go.

"Did we decide what day it is?" I ask. "You know we have to name the day."

"Monday," Monica says. "It's Monday, Mommie."

"No, it's Saturday," Jonathan predictably insists since Saturday is his favorite day.

If it is Monday or any other day of the week, and summer, my remembering will bring into sharp focus the segregated schools Harriet attends. If it is Sunday, I will tell them about preparations Harriet is making for church. My mother is in the center of my remembering. On Sundays, she would awake my sister and me with the aroma of fried sausage, scrambled eggs, grits, and biscuits she made from "scratch" while we slept. Our destination was Sunday School at a Baptist church within walking distance of our home. We would be dressed in the colorful outfits my grandmother had made on an old pedal machine that stood prominently in the kitchen to the right of the back door.

I see again my grandmother laying newspaper on the kitchen table. Again, she is cutting a pattern for a dress she has seen on one of her trips to Main Street. She is laying the pattern on colorful fabric. She is cutting. She is pushing the pedal rhythmically. She is hand stitching. She is calling my sister and me for fittings. She is smiling.

I tell the children again about Sunday School, Easter pageants, and Christmas plays; about the little old ladies who were in charge of the "sunshine band" for young children; about my aunt, their great-aunt, whose voice was all by itself a choir of angels; and about my mother, their grandmother, who could not carry a tune, but who always sang the words with passion.

They like Sunday remembering because I sing old songs for them: "Yes, Jesus loves me. Yes, Jesus loves me. Yes, Jesus loves me, for the Bible tells me."

But today is not Sunday. It is Saturday. Harriet is waking up on Saturday.

"What do you think Harriet is doing?" I ask. "She is just waking up." I yawn and stretch for them. They imitate me.

"Cartoons," Jonathan says after his yawn. "She's watching cartoons." That is what middle-class children do on Saturdays, I tell myself. My children included. They awake at the crack of dawn, and at the crack of dawn media is prepared for them. One cartoon after another flickers on the screen.

"No, Harriet is not watching cartoons," I tell them.

"How come?" Jonathan asks, disappointed.

"Not 'how come,'" I correct him. "What should you say?"

"Why? Why," he says with emphasis on the correct word, "can't Harriet be watching television?"

"Because her mommie and daddy didn't buy her a television," Jonathan says.

"No, that's not the reason," says Monica.

"Well, how come. I mean why can't Harriet be watching television?" Jonathan asks again.

Sad faces.

"Well, she has a television," I tell them.

"Is it a color television?" Jonathan asks.

"No," I answer.

"How come?" they ask in unison and correct themselves in unison, "I mean why?"

"Because color televisions cost a whole lot of money," one of them says. Sad faces again. Monica says, "Harriet's family is poor."

"You are forgetting," I tell them. "Remember? Remember we said that Harriet's family is rich?"

"Rich in love." They are proud that they come in on cue to repeat the phrase handed down from my mother.

"Harriet isn't watching cartoons," I explain, "because cartoons weren't all that important then."

"Well, what is she going to do?" In their world, what else can a young girl do on Saturday except begin the day by watching cartoons?

I tell them about spring cleaning days. Washing windows, scrubbing floors, cleaning the oven, and putting curtains on the stretcher. Each time, they say "stretcher" makes them think about very sick people. Well, they have a point. But stretchers stretched curtains. They were wooden frames filled with small nails that could be adjusted to different sizes. We would wash curtains, soak them in starch, and stretch them, dripping wet, from nail to nail, leaving them to dry outside, propped against the wall underneath the kitchen windows. We would have all of this work completed no later than nine in the morning so that the curtains could get the full morning sun. Our parents valued work and cleanliness.

Jonathan and Monica are much too young to understand such heavy chores. They are responsible only for minor tasks. When they ask whether or not Harriet liked doing all that work, I answer honestly that Harriet was anxious to get outside where she could play games, talk to boys, or go to the Saturday matinee with her friends. But I add that Harriet will learn when she is older what the chores meant to her. In spite of all the hours of play the chores stole from me, I value them. They made my mother, my sister, and me workers together and, in so doing, they gave me a sense of worth. They taught me the meaning of cooperative effort, the joy of accomplishment, and the importance of planning which is all about priorities and about sacrifice as well. My mother, and other adults with her, planned Saturdays, especially spring-cleaning Saturdays, with skill.

The children remember my remembering of these special Saturdays, mainly because my remembering usually includes stories about a horse.

"It could not gallop from your nose to your toes if his life depended on it," I tell them.

"And when Harriet puts the curtains on the stretcher," one of them asks, "is that when the horse comes clippety-cloppety?"

This gives them an opportunity to stand up and imitate the horse. They move around the room, saying "Giddy up," and "Clippety. Cloppety." I let them enjoy themselves for a few seconds, and then I say in a deep voice, "Whoa, horse. Whoa."

In the summer, an Italian marketman came down our driveway every Saturday morning, early morning, with a wagonload of greens, onions, yams, corn, and other vegetables sold at higher prices at the market down the street and across the boulevard named Mississippi. The wagon was old, and so was the horse. And so, too, the marketman. I remember that he had snow-white hair which contrasted sharply to the dirty clothes he always wore. Since our unit was midway through the court, he stopped his wagon almost directly in front of our door. Women from units on both sides of the street came from their kitchens with money in their hands. We had no fear of robberies.

The marketman was grouchy. I remember that. When I was older and processed race differently, I was incensed that he was grouchy. He, an outsider coming into our community to sell his wares! How dare he be grouchy! And why did the women purchase his wares? Why didn't they kick him out of the neighborhood. All they had to do was lean a little too hard on the wagon. It would have collapsed. Or they could have tapped the old horse on his nose. He would have rolled over and died. How did they turn the produce he sold with contempt into dinners that were family feasts, rituals that really brought us together joyous in our own world?

At this point in my remembering, I search for answers. My mother and other women were visible targets of racial and sexual rage and violence. Yet after each hard day in that cruel world, they returned home undiminished. They never gave in to the corrosion of hatred.

What made it possible for them to love in the face of such violence and hatred?

What inspired them to plant flowers, to sing, and to plan days, even nights, for themselves and their families? What prevented them from becoming like the women we rarely talked to; the women who were splintered, scarred, damaged, destroyed. What was their armor? Their secret potion? Their magic?

The answer shapes the way I am rearing my children. The women remained whole because they were certain of their own goodness and equally certain that goodness, in time, wins over evil. It is not by accident that black women poets call these women "sturdy oaks." Like trees in fierce storms, they knew how deep in the soil of goodness their roots were planted and, like giant trees, they reached beyond themselves to embrace others. But the how of their knowing, the source of their certainty, remains a mystery to me.

—⌒◌⌒—

Acclaimed writer, teacher, and scholar of African-American women's literature, *Gloria Wade-Gayles* (1938 –) was born in Memphis, Tennessee, one of two daughters of a stable black family. After earning her doctorate from Emory University in 1981, she taught permanently at Spelman College, earning the rank of full professor in 1989. Before that, she was a visiting professor at Howard University, Morehouse College, Emory University, and Talladega College. Wade-Gayles has published *Anointed to Fly* (1991), *My Soul Is a Witness: African-American Women's Spirituality* (1995), *Rooted against the Wind: Personal Essays* (1996), and *Father Songs: Testimonies by African-American Sons and Daughters* (1997). Wade-Gayles's scholarship rejects traditional approaches to literary criticism by presenting a deeply personal perspective. "When you step outside the expectations of the academy, you take a risk," she says. "But I can't breathe professionally without also breathing personally. My work is a reflection of my identity. It's about going to the art and hearing my own voice, my mother's voice, my grandmother's, my uncle's, my father's." This excerpt is from her memoir, *Pushed Back to Strength: A Black Woman's Journey Home* (1993).

Permissions Acknowledgments

Grateful acknowledgment is given to the following publishers and copyright holders for permission to reprint the following excerpts in *Girls Like Us:*

ISABEL ALLENDE: Excerpt from *Paula* by Isabel Allende. © 1994 by Isabel Allende. Translation © 1995 by HarperCollins Publishers. Reprinted by permission of HarperCollins Publishers, Inc.

MARGARET ATWOOD: Excerpt from *Cat's Eye* by Margaret Atwood. © 1988 by O. W. Toad, Ltd. Reprinted by permission of Doubleday, a division of Random House, Inc. and McClelland & Stewart, Inc.

LAUREN BACALL: Excerpt from *Lauren Bacall: By Myself* by Lauren Bacall. © 1978 by Caprigo Inc. Reprinted by permission of Alfred A. Knopf Inc. and Jonathan Cape (Random House UK).

JOAN BAEZ: Excerpt from the chapter "My Memory's Eye" from *And a Voice to Sing With* by Joan Baez. © 1986 by Joan Baez. Reprinted with the permission of Simon & Schuster.

Song lyrics "Honest Lullaby" appear on the album *Honest Lullaby*. Words and music by Joan Baez. © 1977, 1979 by Gabriel Earl Music (ASCAP). Reprinted by permission of Gabriel Earl Music.

BENAZIR BHUTTO: Excerpt from the chapter "Imprisoned in My Home," from *Daughter of Destiny* by Benazir Bhutto. © 1989 by Benazir Bhutto. Reprinted with the permission of the Wylie Agency, Inc.

TERESA CADER: "The Strand Theatre" © 1980 by Teresa Cader. Reprinted by permission of Teresa Cader.

bell hooks: Excerpt from *Bone Black* by bell hooks. © 1996 by Gloria Watkins. Reprinted by permission of Henry Holt and Company, Inc.

DOLORES HUERTA: *"Una mujer con compacion y gran fortaleza*/A Woman of Fortitude and Compassion" © 1998 by Dolores Huerta. Printed by permission of Dolores Huerta and the César E. Chavez Foundation.

SHIRLEY ANN JACKSON: "Discovering Science in My Backyard" by Dr. Shirley Ann Jackson, 1998. Printed by permission of Shirley Ann Jackson.

GISH JEN: Excerpt from "What Means Switch" by Gish Jen. © 1990 by Gish Jen. First published in *The Atlantic*. Reprinted by permission of Gish Jen.

JACKIE JOYNER-KERSEE: The chapter "My Guiding Light" from *A Kind of Grace* by Jackie Joyner-Kersee. © 1997 by Jackie Joyner-Kersee. Reprinted by permission of Warner Books.

ANNE HITT KEITER: "Summer Mama" © 1974 by Anne Hitt Keiter. Reprinted by permission of Anne Hitt Keiter.

CLAUDIA J. KENNEDY: "Inner Inspiration" by Lt. Gen. Claudia J. Kennedy, 1999. Printed by permission of Lt. Gen. Claudia J. Kennedy.

DORIANNE LAUX: "Rites of Passage" © 1990 by Dorianne Laux. Reprinted by permission of Dorianne Laux.

RITA LEVI-MONTALCINI: Excerpt from the chapter "Turin: Royal City and Home Town" from *In Praise of Imperfection: My Life and Work*. © 1988 by Rita Levi-Montalcini. Translated into English by Luigi Attardi.

DEVORAH MAJOR: "A Line of Storytellers" © 1995 by Devorah Major. Reprinted by permission of Devorah Major.

WILMA MANKILLER: Excerpt from the chapter "Child of the Sixties" from *Mankiller: A Chief and Her People* by Wilma Mankiller. © 1993 by Wilma Mankiller and Michael Wallis. Reprinted by permission of Wilma Mankiller.

AMY TAN: "The Voice from the Wall" from *The Joy Luck Club* by Amy Tan. © 1989 by Amy Tan. Used by permission of Putnam Berkley, a division of Penguin Putnam Inc.

JANE C. WAGNER and TINA DIFELICIANTONIO: The essay "Girls Like Us" © 1998 by Jane C. Wagner and Tina DiFeliciantonio. Printed by permission of Jane C. Wagner and Tina DiFeliciantonio in conjunction with Naked Eye Productions.

ALICE WALKER: "To Hell with Dying" from *In Love & Trouble: Stories of Black Women*. © 1967 and renewed 1995 by Alice Walker. Reprinted by permission of Harcourt Brace & Company and Women's Press. Women's Press permission acquired through David Higham Associates.

GLORIA WADE-GAYLES: Excerpt from the essay "For My Child's Remembering" from *Pushed Back to Strength* by Gloria Wade-Gayles. © 1993 by Gloria Wade-Gayles. Reprinted by permission of Beacon Press, Boston.

FAYE WATTLETON: Excerpt from *Life on the Line* by Faye Wattleton. © 1994 by Faye Wattleton. Reprinted by Permission of Ballantine Books, a division of Random House, Inc.

JUDITH WICKS: "A Table for 6 Billion, Please!"™ © 1998 by Judith Wicks. Printed by permission of Judith Wicks.

JODY WILLIAMS: Original letter © 1990 by Jody Williams. Printed by permission of Jody Williams.

NAOMI WOLF: Excerpt from the chapter "Girlfriends" from *Promiscuities* by Naomi Wolf. © 1997 by Naomi Wolf. Reprinted by permission of Random House, Inc. and Chatto & Windus, a division of Random House UK Ltd.

All photographs that appear in *Girls Like Us* are reprinted by permission of the contributors. Marian Wright Edelman's photo is reprinted by permission of the Children's Defense Fund.

About the Editor

Gina Misiroglu is a twelve-year veteran of the West Coast publishing industry, specializing in the development and editing of lifestyle, current issues, and women's studies titles. Of the many titles Misiroglu has contributed to, she is particularly proud of her co-authorship of *Space Jammin': Michael and Bugs Hit the Big Screen* and her work as editor and contributing writer to *Lay Down Body: Living History in Africa-American Cemeteries*, a reference book on African-American genealogy, history, and folklore. She is currently at work on her second anthology for New World Library.

If you enjoyed *Girls Like Us*, we highly recommend the following books and cassettes:

The Chalice & the Blade: Our History, Our Future by Riane Eisler. In this new, accessible audio adaption of her ground-breaking classic, Eisler eloquently reconstructs a prehistoric culture based on partnership rather than domination. *The Chalice & the Blade* provides new scripts for living, proving that a better future is possible, and is in fact firmly rooted in the drama of our past. (Audio.)

Legends: Women Who Have Changed the World Through the Eyes of Great Women Writers edited by John Miller. In prose and photography, contemporary women artists and writers celebrate courageous women whose work and lives continue to inspire. This provocative salute to both the accomplishments and imperfections of fifty courageous women is a beautiful volume that spans the twentieth century and all the flavors of our diverse culture. (Hardcover.)

Spilling Open: The Art of Becoming Yourself by Sabrina Ward Harrison. The journal pages of a young woman provide an intimate and moving picture of what it means to enter a contemporary adult world filled with contradictions about womanhood. Sabrina Ward Harrison reveals with tender honesty that, in spite of the women's movement, she has more questions than answers about growing up female in today's society. (Paperback.)

The Wisdom of Women edited by Carol Spenard Larusso. This popular collection of writings of women from around the world on topics of life and living portrays a mini-history of women. It includes pieces by Virginia Woolf, Georgia O'Keeffe, Anaïs Nin, Simone de Beauvoir, Rosa Parks, and many others. Highly inspirational. (Hardcover.)

New World library is dedicated to
publishing books and cassettes that inspire
and challenge us to improve the quality
of our lives and the world.

Our books and tapes are available
in bookstores everywhere.
For a catalog of our complete library
of fine books and cassettes, contact:

New World Library
14 Pamaron Way
Novato, CA 94949

Phone: (415) 884-2100
Fax: (415) 884-2199
Or call toll-free: (800) 972-6657
Catalog requests: Ext. 50
Ordering: Ext. 52

E-mail:escort@nwlib.com
Website:http://www.nwlib.com